The Translanguaging Classroom

The Translanguaging Classroom

Leveraging Student Bilingualism for Learning

Second Edition

by

Kate Seltzer, Ph.D.
Rowan University
Glassboro, NJ

Susana Ibarra Johnson, Ph.D.
New Mexico State University

and

Ofelia García, Ph.D.
City University of New York

Baltimore • London • Sydney

Paul H. Brookes Publishing Co.
Post Office Box 10624
Baltimore, Maryland 21285-0624
USA
www.brookespublishing.com

Typeset by Apex CoVantage, LLC, York, Pennsylvania.
Manufactured in the United States of America by Sheridan Books, Inc.

The individuals described in this book are real people or composites based on the authors' experiences. In some instances, names and identifying details have been changed to protect confidentiality. Otherwise, real names and identifying details are used by permission.

Library of Congress Control Number: 2025931808

British Library Cataloguing in Publication data are available from the British Library.

2029 2028 2027 2026

10 9 8 7 6 5 4 3 2

Contents

About the Online Materials

Purchasers of this book may download, print, and/or photocopy the Appendices for educational use.

To access the materials that come with this book:

1. Go to the Brookes Download Hub: http://downloads.brookespublishing.com
2. Register to create an account (or log in with an existing account).
3. Filter or search for the book title *The Translanguaging Classroom, Second Edition*.

About the Authors

Kate Seltzer, Ph.D., Rowan University

Kate Seltzer is an Associate Professor of ESL and Bilingual Education at Rowan University. A former high school English Language Arts teacher in New York City, she now works with schools and pre- and in-service teachers to recognize and build on students' rich language practices while also disrupting their own ideologies about these students and their ways of using language. Her award-winning work on translanguaging, literacy, and teacher education can be found in numerous journals and books. You can learn more about her work at kateseltzer.owlstown.net/.

Susana Ibarra Johnson, Ph.D., New Mexico State University

Susana Ibarra Johnson is an Assistant Professor of Bilingual Education/TESOL at New Mexico State University. Her commitment to improving the education of bilingual students is evident in her diverse and extensive experience. She has served in various roles, including as a professional development specialist, associate researcher for WIDA, director of bilingual multicultural education programs at Bernalillo Public Schools, district biliteracy specialist for Albuquerque Public Schools, and a bilingual education teacher in California, Texas, and New Mexico public schools. However, it is her research that truly stands out. Her work focuses on how translanguaging reshapes traditional conceptualizations of biliteracy with the implementation of translanguaging pedagogy in bilingual education and English-language development contexts. This research is not just academic; it has the potential to significantly improve the education of emergent bilingual students.

Ofelia García, Ph.D., City University of New York

Ofelia García is Professor Emerita in the Ph.D. programs in Urban Education and Latin American, Iberian and Latino Cultures at The Graduate Center, City University of New York. She has published widely in the areas of sociolinguistics, language policy and practices, multilingualism and translanguaging, and the education of bilingual students. García has received Distinguished Scholar Lifetime Awards from the American Education Research Association (AERA) (Social Contexts in Education, 2019 and Bilingual Education, 2017); from the Modern Language Association (MLA) in 2022; and from the Literacy Research Association (LRA) in 2024. In 2023 she was elected to membership in the Academy of Arts and Sciences (2023) and in 2018 in the National Academy of Education (2018). Her website is www.ofeliagarcia.org.

Foreword

When I wrote the foreword for the first edition of this book in 2017, the fall quarter had just begun at Stanford University and I had met the students enrolled in my course, Issues in the Study of Bilingualism, for the first time. The students were eager and interested, and many were clearly dedicated to making a difference as researchers and current and future teachers. In sharing their reasons for enrolling in the class, several students communicated a sense of urgency. They wanted to identify best practices for designing educational programs that would successfully teach science, math, reading, and writing to English language learners. They were eager to help immigrant-origin students to close what appeared to be an ever-widening achievement gap. There was little optimism expressed about schools' ability to make a difference in students' lives and much concern about whether immigrant-origin children could actually be educated in U.S. schools as currently configured.

After introductions, I began my brief lecture by talking about the shifts taking place in the field of bilingualism, about changing epistemologies, and about the excitement of moving forward by questioning the body of knowledge and the thinking that had informed us since *Languages in Contact* (Weinrich, 1953). From the questions my students asked, it was clear they had not yet heard about the *disinvention of languages* (Makoni & Pennycook, 2007), the *multilingual turn* (May, 2013), or *super-diversity* (Vertovec, 2007), and certainly not about *translanguaging* (Canagarajah, 2011, 2013; Creese & Blackledge, 2010; García, 2009, 2011a, 2011b, 2012, 2013, 2014; García & Wei, 2014; Wei, 2010, 2013). Most had heard about code-switching and disapproved of its use, some described their own language use as Spanglish or Chinglish, and the majority of the class fully subscribed to a narrow definition of bilingualism in which bilinguals are seen as two monolinguals in one person. It was clear that there was much work to be done if I wanted to move them gently from their unexamined deficit views about the flaws that they believed characterize immigrant youngsters' language(s) to embracing the richness of their present and future multicompetence. I knew, moreover, that it would be even more difficult to persuade these students that an intense focus on the teaching of bits and pieces of English and the exclusion of their home language in all intellectual activities would not benefit their students in developing their very fine minds.

As was the case every year that I taught that class, I required students to read both foundational works as well as the new literature (about translanguaging, plurilingualism, metrolingualism, and transidiomatic practices). They read about language ideologies, language variation, societal versus individual bilingualism, and the fuzzy boundaries of "named" languages. As a class, we engaged in extensive discussions of language and identity, multilingualism, multiculturalism, and new linguistic landscapes, and we argued about the types of instructional arrangements that might sustain and support bilingualism across generations. I hoped that the students would learn a great deal and possibly begin to question many strongly rooted beliefs and perspectives.

I was painfully aware, nevertheless—and I still am—that carefully selected readings will not change students' everyday teaching. If they are to link these new perspectives on bilingualism to a transformative practice that builds on what we now know about bilingualism, they will need to go beyond the existing theoretical and research literature. They will need to read and carefully study very different works, works that begin with theory and then invite teachers to explore new ways of thinking about language and new approaches in using "named" languages in classrooms to transform their practice. Ideally, such books will describe (1) how new theories can be instituted in everyday classrooms with students who are multicompetent, (2) how youngsters' needs can be identified, and (3) how particular pedagogies can respond to different students' characteristics and strengths. Such books will also provide details about designing classroom practices that meet these different needs and about the types of pedagogies that can develop youngsters' subject matter knowledge and their linguistic repertoires.

The process of translating theory to pedagogical practice is a difficult one. Teachers cannot imagine what they have not seen. Once they are socialized into their disciplines, professional identities, and accompanying language ideologies, they cannot change their practice unless they have a solid understanding of the alternatives. Teachers may agree that established approaches have been ineffective. However, moving from that conclusion to an actionable understanding of what to do and how to do it requires detailed descriptions of what steps to take, as well as models of practice accompanied by commentaries relating particular pedagogies to their broader personal beliefs and their views on children's languages and abilities, curricular demands, policy expectations, and assessment challenges.

The Translanguaging Classroom: Leveraging Student Bilingualism for Learning in both its first and the second edition provides precisely this important link between new theoretical perspectives on bilingualism and actual classroom practice. It is an important book that has and will continue to significantly shift and problematize our current approaches to teaching immigrant-origin students in the years to come. I continue to believe, moreover, that, because of this book, how researchers and educators view the use and role of language in the education of *all* children, especially language-minority children, will change dramatically as the ideas and practices presented here are discussed, debated, and implemented. At a time when we are engaged in a national conversation about race, inequality, poverty, opportunity, and immigration, this book brings us a groundbreaking and daring pedagogical vision. It invites us to re-examine and change the common-sense everyday classroom practices that we, as teachers and researchers, have used or recommended for (1) the teaching of content and language to immigrant-origin children in regular *and* bilingual education programs, and (2) the teaching of monolingual-English-speaking children who hope to acquire a language other than English (LOTE) in two-way, dual-language bilingual programs.

I purposefully refer to the book as presenting a view that is both groundbreaking and daring. I chose *groundbreaking* because the conceptualizations of language that underlie the pedagogical practices proposed here will be both new and unprecedented for many educators. I chose *daring* because the views and perspectives on linguistic multicompetence that inform the proposed approaches to instruction directly challenge established orthodoxies about bilingualism, bilingual children, and the use of two languages in education.

The translanguaging pedagogy described in detail in the text builds directly on García & Wei's (2014) book-length work on translanguaging and its role in education, which defines translanguaging as "an approach to the use of language, bilingualism, and the education of bilinguals that considers the language practices of bilinguals not as two autonomous language systems, as has been traditionally the case, but as one linguistic repertoire with features that have been societally constructed as belonging to two separate languages" (p. 2). In this book the authors describe translanguaging as "a way of *thinking about* and *acting on* the language practices of bilingual people." They then present a step-by-step guide for a pedagogy that builds on bilingualism itself—in all of its richness and complexity—and that invites teachers to see dual-language competency as a repertoire of diverse and complex language practices that can be used and developed in multiple ways in everyday classrooms.

Thinking and *acting differently* about the language practices of bilingual people is fundamental to bringing about change. And change is imperative! Immigrant-origin children in particular are facing increasingly difficult challenges. For a number of years, those of us who work on the education of these children have continually looked for ways to call attention to the challenges facing youngsters variously classified as English language learners (ELLs) (Linquanti & Cook, 2013) as they struggle to "learn" English at the same time that they are learning challenging content. We have tried, for example, to describe ELL ghettos to those who, because they do not work in schools, imagine that "teaching" English is a straightforward, race-neutral, apolitical activity. We have also struggled to describe the disappointed faces of students who thought they would have the opportunity to learn, to excel, and to compete academically and their discouragement at being limited to meaningless drills on bits and pieces of language for hours at a time. Unfortunately, as many who spend time in classrooms with ELLs know too well, in many classes and in many schools, there is no access to age-appropriate subject matter content for students classified as ELLs, only hours of worksheets and activities that keep them both busy and quiet. They are tested endlessly, and their progress is evaluated narrowly.

This book challenges the status quo and the well-meaning pedagogies that provide few challenges for pobrecito students. It assumes that students arrive with valuable linguistic capabilities that can be leveraged to develop their fine minds and to further expand their academic and personal competencies by using their full existing language repertoires at all times. It rejects deficit perspectives and approaches to teaching bilingual students, whether emergent or established, and insists on recognizing that their multiple ways of being and speaking are an essential part of their cultural ways of knowing.

In very important ways, *The Translanguaging Classroom: Leveraging Student Bilingualism for Learning* is by far the most compelling example proposed to date of a *culturally sustaining pedagogy* as defined by Paris (2012, p. 95):

> The term *culturally sustaining* requires that our pedagogies be more than responsive of or relevant to the cultural experiences and practices of young people—it requires that they support young people in sustaining the cultural and linguistic competence of their communities while simultaneously offering access to dominant cultural competence. Culturally sustaining pedagogy, then, has as its explicit goal supporting multilingualism and multiculturalism in practice and perspective for students and teachers. That is, culturally sustaining pedagogy seeks to perpetuate and foster—to sustain—linguistic, literate, and cultural pluralism as part of the democratic project of schooling.

As Paris (2012) argues, our search for asset or resource pedagogies, that is, for pedagogies that resist deficit perspectives and seek to honor, explore, and build on the cultures and experiences of minoritized students, has been a long and challenging one. All of us, including scholars deeply committed to equity, have found it difficult to convince others to question the deeply embedded notion that students' heritage and community practices are incompatible with opportunity and academic excellence. Too often, proposed pedagogies for cultural responsiveness or relevance have not necessarily invited students to value what they bring or to proudly continue to use features of their full linguistic repertoires in both formal and informal oral and written production for a variety of purposes in and out of school.

This book is different. It explicitly takes the position that past scholarship on language has misunderstood the nature of bilingualism and bilingual practices. It insists that students be invited to foster, maintain, and develop their complex repertoires. It invites teachers to reject static views of Language A versus Language B kept separate and pristine. It urges them to engage thoughtfully and joyfully with the richness of multicompetence in children's lives.

Educators and researchers will learn much from this timely and significant book and from the implementation of the *linguistically sustaining pedagogies* presented here. As these pedagogies are implemented, I am confident that the field will engage in challenging and important conversations and debates about the theories and ideologies that are uniquely presented and problematized in this volume. As my class at Stanford made enormously evident, our understanding of "bilingualism" has shifted in important ways. We now know more, and we now question many established views that had prevented us from seeing the complexity and potential of linguistic flexibility and range. In the case of my students, most of whom are deeply committed to social justice, making a difference in students' lives across their professional careers will require their constant examination and problematization of both established and current theories. It will also require, as Paris (2012) suggested, a clear change in *stance, terminology,* and *practice.* How we think, how we talk, and how we act matters. I applaud the authors for providing us with a guide for moving forward and sincerely thank them for their deep commitment to the complex, multicompetent voices of the children of the world.

Guadalupe Valdés
Palo Alto, California

Preface

A NOTE ABOUT THIS SECOND EDITION

The second edition of *The Translanguaging Classroom: Leveraging Student Bilingualism for Learning* includes several changes that are important to note. When we wrote the first edition, Kate had just left her position as a classroom teacher and was starting her doctoral work with Ofelia as her advisor. Susana was working with WIDA as an Associate Researcher and was also a doctoral student. Ofelia was a Professor at the CUNY Graduate Center. We became a collaborative trio as we discussed what teachers needed to understand about translanguaging if they were to change practices and transform language education, and so this book became reality.

In the almost 10 years that have elapsed since we started preparing the first edition, Kate and Susana have become accomplished scholars on their own, working with their own students and numerous other scholars. Ofelia has retired. Thus, it was important for us to change the order of authorship. While Ofelia continues her seminal work on translanguaging in other ways, it is Kate and Susana who are moving it forward with teachers and in the classrooms where they continue to work. The author order in this second edition ensures that the work is projected into the future.

Over the years, we have received feedback from many educators working with the first edition of *The Translanguaging Classroom.* We listened, and have made changes that reflect what we've heard. We have removed parts of the first edition that were not as useful to educators or that they found confusing. We also have included new content and connections in sidebars within the chapters, which we hope will serve as helpful resources. In addition, given the availability of multimedia and other work on the Internet, this edition has a companion website, where more resources can be found and accessed. Lastly, and perhaps most importantly, we have included throughout the book testimonials from the educators whose feedback has shaped this second edition; we hope their voices resonate with you as much as they have with us.

In the years since we started working on the first edition of this book, much critical language scholarship has emerged, and translanguaging scholars have insisted on its decolonial purposes. The work on raciolinguistic ideologies spearheaded by Nelson Flores and Jonathan Rosa has also shaped today's understandings of translanguaging. If you read the first edition, you know that these critical orientations were always there; now they are explicitly named, along with the work of the many scholars who have and continue to develop these connections. Relatedly, this second edition features a new Afterword by Nelson Flores, whose criticality and contributions to this book and to our field are immeasurable.

Finally, the first edition was published by Caslon, and Rebecca Field played an important role in shaping it. Brookes Publishing acquired the rights for this second edition, and we're grateful to Liz Gildea, and many other members of the Brookes team, for moving it forward.

THE BOOK

If you have chosen to read *The Translanguaging Classroom: Leveraging Student Bilingualism for Learning,* you are probably an educator—a teacher, a curriculum developer, a professional development provider, a school administrator, or other school personnel. And, like most educators, you probably have students in your classrooms and schools who speak languages other than English (LOTE), and you are interested in how to further their education, including their English language and literacy development. This book is for you.

This book shows teachers, administrators, consultants, and researchers how **translanguaging**, a way of thinking about and acting on the language practices of bilingual people, may hold the key to successfully educating bilingual students. The translanguaging pedagogy that we put forward in this book is purposeful and strategic, and we demonstrate how teachers can use translanguaging to do the following:

1. Support students as they engage with and comprehend complex content and texts.
2. Provide opportunities for students to develop their linguistic practices for a variety of purposes and contexts, including those deemed academic.
3. Support students' bilingual identities, socioemotional development, and critical consciousness and disrupt ideologies that render bilingual students as deficient.
4. Make space for all students' language practices and ways of knowing, and in so doing build a classroom and society that is inclusive of linguistic, racial, gender, and ability differences.

You will notice that these purposes are slightly different from those in the first edition. We have chosen to sharpen our focus and name *transformative social purposes* for translanguaging that include and go beyond classroom instructional practices. These four purposes frame the translanguaging pedagogy, and they work together to advance the primary purpose of translanguaging—social justice—ensuring that bilingual students, especially those who come from minoritized groups, are instructed and assessed in ways that provide them with equitable educational opportunities.

With that said, we have not abandoned our focus on classrooms, and in Chapter 1 we describe four reasons for opening up translanguaging spaces in *instruction*:

1. To assess or document what students know and can do
2. To scaffold instruction and provide support to individual students
3. To deepen understandings
4. To transform individual and classroom subjectivities

Translanguaging classrooms are aligned with the global and local realities of the twenty-first century. These dynamic classrooms advance the kinds of practices that college and career-readiness standards demand, as they enhance bilingual students' critical thinking and creativity. Teachers learn to expand and localize their teaching in ways that address all content and language standards and integrate home, school, community, and societal practices and understanding. Translanguaging classrooms also allow teachers to carry out the mandates of the growing number of states that are adopting Seals of Biliteracy to recognize and reward students' bilingual abilities.

WHO SHOULD READ THIS BOOK?

This book has been written specifically with bilingual students in fourth through 12th grades in mind. However, teachers and other educational leaders can use this book to guide teaching, instructional programming, and action-oriented research in any context.

Our primary audience is teachers. Any teacher, whether monolingual or bilingual, and whether involved in a program officially designated as English-medium[1] or bilingual education, can create a translanguaging classroom. You could be a specialized language teacher or professional—a teacher of English as an additional language, bilingual education, home language literacy, or world language[2]—a general education teacher of either children

[1]English-medium classes and programs officially use English for instructional purposes, and they aim for academic achievement and language development in English. Bilingual education classes and programs use two or more languages for instructional purposes, and they aim for biliteracy and academic performance in two languages.

[2]In the United States, "world language" refers to a class focused on the teaching of a LOTE as a subject to language majority students, whereas home language literacy classes teach that language to bilingual students as a subject. English as an additional language teachers can teach only the subject (English literacy) or be classroom teachers of all subjects. Bilingual teachers are classroom teachers teaching subjects through two languages.

or adolescents, or of a specific content area at the secondary level, or even the principal of a school. Teachers and administrators can build instructional spaces that go beyond our traditional understanding about programs for bilingual students.

Most classrooms today are multilingual, with students who speak languages in addition to English. Some of these students are highly bilingual and biliterate (*experienced bilinguals*), whereas others' bilingualism and biliteracy are emerging (*emergent bilinguals*). Some of these bilingual learners have developed strong academic foundations through quality school systems, while others may have experienced limited formal schooling. Regardless of where your students fall along bilingual or educational continua, this book demonstrates innovative ways of educating them.

Because of the important place of bilingual Latinx students in U.S. education, this book emphasizes the context of Latinx students in both English-medium and bilingual instructional settings to help you understand translanguaging classrooms. But because we know that translanguaging is not limited to Spanish–English bilingualism, we also draw on examples from English-medium classrooms that include bilingual students from linguistically and culturally diverse backgrounds. Whether your students are speakers of Spanish, Mandarin, Korean, Karen, Pular, or any other language, the principles for translanguaging in the classroom are the same.

Research and practice on bilingualism at U.S. schools have focused narrowly on English language learners' content and language learning, generally in English-medium classrooms, and have reflected a language-as-problem or deficit orientation. In contrast, *The Translanguaging Classroom: Leveraging Student Bilingualism for Learning* takes a much broader approach. We focus on all bilingual students, including those who are emergent bilinguals as well as those who are seen by the academic mainstream as English speakers but speak languages other than English at home. We show teachers how to identify and build on the varied bilingual performances of all bilingual students, whether or not they perform well academically in English or another language, and whether they are learning in English-medium, bilingual, or LOTE classrooms.

We bring the translanguaging pedagogy to life through vignettes from three very different classrooms:

- A fourth-grade dual-language bilingual education classroom of students who speak English, Spanish, or both at home, taught by a bilingual (Spanish–English) teacher in New Mexico
- An 11th-grade English-medium social studies classroom of students who mostly speak English, Spanish, or both at home, though others speak additional languages, taught by a monolingual English-speaking teacher in New York City
- Seventh-grade English-medium math and science classrooms that include emergent bilinguals who speak Spanish, Cantonese, Mandarin, French, Tagalog, Vietnamese, Korean, Mandingo, and Pular (Fula) at home, co-taught by English monolingual math and science teachers and an ESL teacher in California

These rich and varied cases clearly demonstrate how teachers can adapt the translanguaging pedagogy that we introduce in this book for all students, whatever their bilingualism looks like, in whatever instructional context.

WHAT ARE THE KEY COMPONENTS OF A TRANSLANGUAGING PEDAGOGY?

The central innovative concept in this book for teachers is *translanguaging*, which García (2009) describes as "an approach to bilingualism that is centered not on languages, as has been often the case, but on the practices of bilinguals that are readily observable" (p. 45). An additional, much-cited definition is "the deployment of a speaker's full linguistic repertoire without regard for watchful adherence to the socially and politically defined boundaries of named languages" (Otheguy et al., 2015, p. 281). This book builds on this approach in three important ways. First, we describe the **translanguaging corriente**, the natural flow of students' bilingualism through the classroom. Second, we explore bilingual students' **dynamic translanguaging performances**, which allows teachers to look holistically at their language performances in specific classroom tasks from different perspectives at different times, setting learning in motion. Third, we introduce a **translanguaging pedagogy** for instruction and assessment that teachers can use to purposefully and strategically **leverage** the translanguaging corriente produced by students.

Translanguaging classrooms have two important dimensions. First, teachers observe students' languaging performances and then describe and assess their complex language practices. Second, teachers adapt and use the translanguaging pedagogy for instruction and assessment to leverage the translanguaging corriente for learning. These two dimensions have at their core three important principles:

1. Bilinguals use their linguistic repertoires as resources for learning and as flexible identity markers that point to their innovative and changing ways of knowing, being, and communicating.
2. Bilinguals learn language through their interaction with others within their home, social, and cultural environments.
3. Translanguaging is fluid language use that is part of bilinguals' sense-making processes.

Translanguaging Corriente

We suggest that the translanguaging corriente, produced and driven by the positive energy of students' bilingualism, flows throughout all classrooms. Metaphorically, we think about the translanguaging corriente as a river current that you can't always see or feel but is always present, always moving, and responsible for changes in the (classroom) landscape. Sometimes the translanguaging corriente flows gently under the surface, for example, in classrooms where teachers do not generally tap into students' home language practices for learning. At other times the translanguaging corriente is much stronger, for example, in bilingual classrooms or English-medium classrooms that do draw on students' home language practices.

To feel the translanguaging corriente, all you have to do is take a step back from your daily routine to really listen. Listen to what your students say to you and their peers, inside the classroom, in the hallways and the cafeteria, and on the playground. If you listen hard enough you might be able to perceive their **intrapersonal voices** (the unvoiced dialogues they have in their heads with themselves or friends). Listen also to the conversations that take place when their families and peers are present; try to hear what is being said and how it is said, as well as what is not being said and why. Listening in this way allows you to perceive your students' voices anew and puts you in touch with the translanguaging corriente, even if it is not obviously at the surface of your classroom.

In this book the translanguaging corriente runs through the content it communicates; we have chosen to use words in Spanish in this predominantly English-language text, without any italics. We do this to indicate that, for us, the Spanish features we use are not alien or foreign; they are simply part of our narrative, always present and part of us, even when we are writing in English. We translate some documents in the Appendix into Spanish because, as we said earlier, Latinx students make up the largest population of U.S. bilingual students and represent the majority of the students featured in the classrooms in this book. However, you can translate the English text in these documents to any of the languages in your classroom as one means of leveraging the translanguaging corriente in your classroom.

Dynamic Translanguaging Performances

The notion of the translanguaging corriente moves us from the concept of linguistic *proficiency*, which is assumed to develop along a relatively linear path in more or less the same way for all bilingual learners, to one of linguistic *performance*. The focus on students' dynamic translanguaging performances enable teachers to do the following:

- Gauge the students' different linguistic performances on different tasks and from different perspectives

- Distinguish between **general linguistic performance** (bilingual students' ways of performing academic tasks—e.g., express complex thoughts effectively, explain things, persuade, argue, compare and contrast, recount events, tell jokes—without regard to the language used to express these tasks) and **language-specific performance** (bilingual students' use of features corresponding to what society considers a specific language or variety)
- Leverage the translanguaging corriente for learning in their classes

Teachers in translanguaging classrooms document their students' language performances on specific classroom-based tasks—in any language.

Translanguaging Pedagogy: Stance, Design, and Shifts

The translanguaging pedagogy in this book encompasses both instruction and assessment and is structured into three interrelated strands: the *translanguaging stance, design*, and *shifts*.

A stance refers to the philosophical, ideological, or belief system that teachers draw from to develop their pedagogical framework. Teachers with a translanguaging stance believe that bilingual students' many different language practices work **juntos**, not separately, as if they belonged to different realms. Thus, the teacher believes that the classroom space must promote collaboration across content, languages, people, and home, school, and community. A translanguaging stance sees the bilingual child's complex *language repertoire* as a resource, never as a deficit.

Designing translanguaging instruction and assessment involves integrating home, school, and community language and cultural practices. The movement is created by the interaction between the translanguaging corriente and the teacher and students' joint actions, which enable bilingual students to integrate *all* of their linguistic and other meaning-making practices. Designing translanguaging instruction also means planning carefully (e.g., the grouping of students; elements of planning—essential ideas, questions, and texts; content, language, and translanguaging objectives; culminating projects; design cycle; pedagogical strategies). The translanguaging design is a flexible framework that teachers in English-medium and bilingual classrooms can use to develop curricular units of instruction, lesson plans, and classroom activities. The flexible design is the pedagogical core of the translanguaging classroom, and it allows teachers and students to address all content and language standards and objectives in equitable ways for all students, particularly bilingual students, who are often marginalized in mainstream classrooms and schools. Designing assessment to set the course of the translanguaging corriente means including the voices of others, taking into account the difference between content and language and between general linguistic and language-specific performances, and giving students opportunities to perform tasks with assistance from other people and resources when needed.

Because the translanguaging corriente is always present in classrooms, it is not enough to simply have a stance that recognizes it and a design that leverages it. At times it is also important to follow the dynamic movement of the translanguaging corriente. The translanguaging shifts are the many moment-by-moment decisions that teachers make all the time. They reflect the teacher's flexibility and willingness to change the course of the lesson and assessment, as well as the language use planned for it, to release and support students' voices. The shifts are related to the stance, for it takes a teacher willing to keep meaning-making and learning at the center of all instruction and assessment to go with the flow of the translanguaging corriente.

USING THIS BOOK

We have three purposes for this book. First, we want educators and researchers to see a clearly articulated translanguaging pedagogy in practice. The examples from three very different classrooms stimulate concrete thinking about students, classrooms, programs, schools, practices, and research in different bi/multilingual communities. Second, we want to guide teachers' efforts to adapt the translanguaging pedagogy put forth in this book to any translanguaging context. Third, we provide the foundation for teachers and researchers to gather empirical evidence in translanguaging classrooms, which will help refine theory and strengthen practice.

We provide templates and examples from our focal bilingual and English-medium classrooms to assist you in designing instructional units, lessons, and assessments that identify and build on the translanguaging corriente in your classroom, school, and community context. When teachers enact a translanguaging stance, implement a translanguaging design for instruction and assessment, and intentionally shift their practices in response to student learning, they help fight the English-only current of much U.S. educational policy and practice and advance social justice.

We have organized the book into three parts:

Section I: Dynamic Bilingualism at School

This part of the book focuses on the "what" and "why" of translanguaging.

Section II: Translanguaging Pedagogy

This part of the book focuses on how to create a translanguaging pedagogy.

Section III: Reimagining Teaching and Learning Through Translanguaging

This part of the book focuses on how a translanguaging pedagogy works to enhance students' performances in different standards and literacy, develop their socioemotional identity, and advance social justice.

In each chapter, learning objectives lay out what readers will learn and be able to do with chapter content materials. This is then followed by the core of the chapter—vignettes of classroom practices, tools, templates, and/or frameworks. Each chapter ends with questions and activities that educators can use to reflect on aspects of translanguaging classrooms, as well as "take action" in their contexts. As a whole, the taking action questions guide educators to develop a translanguaging pedagogy in their own specific contexts. They also assist practitioners in developing, implementing, monitoring, and evaluating their translanguaging pedagogy in practice. We encourage you to work through these questions and activities with a close community of fellow educators so that you can support one another as you explore and take up the translanguaging corriente in your classroom.

We invite you now to become a reflective practitioner and let yourself be swept up by the translanguaging corriente, as we explore its meaning in instruction and how to teach by capitalizing on its ebbs and flows. We hope that together we will:

- Listen to and deepen our perceptions of the translanguaging corriente that *already* exists in classrooms and schools.
- Learn how to intentionally, purposefully, and strategically navigate the translanguaging corriente in both instruction and assessment by integrating the translanguaging stance, design, and shifts.
- Demonstrate ways that bilingual students and teachers leverage the translanguaging corriente to learn and access content, develop linguistic practices for a variety of purposes, foster secure socioemotional identities and critical consciousness, and make space for all students' language practices and ways of knowing.
- Become more critical as we take up the stance of reflective practitioner and/or critical researcher and work toward social justice.
- Confront the kinds of challenges educators may face in translanguaging classrooms and reflect on how to navigate them.
- Launch an action-oriented, social justice agenda to strengthen translanguaging pedagogy, practice, and research in diverse multilingual contexts.

Acknowledgments

This book was the result of much negotiation among ourselves and with the editor of the first edition, Rebecca Field of Caslon. Although the process was difficult at times, Rebecca pushed our thinking, our words, and the manuscript itself. Gracias, Rebecca. We are also very grateful to our new team at Brookes, particularly Liz Gildea, Ashley Wagner, Rachel Word, and many others who understood and supported our vision for this second edition.

We do not forget the insights gained from generous contributors and reviewers of the first edition. For this second edition, we have additional people to acknowledge and thank. We are grateful to the many teachers, administrators, coaches, teacher educators, and scholars who have lent their voices to the testimonials included in this edition. We thank Guadalupe Valdés, again, and Nelson Flores for their important contributions to the book, to our thinking, and to our field. We also thank the students, teachers, and colleagues whose partnership and work has continued to push us to think about the critical, transformative potential of translanguaging pedagogies.

Kate: To my former students and to the teachers I work with who have and continue to deepen my understanding of la corriente. To my parents and grandparents, whose languages have been in my heart since before I can remember. And to Jimmy, Aaron, and Ada, forever.

Susana: For Andrew, Aaron, Juanita and Reuben—son mi amor, mi vida y mi esperanza.

Ofelia: Para todos mis colegas que han avanzado understandings of translanguaging. Y sobre todo para mi compañero de vida, Ricardo, who has taught me about the many corrientes of translanguaging, as we listened to our children's and grandchildren's translanguaging juntos.

I

Dynamic Bilingualism at School

1

Translanguaging Classrooms: Contexts and Instructional Purposes

LEARNING OBJECTIVES

After reading this chapter, you will be able to:

- See translanguaging classrooms in action.
- Explain how translanguaging can be used by teachers in different types of classroom contexts.
- Summarize the instructional reasons for translanguaging.
- Begin to create a profile of your own translanguaging classroom.

One of the best ways to understand translanguaging is to see and hear it in action. Many of the teachers we have worked with have "aha moments" when they stop and listen to the ways students use language in their classrooms. For example, two students negotiate in Spanish how to solve a math problem posed to them in English. One student with more experience in English quietly explains directions to a newly arrived student from China. A group of students joke with one another using word play, gestures, and English/Spanish puns. Once you take up this new lens for observing your bilingual students, you will notice new and exciting things about the "way they language," which can guide the ways you plan, teach, assess, and advocate for their needs. Our use of the verb "to language" (e.g., "languaging," "translanguaging") reflects our understanding of doing language as a dynamic communicative practice.

Translanguaging, according to García (2009), "is an approach to bilingualism that is centered not on languages as has been often the case, but on the practices of bilinguals that are readily observable" (p. 45). A translanguaging classroom is any classroom in which students are invited to deploy their full linguistic repertoire, not just the particular language(s) that are officially used for instructional purposes in that space. The attention in these classrooms is focused on the students and the ways in which they make meaning of instruction and their lives, not simply on a language to be learned. These students are diverse; they could be members of racialized groups, could come from homes in which other languages are spoken, could use linguistic features that are validated by schools, could be Deaf, could have a disability. The important thing to remember is that a translanguaging classroom can be developed anywhere we find students who use different language practices.

This book focuses on classrooms where children are, or are becoming, bilingual. In the United States this includes classrooms that use only English as the official language for instruction (i.e., what are seen as mainstream English-medium classrooms and **English as a second language [ESL]** classrooms, whether **pull-out**, **push-in**, or **structured English immersion** programs), as well as bilingual classrooms that use two languages as medium of instruction (i.e., dual-language bilingual, transitional bilingual), or classrooms where the focus of instruction is the development of what are called world languages or **heritage languages**. In this book, all students in these translanguaging classrooms are referred to as *bilingual students,* by which we mean **emergent bilinguals**, who are at the early stages of bilingual development, as well as more **experienced bilinguals**, who can use two or more languages with relative ease, although their performances vary according to task, modality, and language. The use of the term *emergent bilingual* in this book includes students who are officially designated by schools as "English language learners (ELLs)," as well as English speakers who are learning other languages (e.g., Spanish, Arabic, Mandarin). We do not use the term *ELL* because it renders the **language(s) other than English (LOTE)** in the emergent bilinguals' developing linguistic repertoire invisible. We do, however, use this term when it refers to the official school designation. Another term increasingly used by educators to talk about these students is "multilingual learners." Though there are myriad terms and acronyms to describe these students, this book encourages you to be intentional about your use of them. Describing students through *asset-based* terms and rejecting those that erase their existing language practices and identities is part of creating translanguaging classrooms, which is described next.

TRANSLANGUAGING CLASSROOMS

A **translanguaging classroom** is a space built collaboratively by the teacher and bilingual students as they use their different language practices to teach and learn in deeply creative and critical ways, as they develop their bilingualism. The term translanguaging comes from the Welsh *trawsieithu,* coined by a Welsh educator, Cen Williams (1994, 2002), who developed a *bilingual* pedagogy in which students were asked to alternate languages for the purposes of receptive or productive use. For example, students might be asked to read in English and write in Welsh and vice versa to deepen and extend their bilingualism.

Since Colin Baker translated the Welsh term to English in 2001, translanguaging has been extended by many scholars to refer both to the complex language practices of bilingual and multilingual individuals and communities and to the pedagogical approaches that draw on those practices (García & Wei, 2014). As mentioned above, García (2009) explains that translanguaging "is an approach to bilingualism that is centered not on languages as has been often the case, but on the practices of bilinguals that are readily observable" (p. 45). From a linguistics perspective, Otheguy et al. (2015) define translanguaging as "the deployment of a speaker's full linguistic repertoire without regard for watchful adherence to the socially and politically defined boundaries of named languages" (p. 281). According to Flores and Schissel (2014, pp. 461–462):

> Translanguaging can be understood on two different levels. From a sociolinguistic perspective it describes the fluid language practices of bilingual communities. From a pedagogical perspective it describes a pedagogical approach whereby teachers build bridges from these language practices and the language practices desired in formal school settings.

The focus in this book is on pedagogy, or the art, science, method, and practice of teaching.

Translanguaging is the norm in translanguaging classrooms—regardless of the official language of instruction of the class. This book provides the framework for a translanguaging pedagogy that shows educators how to **leverage** the language practices of their bilingual students and communities while addressing core content and standards of language development that are consonant with what the different bilingual students can do. We illustrate this pedagogy in action with three case examples, which follow, that together represent the kinds of diversity we find among students, teachers, language policies, program types, and grade levels in schools. As you read, think about the actual language practices of your students relative to the official language policy of your school.

Interested in seeing how more teachers open up translanguaging spaces across programs and language backgrounds? Check out the web series "Teaching Bilinguals (Even If You're Not One)" from the CUNY-New York State Initiative on Emergent Bilinguals project! You can access this web series via the Brookes Download Hub.

Carla's Elementary Dual-Language Bilingual Classroom

Carla teaches a fourth-grade dual-language bilingual[1] class in Albuquerque, New Mexico, and all of her students come from homes where Spanish, as well as English, and sometimes Indigenous languages are spoken. This elementary school program aims for bilingualism, biliteracy, and academic achievement in two languages. Carla was born in Puebla, Mexico, and came to New Mexico at the age of 10 with her family. She is bilingual and studied Spanish in high school and at college as she pursued her bilingual education certification.

Most of Carla's students are Spanish-speaking bilinguals, though their individual profiles are very different. ***Moisés***, for example, emigrated from Mexico to the United States 2 years ago and is considered a newcomer. Moisés is officially designated as an ELL, but we refer to him as an emergent bilingual. Though Moisés is developing his Spanish and English practices in Carla's classroom, he prefers speaking Spanish. ***Ricardo***, like Moisés, is considered a newcomer and is officially designated ELL. Ricardo is in the process of learning English. At home he speaks Spanish and Mixteco, the Indigenous language he spoke with his family and community in Mexico. At different points on the bilingual continuum are ***Erica*** and ***Jennifer***, who were both born in the United States. Erica prefers to speak English, though her family does speak some Spanish at home, while Jennifer, a more experienced bilingual, feels comfortable using both languages to carry out academic tasks. Jennifer has also been diagnosed as having a learning disability and has an Individualized Educational Program (IEP). As is evident, not all of Carla's students are classified as ELLs (or emergent bilinguals). Her students' bilingual performances are varied, and the students have a wide range of strengths within and across languages.

Although Carla was always comfortable translanguaging and saw its value in communicating with different family members, she was taught never to use it for instruction. Her teacher education program in bilingual education advocated that, unless there was a clear and separate space for Spanish, English would take over instruction and there would be little development of Spanish. In studying the dual-language model, she was told that teachers were never to put the different language practices alongside each other. She was taught to make sure that writing in English and Spanish never appeared together and to dedicate different parts of the room to the two languages. At the beginning of her career, she taught strictly in Spanish in the morning and in English in the afternoon and corrected students when they spoke the "wrong" language at the "wrong" time. She never brought multilingual resources into the classroom—she used Spanish resources during Spanish time and English resources during English time.

When Carla first encountered the concept of a translanguaging pedagogy, she questioned and resisted it. However, she quickly realized that despite all her strict rules about English here and Spanish there, her students were always using features from Spanish and English to make meaning, albeit surreptitiously. For example, during English time, they often whispered to each other in Spanish; when Carla approached, the discussion would simply stop. Carla decided instead to bring the students' language practices to the forefront and build on them in the classroom. Rather than "policing" which language was used where (Flores, 2020), she encouraged students to use their entire language repertoire to learn and demonstrate what they had learned. Though she maintained an official space for English and an official space for Spanish to provide opportunities for language development, she now opened up spaces for translanguaging in instruction. For example, she realized that Moisés and Ricardo benefit from having a translanguaging space because it scaffolds instruction, making it possible for them to engage with the classroom instruction when Carla is teaching

[1]We use the term **dual-language bilingual education** intentionally. In New Mexico, this type of bilingual program is often referred to as one-way dual-language education. In some education districts, this type of program is referred to as a developmental bilingual education program, or as a developmental-maintenance bilingual education program. We do not use the term "one-way" because in practice we find tremendous variation in the ways that emergent and experienced bilingual students from the "same" language background use languages in their everyday lives. We also include the word *bilingual*, which has largely disappeared from discussions about dual-language education in response to the backlash against bilingualism and bilingual education. In fact, it is not uncommon to hear bilingual educators say that dual-language education is not bilingual education, a stance with which we disagree. Our use of bilingual emphasizes that dual-language education is bilingual education.

in English. She also noticed that, at times when the instruction is in Spanish, it is Erica who benefits from a translanguaging space. Erica deepens her understanding of what she is reading in Spanish during guided reading because she is allowed to use her full linguistic/semiotic repertoire to ask questions of the group and tell her own stories. Sometimes Erica uses gestures and drawings, besides features from English and Spanish, to share her experiences.

At the center of Carla's literacy and language instruction during her (bi)literacy block is the sharing of human experiences, especially those of the neighborhood and land, el barrio y la tierra. The experiences of the New Mexico barrio where Carla's school is located are deeply connected to the tierra because many of her students' parents are farm workers. Carla introduced a translanguaging space into her dual-language bilingual classroom through what she called "Cuéntame Algo," which she describes as a time for bilingual storytelling when a translanguaging literacy activity takes center stage. Her instructional unit "Cuentos de la tierra y del barrio" focuses on stories of how students, families, and the local community are tied to their land and, by extension, to their traditions. Students discuss cuentos (stories) written by Latinx bilingual authors about land and traditions, as well as those told to them by family and community members, including abuelitos and abuelitas, grandparents whom Carla invites to her classroom. They also discuss video clips, music and other multimodal texts, as well as their own experiences and those of barrio residents in order to connect them to their land more closely.

Stephanie's High School Social Studies Class

Stephanie is an 11th-grade social studies teacher in New York City, and English is the official language used for instructional purposes in her classroom. Thus, Stephanie's classroom provides an example of a translanguaging classroom in an English-medium context. She is a White woman of Polish descent, and though she knows some Spanish words that she has learned from her students, she does not consider herself bilingual. Stephanie was trained as a history teacher but found that once she entered the classroom, she also had to teach content area literacy.

The linguistic diversity in Stephanie's English-medium classroom is rich. Most, though not all, of Stephanie's students are Spanish-speaking Latinx who perform differently in language and literacy in Spanish and English. Some of them speak Indigenous languages, such as Mixteco and Quechua. Some are Black students who have different ways of speaking English, including what are often seen as different varieties—Black English, Jamaican English, African English, etc. A few of her Latinx students are officially designated as ELLs. Some of these emergent bilinguals (to use our preferred term), like ***Noemí***, are newcomers with solid educational backgrounds and strong oracy and literacy in Spanish. Other newcomers, like ***Luis***, have had inconsistent schooling in the countries they came from and struggle to meet grade-level expectations in literacy and numeracy. Other emergent bilinguals, like ***Mariana***, have received most or all of their education in the United States but were labeled as ELLs when entering school and have yet to test out of this status. Although Mariana is now classified as a **long-term English language learner (LTELL)**—meaning she has been enrolled in a U.S. school and received English language services for 6 or more years without being reclassified as "English proficient"—she generally uses English at school. In fact, many of her teachers do not even realize she is still officially considered an ELL.

It is important to emphasize that there is also considerable linguistic and cultural diversity among Stephanie's "English-speaking" students. Because many of the bilingual Latinx students are not designated as ELLs, their bilingualism tends to go unnoticed. Stephanie, however, knows that these students have a wide range of experiences with oral and written Spanish and English. Some, like ***Eddy*** and ***Teresita***, were born in the United States and have different degrees of comfort with using Spanish. There are also some students in her class who are Black, some from the Anglophone Caribbean, and their English also includes features that are not perceived as "standard" or "appropriate" for academic purposes.

As a social studies teacher, Stephanie is expected to prepare her students to meet the New York State Social Studies Framework and to pass a final assessment in the 11th grade social studies curriculum—U.S. history and government. But Stephanie has to do much more than simply teach the content of the U.S. history curriculum, the history of the United States from its colonial foundations to the present. Content standards are expressed through language: reading, writing, speaking, and listening. Stephanie is expected to make sure her students can read social studies texts in English so that they can identify key ideas in texts, evaluate their premises, and integrate information from diverse sources. Her students are also expected to write argumentative and information texts in English, conduct research, integrate information and concepts from different sources, as well as engage in discussions with peers in English. Although achievement tests in New York State (the Regents exams) are translated into the five most common languages of students—Chinese, Haitian Creole, Korean, Russian, and Spanish—only Noemí, with strong Spanish literacy skills, will be able to take advantage of this accommodation to take the U.S. history exam. And even for her, reading and writing only in Spanish about topics that she studied and discussed in English will be difficult. The rest of the students in Stephanie's class may be good U.S. historians, but their understandings will be assessed using only features of "standard" or "academic English," an ideological construct that is often perceived as distinct from the students' own language practices (Flores & Rosa, 2015; Lippi-Green, 2012).

When she first started teaching, Stephanie realized quickly that her students were capable of thinking critically and understanding deeply. How could she work with the students' strengths and creativity and enable them to show what they know in ways that were acceptable on the assessments that they were required to take? When she learned about translanguaging, she realized that she could create spaces in her classroom to leverage the many different meaning-making resources available. Without knowing it, she had already set up her classroom in ways that made it possible to capitalize on translanguaging. She always organized students into groups that had mixed strengths so they could help each other in the project-based activities of her thematic, often interdisciplinary, units. In these groupings she noticed that peers helped each other using Spanish as well as English, and she realized that students were using all their language resources, including gesturing, role playing, and even drawing. And of course, all were also using what is considered Black Language.[2] She realized she could encourage the students' translanguaging interaction to enable all of them to engage with the learning activity, but also to transform the subjectivities of inferiority that many students held about themselves when they entered her class. In opening up translanguaging spaces in this classroom, Stephanie saw the transformative potential of translanguaging with regard to the students' perceptions of themselves—her students began to view themselves as strong learners with capabilities in multiple languages.

Since learning about translanguaging, Stephanie has made a strong effort to build a robust **multilingual ecology** in which all her students can thrive. For example, although her classroom is not officially bilingual, Stephanie works with bilingual staff members and student volunteers to translate and create multilingual materials and actively seeks out Spanish language resources, and she has become aware of students who also speak other Indigenous languages as well as the language and cultural practices of her Black students. She has a large collection of books written by Black and Latinx authors. To build a collaborative spirit among all her students, Stephanie seeks out history texts that tell the story of the combined contributions of Black Americans and Latinx to U.S. history, such as Ortiz's (2018) *An African American and Latinx History of the United States*. Stephanie also has a shelf full of bilingual dictionaries that students can use at any point in the lesson, and she has supplementary U.S. history textbooks in Spanish that students are encouraged to use. She also has iPads, which newcomers use frequently to access the Spanish version of their history textbook, and she has taught her students to use Google Translate.

Stephanie is passionate about helping her students see connections across different content areas. While schools separate topics into "subjects" like social studies or science,

---

[2]Though many terms have been used to describe these language practices (e.g., AAE, AAVE, Black English), we have chosen to use Black Language, following language and literacy scholar Dr. April Baker-Bell.

Stephanie believes that one cannot be understood without the other. Thus, many of Stephanie's units focus on history but bring in interdisciplinary connections. For example, one of Stephanie's interdisciplinary units, "Environmentalism: Then and Now," is a historical study of the U.S. environmental movement. Students learn about the history of this social movement by reading their textbooks and supplemental readings from websites, newspapers, and magazines. They also listen to podcasts and radio interviews, watch clips from documentaries, and look at visual art. Stephanie also invites community experts, such as the 11th-grade science teacher and the leader of a local nonprofit.

Though the textbook does not focus heavily on the environmental movement, Stephanie places this movement within a larger historical context, from its beginnings during industrialization, to social action campaigns in the 1960s and 1970s, to today's political conversation on climate change. Because she knows that her students excel when their understanding is "brought home," the unit culminates in students designing a plan of action that would make the school or local community more environmentally sustainable.

Justin's Role as a Middle-School English as a Second Language Teacher

Justin provides push-in ESL services in English-medium eighth-grade math and science classrooms in Los Angeles, California. Justin speaks English and Mandarin Chinese (following 3 years of studying Chinese in Shanghai). His students are speakers of many languages, including Spanish, Cantonese Chinese, Mandarin Chinese, Korean, Mandingo, Tagalog, Vietnamese, and Pular (Fula). The students who speak Fula and Mandingo also speak French, the colonial language. Because there are multiple speakers of Spanish, Cantonese, Mandarin, French, Tagalog, and Vietnamese in this classroom, Justin and the math and science teachers work together to group students according to their home languages and mixed English language abilities.

Although most students in Justin's class have at least one other student with whom they can collaborate to make meaning of the texts, there is great diversity among them, even among those with the same language background. For example, ***Yi-Sheng*** arrived recently from Taiwan. Unlike some of the other students from mainland China, Yi-Sheng has not received any instruction in using Latin script, so she needs lots of writing practice. ***Pablo*** came not from Mexico, the country of origin of most of the Latinx students in the class, but from Argentina, and attended private English after-school classes before coming to Los Angeles. ***Fatoumata*** came from Guinea a year and a half ago. She had not gone to school regularly in Africa, so she struggles with literacy in French, the language of instruction in Guinea. She is not the only Pular-speaking student in Justin's classroom, although West African children in the class often speak to each other in French. ***Danilo*** is from the Philippines and speaks Tagalog. Although he has strong literacy in his home langugage, it is only emerging in English. There is also only one Korean student in the class, ***Jee-hyae***.

Justin's role as an ESL teacher in the content classrooms has been to support students so that they could meet the demands of the California CCSS and the California ELD Standards. He often obtains supplementary written material in the languages of the students and brings it to class. He uses Google Translate to write worksheet instructions in the students' languages. Justin also encourages students to use iPads to look up words and translate passages, and he often uses the iPad to make himself understood in students' languages. Because Jee-hyae is the only Korean student in the class, Justin spends lots of time using Google Translate, trying to make the material accessible to her. He also makes sure to help her engage in translanguaging on her own, telling her to use her intrapersonal inner speech to brainstorm, prewrite, and annotate texts in Korean. Though Justin won't understand what Jee-hyae writes, he makes it clear that the language she brings with her is useful and necessary to her learning and her development of English. Justin also often seeks help from other Korean-speaking students in the school. Because students in this classroom often write in their home languages, Jee-hyae has discovered that she knows some of the Chinese characters the Cantonese and Mandarin speakers use because she learned some of them in her Korean school.

For Justin, the main purpose of opening up a translanguaging space is to be able to assess and document what his students know about math and science. For example, Pablo and Jee-hyae have a great grasp of the math and science content, although they cannot show what they do know through English only. This is very different from the situation of Fatoumata, for whom the English language is not the only thing holding her back from comprehending the math and science content.

INSTRUCTIONAL REASONS FOR TRANSLANGUAGING

The translanguaging pedagogy put forward in this book is purposeful and strategic. In the translanguaging classrooms profiled in this chapter, Carla, Stephanie, and Justin had *four instructional reasons* for creating a translanguaging space in their classrooms. Three of these reasons—*to scaffold, to assess or document*, and *to transform*—were originally proposed by Sánchez et al. (2017) to extend the rigid language-specific boundaries of many dual-language bilingual education programs in the United States. We have added a fourth reason—*to deepen understandings*—as an important instructional consideration for teachers of bilingual students. The following list outlines each of these four instructional reasons for creating translanguaging spaces.

1. *To scaffold* instruction and provide support to individual students. The teachers know which students need the lessons scaffolded and for what purposes, as well as when to provide the scaffold and when not to. For example, Carla often provides newcomers to English with a text in Spanish so that they can engage with the lesson. Other times, she provides them with videos to offer more contextualization. These uses of translanguaging can be seen as **translanguaging rings**, that is, lifesaver rings that are put on individual students and that are taken off when they can navigate the communicative waters of the classroom without such assistance.

2. *To assess or document* what students know and can do. Especially with emergent bilinguals, it is often not possible to distinguish what content they know when they are being asked to perform with language practices and features that are new to them. For example, for Justin to evaluate Pablo's understandings of mathematical concepts, he must enable Pablo's use of translanguaging so that he can show his mathematical understanding. Without this translanguaging space, Justin would have no idea of Pablo's content knowledge.

3. *To deepen understandings.* To truly engage with texts in one language, bilingual students must bring their whole being and all their experiences—including their language practices—into this endeavor. For example, Stephanie often groups students with different language practices at the same table so that they can discuss texts that are encoded in one language with their entire language repertoire. In so doing, students can make meaning of the texts for themselves. At the same time, in exchanging their individual meanings, they are deepening and expanding the meaning of texts for the entire classroom.

4. *To transform* individual and classroom subjectivities. For instance, when Stephanie has students listen to each other and use their full multimodal repertoire, as well as when she acknowledges her students' strengths and potential, she engages in transforming the subjectivities of students who have previously been identified as inferior. As individual students' subjectivities are transformed, the classroom space itself is transformed. Students develop strong relationships with each other, and their increasing sense of belonging in this classroom transforms their potential as agentive beings able to learn, succeed, and work for a more equitable and inclusive society.

For teachers, the reasons for creating a translanguaging space have a special connection to instruction itself. But as we will see in Chapter 2, there is more to translanguaging than simply improving instruction for bilingual students. The next chapter addresses the broader *social purposes* of translanguaging pedagogy. These purposes go beyond the classroom and are strongly tied to the advancement of social justice, that is, to the transformative potential of translanguaging.

CONCLUSION

It is important to remember that translanguaging classrooms can be of any type—bilingual (dual language or transitional) or English-medium (ESL programs or mainstream classrooms)—and that they can serve young children as well as older students. Translanguaging also can be used by any teacher: bilingual or monolingual teachers; elementary, middle school, or high school teachers; "official" language teachers (English or a language other than English); or content teachers.

The translanguaging classroom is purposeful and strategic, not chaotic and messy. Of course, the ways that teachers design their translanguaging pedagogy will vary according to their own bilingual experiences and relative to the school and community context in which they work. Translanguaging spaces are created by teachers strategically, and sometimes moment-by-moment, as they scaffold instruction, assess and document what students know and can do, deepen understandings of texts, and transform individual and classroom subjectivities. When teachers effectively leverage students' bilingualism for learning, they are ensuring that bilingual students and their resources are at the center of their instruction. By focusing on the bilingual students, they begin to level the educational playing field.

REFLECTION QUESTIONS AND ACTIVITIES

1. What challenges does translanguaging introduce to your understanding of how bilingual students are taught?
2. Compare and contrast Carla's and Stephanie's uses of translanguaging. Why do you think those differences occurred? You might think about their personal backgrounds, the grade levels they teach, and their classroom contexts.
3. Watch any of the videos referenced earlier in the chapter from the web series "Teaching Bilinguals (Even If You're Not One)." How do different teachers purposefully and strategically make space for students' translanguaging and to what effects?

TAKING ACTION

1. Begin a preliminary profile of a translanguaging classroom. This can be your own classroom, or it can be one that you are focusing on for action-oriented classroom research. Use the profiles from Carla's, Stephanie's, and Justin's classes as models (see Table 1.1).
2. Who are your bilingual students? Choose several bilingual students that together reflect the range of linguistic variation in your class. Describe your understanding of their sociolinguistic histories/practices.
3. Who is the teacher? Describe their sociolinguistic history and practices.
4. What language(s) are used for instructional purpose in the class?
5. What are the content, language, and literacy goals for the instructional program serving these bilingual students?
6. Investigate the type of program for emergent bilinguals implemented in your context. (You can find definitions of different types of programs in the glossary.)
    - What is the official language policy of the program?
    - What content and language development standards are used in the program?
    - Who are the target populations of the program?
    - What are the goals of the program?
    - How is the program structured to meet those goals?
    - How are students performing relative to those goals?

Carla	Stephanie	Justin
Teacher in a 4th-grade dual-language bilingual classroom	Teacher for an 11th-grade social studies class, English-medium	Provides push-in ESL services for English-medium middle school math and science classrooms
Albuquerque, NM	New York, NY	Los Angeles, CA
Instructional Unit: *Cuentos de la tierra y del barrio*	Instructional Unit: *Environmentalism: Then and Now*	Instructional Unit: *Geometry in Our World*
Cuéntame Algo—space for bilingual storytelling dedicated to human experiences, particularly those of el barrio y la tierra		Culminating Project: bilingual children's book explaining a geometric concept
Moisés • Newcomer, emigrated from Mexico two years ago • Emergent bilingual • Developing Spanish and English practices, prefers Spanish Ricardo • Newcomer, recently arrived from Mexico • Emergent bilingual • Speaks Spanish and Mixteco at home Erica • Born in the United States • Speaks some Spanish at home, prefers English Jennifer • Born in the United States • Comfortable with English and Spanish • Has an IEP and is diagnosed as having a learning disability	Noemí • Newcomer, recently emigrated from Ecuador • Emergent bilingual • Strong educational background in Spanish Luis • Newcomer, arrived recently from El Salvador • Emergent bilingual • Inconsistent schooling Mariana • Received most of her education in the United States • Emergent bilingual yet to test out of ELL status (long-term ELL) • Generally uses English at school Eddy • Born in the United States • Experienced bilingual Teresita • Born in the United States • Strong reader and writer in English and Spanish	Yi-Sheng • Newcomer, arrived recently from Taiwan • Emergent bilingual • Has not received any prior instruction in using Latin script, however, her performance in Mandarin is at grade-level Pablo • Born in Argentina • Attended private English after-school classes before coming to Los Angeles Fatoumata • Newcomer, came from Guinea 1.5 years ago • Speaks Pular (Fula) and French • Attended school irregularly, struggles with literacy in French Danilo • Born in the Philippines • Emergent bilingual • Speaks Tagalog • Strong reader and writer in his home language Jee-hyae • Speaks and writes in Korean • Knows some Chinese characters from her education in Korea

2

Translanguaging Classrooms: Transformative Social Purposes

LEARNING OBJECTIVES

After reading this chapter, you will be able to:

- Consider the transformative social purposes of a translanguaging classroom.
- See concrete examples that illustrate the transformative social purposes of translanguaging pedagogy in practice.
- Understand how translanguaging classrooms can serve the overarching purpose of social, racial, and **cognitive justice**.

As explored in the last chapter, the reasons for a translanguaging pedagogy start with improving the instruction of bilingual students, but the purposes for enacting it go beyond the walls of schools. A translanguaging pedagogy is strongly tied to the *advancement of social, racial, and cognitive justice,* that is, to the transformative potential that these practices have to disrupt the power hierarchies and ideologies that construct bilingual speakers as inferior and deficient (García et al., 2021).

Centering bilingual children's linguistic practices in classrooms is not enough. Teachers must understand the relationship between how schools define language (as a system of standard linguistic structures that parallel the ways of speaking of White, middle-class, monolingual people) and racism, sexism, and ableism. Sánchez and García's (2022) *Transformative Translanguaging Espacios* described how translanguaging pedagogies have the potential to reconfigure power, disrupt established knowledge, and develop students' critical consciousness. Based on Freire's concept of conscientização (1970), scholars working on the education of bilingual students have claimed that **critical consciousness**, that is, the ability to reflect and act on their sociopolitical and socioeconomic conditions, is a necessary goal of any bilingual education classroom (Palmer et al., 2019). As Cervantes-Soon (2018) has said, a translanguaging practice may be a way of making visible

> the coloniality of power masked as modernity with all of its systems of racist and heteropatriarchal oppression and the colonial blindness prevalent among most educators, which perpetuates Eurocentrism and settler colonialism as the dominant ideological frameworks of U.S. education. (pp. 865–866)

By including the epistemologies and ways of knowing and languaging of diverse groups other than Eurocentric ones, translanguaging contributes to cognitive justice (Santos, 2018), rendering language practices other than those that correspond to named standardized languages as *also* "appropriate" and "academic."

Because race and language have been co-constructed as categories of exclusion, racialized bilingual students' language practices are often constructed as deficient by "white listening subjects" with institutional privilege. This is what Nelson Flores and Jonathan Rosa (2015) call **raciolinguistic ideologies**. That is, it is not language itself, but social categories, and race in particular, that produce the *perception* of language that is then negatively evaluated. Rather than attempt to remediate the practices of racialized bilinguals, Flores (2020) proposes that what needs remediation are "the listening/reading practices that continue to inform mainstream representations of these practices" (p. 28). Translanguaging pedagogical practices thus engage students in reflecting on the richness of their linguistic repertoire, as they become critically conscious of the reasons why they have been made to feel linguistically inadequate.

In considering the transformative purposes of translanguaging, we do not simply focus on transforming the structural inequalities and histories of exclusion in the education of bilinguals. As Martínez and his colleagues (2022) say, "If we insist on excessively narrow criteria for what counts as 'transformative,' we miss the transformative potential that is reflected in the everyday actions of students and their teachers" (p. 110). Thus, we identify and then see in action how teachers engage in translanguaging in conjunction with the overarching purpose of social, racial, and cognitive justice: by leveraging students' translanguaging for learning, teachers help level the playing field for bilingual students at school. Four elements of this larger purpose are highlighted in this chapter:

1. Supporting students as they engage with and comprehend complex content and texts
2. Providing opportunities for students to develop their linguistic practices for a variety of purposes and contexts, including those deemed academic
3. Supporting students' bilingual identities, socioemotional development, and critical consciousness and disrupting ideologies that render bilingual students as deficient
4. Making space for all students' language practices and ways of knowing, and in so doing building a classroom and society that is inclusive of linguistic, racial, gender, and ability differences

In addition to advancing social, racial, and cognitive justice, these four translanguaging purposes work together to advance bilingual students' sense of self, their racial and critical consciousness, as well as their participation in building a more inclusive classroom and society.

To understand how teachers enact these *critical* translanguaging pedagogies with the goal of building a more socially, racially, and cognitively just society, we return to the translanguaging classrooms of ***Carla***, ***Stephanie***, and ***Justin***, the teachers we introduced in Chapter 1.

> *I call this book my translanguaging bible because it goes beyond language practices to evaluating beliefs and recognizing the role of socioemotional well-being and social justice in the translanguaging classroom. The in-service teachers in our program constantly "feel the pressure" of following a "traditional" language separation approach. Still, by embracing translanguaging, they recognize that their students should not leave their identities behind and have become comfortable with linguistic flexibility. These teachers advocate for incorporating students' whole linguistic repertoires and experiences in their classrooms. They see translanguaging as an ally to ensure their students' voices are front and center in their contexts.*
>
> —*Dr. Sandra Rodriguez-Arroyo, Associate Professor, ESL/Bilingual Education, University of Nebraska Omaha*

SUPPORTING STUDENTS AS THEY ENGAGE WITH COMPLEX CONTENT AND TEXTS

When we make space for students to use all the linguistic resources they have developed to maneuver and navigate their way through complex content, myriad learning opportunities open up. Rather than watering down our instruction, which risks oversimplification and robs students of opportunities to engage in productive grappling with texts and content, translanguaging better enables us to teach complex content, which in turn helps students learn more successfully.

Moll (2013) describes the importance of working with bilingual students in what he calls the **bilingual zone of proximal development**, in which assistance is offered to students bilingually to mediate their learning and stretch their performance. As we will see, there are many ways of doing this. Students can work in home language groups to solve difficult problems or analyze a complex text. They can talk to one another about content using their own language practices in ways that help them better understand that content. Because learners develop knowledge *interpersonally*, it is important for them to enter into relationships with others whose language repertoire overlaps with theirs so that they can deeply understand the classroom texts. Knowledge is also developed *intrapersonally*, as students try out new concepts and new languaging in internal dialogue and private speech. Because bilingual students have a voice that includes their home language practices, they need to be encouraged to draw on all of the resources in their linguistic repertoire for learning.

Unfortunately, we don't often find languages other than English being used as resources for learning challenging content and engaging with complex texts in U.S. classrooms serving bilingual students. Instead, teachers generally tell students to only use English; bilingual students (particularly emergent bilingual students) often learn that only English counts. This is especially the case for Spanish-speaking students who are told "speak English," "don't speak Spanish"; "think in English," "don't think in Spanish." As a result, Spanish-speaking Latinx students often learn to see their cultural and linguistic practices only as home and community practices that are not to be used in academic environments. In so doing, bilingual Latinx students are silenced, using only part of their linguistic repertoire and accessing only a small percentage of the adults, peers, and texts that are important to them in acquiring content knowledge. Leveraging translanguaging can help bilingual students overcome this silence and engage with and understand complex content and texts.

Schools must find ways of ensuring that all students, not just those whose language practices align with those used in school, understand challenging content and texts. Translanguaging enables educators to more equitably provide opportunities for students to engage with complex material, regardless of language practices. In this way, translanguaging at school is inextricably linked with social and **racial justice**. For example, in a lesson from the Environmentalism: Then and Now unit that Stephanie designed for her 11th-grade English-medium class, students were asked to analyze statistics about air pollution and asthma, issues that disproportionately affect Latinx, Black Americans, and other residents of urban areas. They were also asked to make a connection to the previous day's lesson on the Clean Air Act of 1970. Stephanie included statistics about asthma rates among Latinx, as well as the map in Figure 2.1, which illustrates which counties did not meet air pollutant standards.

After analyzing the statistics and the map, Stephanie asked students, organized into small groups, to come up with some kind of connection—how did these two pieces of data tell a story about the issue? Although the official language of instruction was English, Stephanie told students that they could discuss the statistics, the map, and the answers to her question using all the resources they had in their repertoire; that is, they could use all their language practices as well as other multimodal practices that are used in communication, such as gestures and drawing. They were also told they could write their responses in their own English and/or their own Spanish. She also told students they were expected to share with the whole class. This vignette shows us what happened next:

After examining the map and discussing it with his group, Luis, who recently came to the United States from El Salvador, shared in Spanish with the whole class that "las áreas oscuras están cerca de ciudades como Nueva York y Los Ángeles. Muchos Latinos viven en esas ciudades." [The dark areas are near cities like New York and Los Angeles. A lot of Latinx live in those cities.] Mariana, who was in Luis's group, translated, adding, "Yes, Latinos, and also African Americans live in the dark areas on the map. Like in New York and Los Angeles." Some students nodded, and others wrote down the comment in

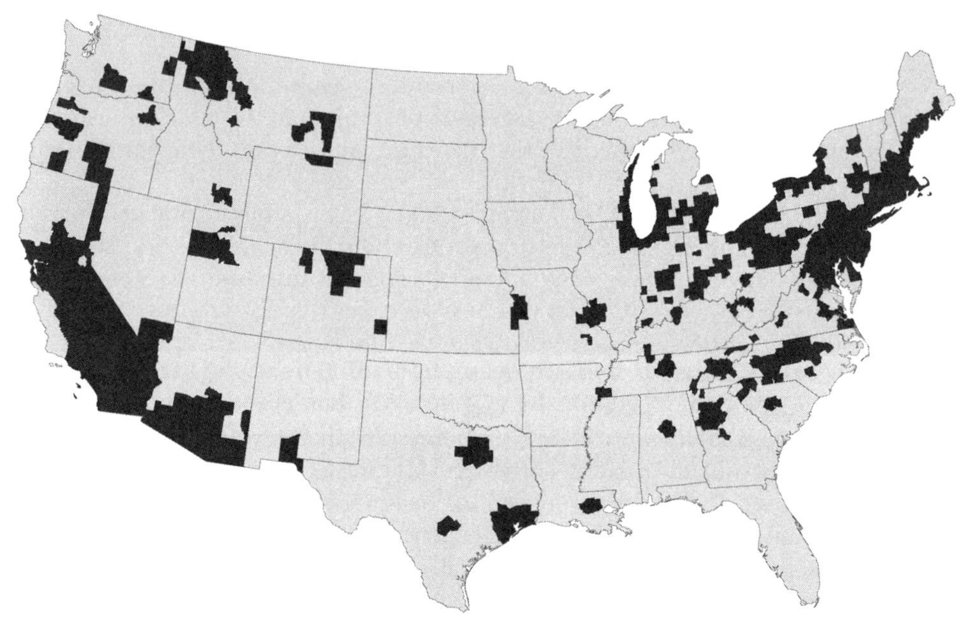

Based on U.S. EPA data as of April 15, 2004.

Figure 2.1. Shows counties in the United States that do not meet air pollutant standards.

Spanish or English next to their own in their notebooks. Eddy added in English that "cities have more pollution than other places." Stephanie then summed up the two comments in English, restating, "It sounds like what you're saying is that if most Latinx and African Americans live in cities, and cities have more air pollution than rural or suburban areas, that this might be a cause of increased asthma in Latinx and African Americans." Students nodded and voiced their agreement.

The kind of linguistic flexibility we see here—using all the students' language practices to discuss, negotiate, and finally write down connections; sharing out their learning in both languages—helped all of the students in Stephanie's classroom engage with texts, synthesize a complex issue, and demonstrate their learning. It also helped them dig into and demonstrate sophisticated understandings of social and racial injustices. As we can see from the students' comments, the translanguaging they had done in groups allowed them to access the content and underlying social phenomena, despite the fact that, for example, Luis was a less experienced English user than Eddy or Mariana. Without translanguaging, which was both an explicit part of Stephanie's instructional design and a natural occurrence among students in their small groups, this kind of intellectually rich conversation would not have taken place.

Carla also uses translanguaging to engage her bilingual students with complex content and texts. However, because an important goal of Carla's instruction is biliteracy, translanguaging in her classroom looks quite different from what we saw in Stephanie's class. During the translanguaging space that Carla calls Cuéntame Algo, students engage in studies of Latinx bilingual authors who use translanguaging in order to make bilingual experiences and characters come to life. Students are encouraged to use all their language practices, which include English, Spanish, and sometimes Indigenous languages, role playing, and drawing, to discuss and make meaning of these stories. Sometimes texts are chosen with English as the main language, but other times Spanish is the main language of the text. As students engage with texts in one language, the reading of the text becomes multilingual and multicultural because students bring their life experiences to the reading. Besides reading and discussing, students are encouraged to design texts (orally and in writing) that reflect the dynamic bilingual language use of communities, both when they communicate among themselves and when they communicate with others who may not share their language practices.

For example, in a lesson from her unit on Cuentos de la tierra y del barrio, Carla and her students used the Cuéntame Algo space to do a read-aloud and shared reading of *Three Wise Guys: Un Cuento de Navidad* by Sandra Cisneros:

CARLA READ EN VOZ ALTA:

> The big box came marked *do not open till xmas*, but the mamá said not until the Day of the Three Kings. Not until Día de los Reyes, the sixth of January, do you hear? That is what the mamá said exactly, only she said it all in Spanish. Because in Mexico where she was raised, it is the custom for boys and girls to receive their presents on January sixth, and not Christmas, even though they were living on the Texas side of the river now. Not until the sixth of January.

Carla engaged students in telling her about el *Día de los Reyes*. Some of the students did so in English, some in Spanish, and some in both languages.

To get students to engage with the text in a deeper, more nuanced way, she set forth the following activity:

Carla took a large sheet of chart paper and drew la corriente del Río Grande. On one side she wrote a sentence the author had written in English. She then asked the groups to translate into Spanish what the author would have said if she were on the Mexican side of the Río Grande. While they worked, one group grew louder. Carla asked what the matter was, and one of them said, "Maestra, es que mi familia on the other side also speaks English. And on this side también hablamos español." A whole class discussion then ensued about bilingual language practices along the U.S.–Mexico border and when and how to use them.

Rather than stop with simple comprehension of the story, the shared reading of this class was the jumping-off point for students' engagement with Cisneros's text. Carla's explicit focus on the language of the book, and how different contexts and characters use different language practices, helped students connect with the story on a much deeper level. Carla also tapped into students' bilingualism, asking them to translate sentences from the book from one language to the other. This not only helps students with the close reading of a text but also helps them to learn new vocabulary and make connections between their linguistic practices. Carla encourages students not to produce a literal translation, but to transform the text as they render it in the other language.

When students came to the realization that their familia on both sides of the border spoke both languages, they began a larger, critical conversation about language practices in borderlands like Texas. This connection and intellectual exchange would not have been possible without the translanguaging that students experienced in the Cuéntame Algo space. Similar to Stephanie's lesson, Carla's explicit use of translanguaging helps her students engage more deeply with a text, but it also helps them develop critical consciousness. By introducing the two languages within geographical and national borders, Carla moves her students to recognize that named languages, like English and Spanish, belong to people who use them as part of their own repertoire and not to nation-states.

Providing Opportunities for Students to Develop Linguistic Practices for a Variety of Purposes and Contexts

"Academic language" is a term we encounter over and over again in schools. Following Valdés (2017) and others, we wish to reframe this term. What some call "academic language" is simply one of many forms of languaging that schools have decided are necessary for academic success. Not surprisingly, it usually reflects the practices of White middle-class speakers. It is important to remind ourselves, though, that bilingual students' own language practices are *also* "academic." Translanguaging can help extend students' existing repertoire and develop the types of linguistic practices that schools require for success on academic measures. For example, translanguaging supports bilingual students' ability to use language to gather, comprehend, evaluate, synthesize, and report on information and ideas and to use text-based evidence, as many of the language standards require. Translanguaging also helps students develop the ability to use language to persuade, explain, and convey real or imaginary experience. Because translanguaging requires collaboration, it also bolsters students' ability to use language socially through cooperative tasks, another important language standard.

Encouraging students to use all the features of their language repertoire, including lexical (words), syntactic (grammar), and discourse (larger chunks of text that hang together as a unit) features, gives them "hooks" on which to "hang" new linguistic features. When adding new linguistic features to students' repertoire, translanguaging can help students make connections to the practices they already use, ask deep questions, and practice and play with language. Translanguaging helps teachers understand that students' own local language practices are also academic and that they are simply helping them add another set of **language features** and practices to their growing, *already academic* repertoire.

When translanguaging is not allowed in schools, bilingual students are placed at a disadvantage because they are assessed on only a part of their linguistic repertoire and are taught in ways that do not fully leverage their language resources. Furthermore, the new language features that bilingual students learn at school do not always become part of their own linguistic repertoire, continuing to represent a "second" language that belongs to others. Thus, this translanguaging purpose is also linked to social and racial justice because it creates the space for fair educational and assessment practices for bilingual students and all racialized students—without the linguistic prejudice that accompanies accepting only the linguistic features of so-called standard English.

The following example from Stephanie's lesson on air pollution illustrates how she and her students use translanguaging to strengthen students' linguistic practices for the purpose of analyzing statistics. The lesson focuses on asthma rates among Latinx, specifically Puerto Ricans.

Stephanie displayed the following statistics and asked one student to read them aloud:

- Puerto Rican Americans have 2 times the asthma rate of the overall Hispanic population.
- Hispanics are 30 percent more likely to visit the hospital for asthma, as compared to non-Hispanic Whites.
- Puerto Rican children are 3.2 times more likely to have asthma, as compared to non-Hispanic Whites.
- Hispanic children are 40 percent more likely to die from asthma, as compared to non-Hispanic Whites.

After the student read the statistics, Stephanie checked the class's comprehension of the English used. Luis said, "Maestra no entiendo" (and pointed to the phrase "more likely"). Stephanie asked students to translate it for Luis, and this turned into a heated discussion. Some translated it as "más me gusta" [I like it more], others as "más como" [more like]. Finally, Stephanie asked Luis to use the translating app on a class iPad, and he immediately came back with "más probable." Stephanie annotated the text with this Spanish phrase. Now all students in the class knew not only what it meant in English, but also how to say it in Spanish.

This simple classroom vignette illustrates two important points. First, bilingual students may think they know the meanings of a word or phrase (e.g., "more likely") in a field-specific text because they know the meanings of each of the words, but these meanings may not be appropriate in this specific context. This vignette also illustrates ways that students' existing language practices are valued and channeled into learning new practices. Because Stephanie is not a Spanish speaker, she encourages her students to help one another and to use resources such as translation apps to better understand this and other texts in English. By annotating an English text with a Spanish phrase, Stephanie is also helping students grow as bilingual and biliterate people, even if she herself is not bilingual and this is not a "bilingual" class.

Furthermore, Stephanie encourages her non-Latinx Black students to think about differences between the ways they use language across contexts. She integrates hip-hop into her lessons and compares songs to written social studies texts that students have to read. Stephanie observes that her English-speaking Black students are also picking up some Spanish words, while her Latinx students are learning about features of Black Language and of Jamaican Creole, spoken by some of the Anglophone Caribbean students in the class. Stephanie's time and focus on language in her content-area classroom demonstrate her belief that teaching students to value their language practices and leverage them as they add features to their repertoire that are used for academic purposes is as important as learning social studies content.

Supporting Students' Bilingual Identities, Socioemotional Development, and Critical Consciousness and Disrupting Ideologies of Deficiency

Translanguaging fosters bilingual students' identities and socioemotional development. First, translanguaging enables all bilingual students to participate actively in daily classroom life. For many students whose ways of languaging differ from the status quo ideal of those considered "native speakers," classroom learning can be difficult and alienating. By making space for students to language on their own terms and participate fully in instructional conversations and work, we are modeling the kind of active participation needed for the creation of a more just world. Second, translanguaging helps students to see themselves and their linguistic and cultural practices as valuable, rather than as lacking. By teaching students to see their language practices as part of a whole, contingent, and ever-changing performance, we are challenging a monolingual version of society and breaking the socially constructed fronteras that stand between languages and that create hierarchies of power. Translanguaging pedagogical practices disrupt ideologies that assign inferiority to those who are linguistically or racially different or those who have different abilities.

We return to Stephanie's "Environmentalism: Then and Now" unit to see this translanguaging purpose in action. To help students build background on the topic of air pollution, Stephanie started the day's lesson by showing students a public service announcement (PSA) about asthma. The PSA, which ran about 30 seconds, depicted a young Latinx male suffering from an asthma attack. Stephanie played the clip twice, once in English and once in Spanish, and asked students to share any questions or connections they had regarding the video clip:

Eddy shared in English that his brother had really bad asthma and has had to go to the hospital several times. Luis jumped in, saying, "Me too! My brother . . . él . . . in El Salvador. . . ." Sensing that Luis was having trouble continuing in English, Stephanie asked him to finish his sentence in Spanish. Luis continued in Spanish, explaining that his brother, who still lives in El Salvador, worked construction and that the dust from the worksite gave him asthma attacks. Stephanie listened, and when Luis was finished, she asked another student in Luis's group, Mariana, to translate what Luis said. Though Mariana understands Spanish, she has told Stephanie that she feels more comfortable speaking English. However, she is a very competent translator, a skill for which, as Stephanie knows, she is often praised by her family.

In this short excerpt, Stephanie's comfort with linguistic flexibility and translanguaging can be interpreted as an act of **social justice** and a way of supporting her students' socioemotional growth. To understand this, consider a different scenario, one that has occurred in far too many English-medium classrooms: Luis, stymied by his emerging English practice, gets frustrated and falls silent, putting his head down on his desk. Other students who are not comfortable sharing in English stare out the window, doodle, whisper to one another, and sneak looks at their phones underneath their desks. And, as can be seen in many schools and classrooms across the United States, these same students are further marginalized when they experience punitive discipline for their disengagement at disproportional rates. Instead of this scene, Stephanie's classroom is one of engagement and shared learning. All students are encouraged to use all their languages to share their ideas, which helps Stephanie understand what they know and can do. In addition, students' out-of-school lives—their stories and skills, such as Mariana's experience as a translator—are honored and drawn on to learn new content. Translanguaging, then, becomes a way of working against the kind of classroom experiences that render too many students silent. By encouraging them to use all their languages and bring forth their life experiences, educators enable students to be themselves, help one another, and succeed academically.

The African American students in Stephanie's class also relate well to the PSA. Many join in the discussion and share their families' struggles with asthma. Together, the Black and Latinx students in Stephanie's class voice their awareness of the toxins in the neighborhoods where they live. They start questioning why. They are developing their critical consciousness, their understanding that there are social, political, and ideological aspects to the content (and language) they are learning. This is the beginning not only of a research project on environmental toxins where students worked through English and Spanish, but also of a letter-writing campaign to their elected officials, in which students used their voices to request information and promote change. In this way, translanguaging pedagogy reaches beyond the classroom to touch those who might take action to listen differently.

We now return to Carla's bilingual class. After reading the story *Three Wise Guys: Un Cuento de Navidad*, Carla asks students to work on translating a piece of the story from English into Spanish: "The mother in the story doesn't speak English. Write the story in a way that the mother would understand." Once student groups had worked together on translating, Carla told them:

> Reflect on the language practices of the characters in the story—the Spanish-speaking mother; the bilingual children, Rubén and Rosalinda; and the father, who speaks English but cannot read it. As you discuss, feel free to use features from both English and Spanish to recapture the bilingual voice of the family in the story and to integrate your own language practices, as the narrator of the story has done.

Through the translation activity and the ensuing discussion, Carla encourages bilingual students' use of translanguaging to make meaning, to develop a bilingual voice in writing, and to deepen their understanding about how all their language practices work together. To this end, Carla has students analyze the ways in which English and Spanish are used in a literary piece written primarily in English, and she has her students practice translation. Through these activities, students learn how translanguaging and translating are transformative acts, changing not only the text but also the text's ability to engage others and give them voice. The students' translation of part of the text into Spanish was not merely an academic exercise; it enabled the students to imagine and hear the Spanish-language voice of the mother who does not say anything in the story itself. Thus, translanguaging allows us to hear voices that may have been excluded. It gives students an understanding of how language use is tied to power, how its use is often employed to produce and reproduce social and racial inequalities, and how bilingual students can rewrite texts to include diverse contributions and perspectives.

Making Space for All Students' Bilingualism and Ways of Knowing and Building an Inclusive Classroom

In addition to improving teaching and learning, translanguaging contributes to the creation of a new kind of classroom, one that takes dynamic bilingualism and bilingual understandings of language as the norm, putting bilingual people and people with linguistic, racial, gender, and ability differences at the center. Shifting focus like this makes space for students to learn and make choices about language that help them traverse the uneven waters of communication in our society. Rather than viewing languages according to rigid power hierarchies, translanguaging can help our students understand languages as practices that are used in different social contexts for different purposes.

Students learn that language use is not neutral but regulated by different social groups for their own purposes. These translanguaging spaces—the intentional moments when teachers allow students to use their entire language repertoire—can help all students become more aware of their expressive potential and how and why we make choices about language. When students gain this kind of critical awareness, they can challenge linguistic hierarchies and rules and see the world through their creative and critical translanguaging perspectives.

Thus, translanguaging makes possible the educational inclusion of all students' ways of knowing and languaging. In giving expression to other ways of being and knowing, translanguaging has the potential to build a more socially just world. Because translanguaging classrooms are inclusive of not only languaging but also life practices, students feel comfortable displaying racial, ability, and gender differences (see Cioè-Peña's 2022 work connecting translanguaging and Universal Design for Learning, and Julián Delgado Lopera's TED talk in the box for connections between language and gender/sexuality). Teachers then work to acknowledge, value, and use these differences through practices that empower all students.

> The social purposes of translanguaging align with broader social and political purposes for inclusion. Writer and activist Julián Delgado Lopera, in their TEDxSoMa talk, draws important connections between the creative linguistic mixing of both bilingual and queer communities. Delgado-Lopera powerfully aligns struggles against "standard" ways of languaging with struggles against gender binaries and heteronormativity. You can access their talk via the Brookes Download Hub.

For example, during a different day's Cuéntame Algo, Carla and her students read *Lluvia de plata* by Sara Poot Herrera, a story about Mariana, a young woman who visits the Tarahumara region in Chihuahua, Mexico, and experiences a cultural and language transformation. To help them better comprehend the story, Carla had students place illustrations onto a backdrop that she created of la Barranca del Cobre (Copper Canyon) overlooking la sierra Tarahumara.

Moisés placed his illustration card on to the backdrop and shared the following:

"Esta parte que leí me gusta porque los trabajadores que construyeron el ferrocarril le llamaban al tren que venía de Kansas a Chihuahua 'si te cansas.' Yo creo que no sabían cómo decir Kansas, entonces para recordar cómo decirlo solamente mencionaban 'si te cansas.'" [This part that I read I liked because the workers that built the railroad would call the train coming from Kansas to Chihuahua "si te cansas" ("if you get tired"). I think they did not know how to say Kansas, so to remember how to say it they would mention "si te cansas."] Everyone started laughing.

Moisés explained how railroad workers adapted the word Kansas [/kǽɴzəs/] to a Spanish word that was similar in pronunciation, cansas [/kansas/]. Although other students laughed, some immediately joined in: "En mi casa nosotros usamos este tipo de palabra . . ." [We use this type of word at home.] And another, "Sí es cierto; he oído algo así también en mi casa." [Yes, it's true; I've heard this also at home.] Some students acknowledged that at home Spanish was often used to remember the sounds of English words. The teacher asked how this was so. Jennifer, the student diagnosed with a learning disability, immediately shared that the Spanish word gel [pronounced "hel"] for hair gel was used by her mother to remember how to pronounce the English word help. Others shared that the Spanish word flor [flower] was used to help recall the pronunciation of the English word floor.

The play-on-word jokes, or chistes, that emerge from words that sound nearly the same in Spanish and English are more than just entertaining; finding a word that creates a chiste takes linguistic and cultural knowledge *across* languages and cultures. The students found the translanguaging moment amusing, yet the humorous moment reflected the complexity of their understanding of language use across contexts and nations. Further, Carla invited this complex understanding into the classroom as a strength and asset on which all her students could draw. By using a text that is culturally and linguistically relevant and that builds on students' translanguaging practices, Carla allowed her students to hear and see themselves and their communities in the text and feel safe enough to experiment with and explore translanguaging. This also permits a student like Jennifer, who has been schooled through approaches aimed at remediating her perceived disabilities, to contribute meaningfully to classroom learning. In so doing, Jennifer feels confident and empowered.

The earlier discussion of Carla and her class's shared reading of *Three Wise Guys: Un Cuento de Navidad* illustrated how a focus on bilingualism and bilingual language practices can foster students' **critical metalinguistic awareness**. In the next vignette, we see how Carla's focus on author Sandra Cisneros's translanguaging helped students engage with a complex text by drawing on their own bilingualism and ways of knowing.

Students continued to read the story beyond what Carla had read out loud in guided reading groups. Carla asked them to pay careful attention to the words Cisneros had chosen to include in Spanish—chicharras (insects), urracas (black/white birds), comadre (woman relative). In their groups, they reflected on and discussed why these words and not others were rendered in Spanish and why the author might have made these choices. Carla then instructed the students to select other words they would have rendered in Spanish if they had been the author.

As bilingual people, Carla and her students have the ability to discuss Cisneros's translanguaged text in a more nuanced, complex way. By drawing their attention to the author's language choices, Carla helps her students grow more critical about language, which in turn helps them grow as bilingual thinkers and writers themselves. The students commented that comadre was probably rendered in Spanish because it is a word from their own culture and community. A discussion ensued about why Cisneros had used urracas and chicharras. One student immediately said, "Because of the *rrrr*" [referring to the rolling double r in Spanish]. They then explored other words in Spanish that have a double r. They looked through the text to see if there were other words in English that would have an equivalent in Spanish that had a double r. This kind of critical metalinguistic analysis of a translanguaged text also demonstrates to students that bilingual languaging is rich and intentional, not messy or impure. When they discussed Cisneros's translanguaging, Carla and her class were also reaffirming their own translanguaging and drawing on their bilingualism to understand that they, too, can produce different texts.

We now turn to Justin's ESL classroom. By focusing not on English and other named languages per se, but on the ways that students use language to make sense of his instruction meant to be in English, Justin builds an inclusive ESL classroom. Students classified as English language learners are often segregated in bilingual classrooms or English as a second language classrooms where they only interact with each other. This traditionally leaves out Black students who are not imagined as bilingual. Even in dual-language bilingual programs that purport to include learners of languages other than English, there are very few Black students (for more on the experiences of Black students in bilingual settings, see Frieson, 2022). The same can be said of world language programs (Anya, 2021).

As the ESL teacher, Justin structures a translanguaging classroom in collaboration with the math/science content teacher with whom he works. They understand that a translanguaging classroom must be inclusive of differences. Thus, for example, they group the students classified as ELLs along with other English-speaking students, including Black and Asian students. In the interactions that occur in this translanguaging classroom during one science lesson, ***Pablo***, the recently arrived Argentinean student, becomes the science expert. Pablo is comfortable with the equipment used in science experiments, while many of his other classmates are not. One day the class is working on a science experiment to see which substances would affect the rate at which ice cubes melt. Pablo understands the science concepts involved in trying out different types of ingredients—salt, sugar, sand. But he does not fully understand the content of what is written on the sheet that was distributed to the class or what he has to do. He also cannot write answers to the questions in English.

The two Black English-speaking students and the Chinese student in Pablo's group are excited about Pablo's grasp of the science concepts, since they do not understand what they are expected to do. Pablo takes the lead by showing them. The other students then try to explain the questions in the worksheet to Pablo by reading them in English. When Pablo does not understand, the other students gesture and draw as Pablo looks up some words in Google Translate. They then write the answers to the questions individually. Although the class is supposed to be in English, Pablo answers the questions mostly in Spanish, using some of the new words he has learned in English. When the students share their work, they are surprised to see that Ming Tao, who speaks English, has used some Chinese characters to remember what the group read together. They all become interested in the Chinese writing system, and Ming Tao explains that he only knows a little, since he only went to a Saturday Chinese school for 4 years when he was in elementary school. Pablo then says, "I also know a little English," and the two Black students respond, "And we only know a little Spanish, and no Chinese!" They then ask Pablo to teach them some words in Spanish. They all know agua, and they remark on the similarity of sal to salt, as Carlos teaches them to say "azúcar." One of the Black students immediately says, "Azúcar, like Celia Cruz." This causes much laughter and camaraderie, as Justin comes over to the group to make sure they are on task.

In this translanguaging ESL/content classroom Justin understands that for students to learn, he must make space for their language practices and ways of knowing. But his translanguaging pedagogical practices have a higher purpose—to integrate classroom linguistic and cultural practices so that all students are included. This enables students like Pablo to contribute to classroom life *and* develop a secure sense of self. Justin does not see his task as a push-in ESL teacher as simply to work with students classified as ELLs. He works collaboratively with the math/science teacher to make sure that all students are also working collaboratively across language, racial, gender, ability, and cultural groups. The purpose of this translanguaging classroom is to make sure that everyone is included.

CONCLUSION

While Chapter 1 considered the *instructional* purposes for translanguaging, this chapter explored the *social* purposes for translanguaging in classrooms and schools. These two sets of purposes are highly related; by making space in instruction for students to show what they know and can do using *all* of their language and meaning-making resources, teachers also make space for students to participate fully in school while also honing the kind of critical consciousness and strong bilingual identities that will enable them to do so on their own terms. In Chapter 3, we step back from the purposes of translanguaging and consider translanguaging itself, as a lens for understanding language, as a norm in bilingual homes and communities, and as a framework for teaching bilingual students in classrooms.

REFLECTION QUESTIONS AND ACTIVITIES

1. What are the four transformative social purposes of translanguaging classrooms? Why are they important?
2. What is critical consciousness and why is it an important purpose in any translanguaging classroom?

3. How do raciolinguistic ideologies influence the ways we often perceive bilingual speakers? Do you have any of your own experiences with raciolinguistic ideologies?
4. Why is transformation of social inequities a most important purpose of translanguaging classrooms? How does this transformation operate?

TAKING ACTION

1. Explore your own school community. Identify specific social and racial issues that your school community faces, and how (or if) they are being addressed. Evaluate the challenges and successes of how these are being addressed.
2. With a small group of peers, work together to identify raciolinguistic ideologies that shape elements of your context (e.g., policies, practices, ways of discussing bilingual students). Brainstorm how you might disrupt and transform these raciolinguistic ideologies that manifest in your context.
3. Analyze the textbook(s) or other materials you are using for instruction and identify whether a western universal knowledge system is being assumed. Identify how it is that this results in cognitive injustice for some students.

3

Language Practices and the Translanguaging Classroom Framework

LEARNING OBJECTIVES

After reading this chapter, you will be able to:

- Consider the uses of language through the lens of translanguaging.
- Explain what it means for a bilingual student to draw on the full features of their linguistic repertoire.
- Compare and contrast the notions of dynamic bilingualism and additive bilingualism.
- Understand the translanguaging corriente and what it represents.
- Use the translanguaging classroom framework to explain how the translanguaging corriente sets learning and teaching in motion.
- Begin to identify evidence of the translanguaging corriente in your context.

This chapter introduces the translanguaging classroom framework, which educators can use to understand translanguaging classrooms like ***Carla***'s, ***Stephanie***'s, and ***Justin***'s. First, however, we must think about how language is used by different speakers in context. When looking closely at the actual language practices of bilinguals, variation, dynamism, and complexity are revealed. The flow of students' bilingual practices, called in this book the **translanguaging corriente**, is at work in all aspects of classroom life. For example, when bilingual students engage with texts, they do so while leveraging all their linguistic and other meaning-making resources such as gestures, role play, and drawing, even if those texts are rendered only in English or only in Spanish or another language. When bilingual students write or create something new, they may filter certain features of their linguistic repertoires to create the *product,* but the *process* will always involve their translanguaging.

When we view students' bilingualism in this way—as a fluid, ever-present current that they tap into to make meaning—we perceive bilingual students differently. This shift in perspective opens new possibilities for teaching and assessing bilingual students. The translanguaging classroom framework proposed in this chapter helps teachers imagine translanguaging pedagogical practices that leverage students' **dynamic bilingualism**, that is, their translanguaging, for learning.

REFLECTING ON THE MEANINGS AND USES OF LANGUAGE

School practitioners often think of language solely as the standardized variety that is present in textbooks or used in assessments. We think we teach in "English," or "Spanish" or "Chinese" or "Korean" or "Russian." But the reality of language is a lot more complex than names of languages indicate.

Think, for example, of how language is used when speaking, reading, talking to a family member, disciplining a child, teaching a class, or working with an individual student. The ways we use language are different, and the features (the words, sounds, word order, etc.) of "English" or "Spanish" or "Chinese" vary depending on the context of use.

Think also of the language practices of different 6-year-old students, or of high school students with diverse experiences. Their so-called "English" or "Spanish" or "Chinese" would vary, even among students in the same age group. Students use language differently, depending on who they are, what they are doing, what they are feeling, and with whom they are interacting. Now think of how different groups of English speakers (e.g., African American, British, Texan, South African) or Spanish speakers (e.g., Mexican, Cuban, Puerto Rican, Peruvian) use the "same" language. Their so-called "English" or "Spanish" would also be very different, reflecting the language practices used in their communities and families. It is important to remember that the linguistic features used by monolingual speakers of any language are never exactly the same. That is, everyone uses language differently, even when it is considered the "same" language or "one" variety.

If it cannot be said that there is a single English or Spanish for those who are monolingual, how much more complex is it to think about the language practices of bilinguals? In order to create linguistic environments that nurture all students, it is important to start with this question: how do bilinguals use language?

Although all speakers use language differently, bilinguals have more choices to make because their **language repertoire** includes many more language features. **Language features** include phonemes (sounds), words, morphemes (word forms), nouns, verbs, adjectives, tense systems, pronoun systems, case distinctions, gender distinctions, syntactic rules, and discourse markers (e.g., marking transitions, information structure). Though from a societal point of view bilinguals are said to use two languages, from their own perspective bilingual speakers draw from *one* language repertoire—*their own*. This language repertoire includes linguistic features that are associated *socially* and *politically* with one **named language** or another (English, Spanish, Chinese, etc.) but that exist within, and are thus shaped by, the speakers' own lived context.

This book radically changed my approach to multilingualism and education. It has deepened my understanding of the concept of named languages and empowered me to problematize it. It has opened my eyes to the fact that language has always been about so much more than rules and systems. To work with language is to work with real lives.

—Sarah Campbell, language teacher and teacher educator, Uppsala University, Sweden

One Bilingual Repertoire vs. Two Monolinguals in One

Recall the students who we met in Carla's dual-language bilingual elementary classroom and in Stephanie's English-medium high school classroom. ***Jennifer***, a student in Carla's class, and ***Eddy***, a student in Stephanie's class, were born in the United States, and they speak a variety of Spanish that includes very different features than that of ***Luis*** (Stephanie's class), who recently arrived from El Salvador, or ***Ricardo*** and ***Moisés*** (Carla's class), who recently arrived from Mexico. The Spanish that Jennifer and Eddy speak is said to have features of "English," whereas what Ricardo speaks is said to have features of "Mixteco," an Indigenous language spoken in Mexico and in Ricardo's home.

In Carla's class, Jennifer and Moisés are asked what they like about the school playground. Jennifer replies, "Me encanta por los swings." [I love it because of the swings.] In contrast, Moisés answers, "Me encanta por los columpios." [I love it because of the swings.] For Jennifer, the word "swings" is neither English nor Spanish, although for dictionaries and nations it may be. It is simply part of her language repertoire, the word she uses

Figure 3.1. Depicts the language repertoire of bilinguals. Fn, (linguistic) features.

to communicate with the other bilingual Latinx children with whom she plays on the playground. Jennifer has one language repertoire, as illustrated in Figure 3.1 (upper box), with entwined linguistic features (Fn) that she often uses to make meaning but that countries, schools, dictionaries, and grammar books classify as different languages (Spanish and English in the lower boxes of Figure 3.1). School (and other monolingual contexts) would want her to use only Spanish, or only English, as if she were two monolinguals in one. However, as Grosjean (1982) emphasized, the notion of two monolinguals in one is impossible.

Although Jennifer has learned to distinguish which linguistic features of her repertoire to use in different communicative settings (i.e., when she uses English and when she uses Spanish), she is also capable of languaging with all the features of her repertoire. This occurs often when she speaks with her bilingual family. We can then say that Jennifer has one linguistic repertoire. However, that repertoire, seen from an external sociopolitical perspective, is divided into two named languages. In school, for example, she is expected to perform according to standard definitions of language, and in her bilingual classroom she has to select only those features in her repertoire associated with English during "English time," Spanish during "Spanish time," and suppress the rest. But when she plays and speaks with her bilingual friends, she is free to use her full linguistic repertoire. Seeing bilingualism in this way is very different from traditional concepts of bilingualism.[1]

Dynamic Bilingualism vs. Additive Bilingualism

Traditionally, bilingualism has been described from a monolingual external perspective simply as the addition of a language. Figure 3.2 presents this traditional conceptualization of **additive bilingualism**, in which a second language (L2) is added to a first language (L1), each with its own autonomous and bounded linguistic features.

But Jennifer's bilingualism is not just additive; it is dynamic, the linguistic features of what are considered two languages functioning in interrelationship and adapting to the communicative circumstance at hand (see García, 2009). Jennifer deploys all the features of her entire language repertoire to communicate and make meaning, thus transgressing traditional societal and national definitions of what language should be and the ways in which language should be used.

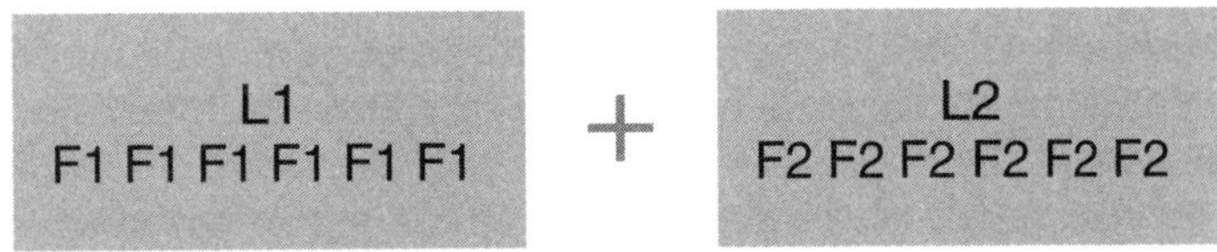

Figure 3.2. Depicts traditional understandings of bilingualism as the sum of two monolingualisms. L1, first language; L2, second language; F1, features of first language; F2, features of second language.

[1]See García and Wei (2014) for further discussion.

Furthermore, Jennifer's bilingualism cannot be understood simply in terms of L1 or L2 languages. Jennifer learned to speak Spanish first because her grandmother raised her and spoke to her in Spanish, but her mother also spoke English to her as she was growing up. Although Jennifer can say that she learned Spanish first, Spanish is not her L1 because she feels more confident in English, uses it more, and identifies with it first. Jennifer's bilingualism is not made up of the simple addition of L1 + L2, but of the dynamic interaction of language features that she uses to communicate appropriately in different situations.

García (2009) conceptualizes students' dynamic bilingualism with the image of a banyan tree, with features that are always interdependent and that together form one intricate communicative repertoire that bilinguals learn to adapt to monolingual contexts. García also uses the image of the all-terrain vehicle to explain how bilinguals use the features of their language repertoires to adapt to different communicative situations. This contrasts with the traditional view of bilingualism, seen as two wheels of a bicycle that are always balanced and move in the same direction.

Rather than thinking about languages as fixed entities with strict boundaries between them, translanguaging extends the potential of bilingualism to all students. Considering language beyond the strict boundaries imposed by institutions means that any student can be included in the translanguaging classroom. This opens space for the inclusion of minoritized English speakers like African Americans, as well as students with disabilities, to develop their bilingualism and expand their linguistic repertoires.

By looking at the ways in which those with language differences deploy their different resources to communicate, instead of focusing on the exclusive use of standardized named languages, translanguaging disrupts the co-construction of race and language that became a tool in colonial processes of domination. Translanguaging disrupts what Walter Mignolo (2000), the decolonial theorist, has called the colonial logic of language and race that maintains the supremacy of some people over others. It reminds us that language is not an independent linguistic structure that speakers *have*. Rather, language is used in human communicative interactions and is entirely semiotic, that is, speakers select language and other multimodal resources to communicate with a listener who then must infer the message.

Translanguaging vs. Code-Switching

Translanguaging refers both to the complex language practices of multilingual individuals and communities and to the pedagogical approaches that draw on them to build the language practices desired in formal school settings. As noted in Chapter 1, Otheguy et al. (2015) have defined translanguaging as "the deployment of a speaker's full linguistic repertoire without regard for watchful adherence to the socially and politically defined boundaries of named languages" (p. 281). From a sociolinguistic perspective, translanguaging differs from two concepts often applied in relation to bilingual students: code-switching and, in the case of bilingual Latinx, "Spanglish."

Code-switching, commonly understood as alternating between different languages, considers the linguistic behavior of bilinguals according to a monolingual norm; it views their languaging as switching back and forth between language codes that are regarded as separate and autonomous. It considers language only from the *external perspective* defined by nation-states and their schools, and it looks at bilinguals' language behavior as if they were two monolinguals in one. In many ways the practices described as "code-switching" align with the translanguaging practices of bilinguals. But because it starts with monolingualism as the norm, this behavior is considered a linguistic violation and is frequently stigmatized.

Translanguaging, however, refers to the ways that bilinguals use their language repertoires, *from their own perspectives,* and not from the perspective of national or standard languages. The language repertoires of bilingual speakers are made up of features that dictionaries, grammar books, and schools put into two categories: in the case of Latinx students, English and Spanish. Of course, bilinguals learn to use the appropriate features according to the context in which they communicate. However, what is important to realize is that, from the speaker's and local community's (i.e., *internal*) perspective, what they deploy in communication is one unitary linguistic repertoire. Taking into account the unitary nature of the linguistic repertoire of bilinguals, the proposed term "multilingual translanguaging" (MacSwan, 2017; 2022) appears to be another way to reposition code-switching and leave intact the notion of languages as produced by nation-states, ultimately excluding the language practices of real people, especially bilinguals.

Whereas the term code-switching focuses on the alternation of named languages, translanguaging refers to the languaging of people who at times have to suppress features of their individual repertoires. Unlike code-switching, which is considered a simple alternation of language codes, translanguaging goes *beyond* named languages (García & Wei, 2014; Wei, 2011). The act of translanguaging is itself transformative, having the potential to infuse creative bilingual meanings into utterances.

For a helpful overview of the distinction between translanguaging and code-switching, watch Dr. Mike Mena's video, "Translanguaging in 15 Minutes." Mena takes Otheguy, García, and Reid's 2015 article and breaks it down in this short, engaging video. You can access the video via the Brookes Download Hub.

The term "Spanglish" is often used to demean and stigmatize the Spanish of U.S. Latinx as "corrupted" Spanish (Otheguy & Stern, 2011). Translanguaging refers instead to bilingual speakers' creative and critical construction and use of interrelated language features that can be used for learning and that teachers can leverage, regardless of the quality of students' performances in one or another named language. Furthermore, translanguaging can also be used to acquire and to learn how to use features that are considered part of standard language practices, which, of course, have *real and material consequences* for all learners.

Several examples of the transformative creativity of bilinguals were displayed in Carla's classroom in Chapter 2—Cisneros's use of the word "comadre," breathing Latinx life into an English language text, and students relating how their parents use the Spanish homonym "gel" to remind them of the English word "help." Many more examples of this transformative creativity are available throughout this book.

TRANSLANGUAGING CORRIENTE

The metaphor of the translanguaging corriente refers to the "current," or flow, of students' dynamic bilingualism that runs through classrooms and schools. It also refers to the sociopolitical flows that interact with bilingual students' ability to leverage their translanguaging overtly to learn. In translanguaging classrooms, bilingual students make use of the translanguaging corriente, either overtly or covertly, to learn content and language in school and to make sense of their complex worlds and identities. When bilingual students work together to carry out an academic task, they negotiate and make meaning by pooling all of their linguistic resources.

Although all bilinguals engage in translanguaging in one way or another, translanguaging pedagogical practices depend on whether the sociopolitical flows are supportive of differences or not (de los Ríos & Seltzer, 2017; Seltzer & de los Ríos, 2021). Sociopolitical ideologies that perceive bilingual students as deficient and bilingualism as the incomplete acquisition of the two languages impede teachers from working with the students' individual translanguaging corriente. The persistence of raciolinguistic ideologies in society is also tied to sociopolitical corrientes, shaping the listeners' perceptions of the language of racialized bodies. For example, in the United States, bilingual programs are now designated as "dual language," pointing to the wish for complete language separation in pedagogy and the notion of separate language competences. In states where educational authorities have recognized translanguaging as a pedagogical possibility, however, teachers are freer to leverage their students' translanguaging.

A current in a body of water is not static; its course both *depends* on features of the landscape and *forms* these features over time. Likewise, the translanguaging corriente highlights the dynamic and continuous movement of language features that are shaped by, but that also have a hand in shaping, the linguistic landscape of the classroom, often defined from a monolingual perspective. Figure 3.3 represents the translanguaging corriente flowing and changing terrain that is traditionally considered "English" or "home language" territory and

Figure 3.3. An image of a river running through a landscape, which serves as a metaphor for translanguaging.

connecting them. From the surface, we see two separate riverbanks, with each side showing distinct features. Depending on the current, however, the riverbanks shift and their features change. And at the river bottom, the terrain is one; the river and its two banks are in fact one integrated whole.

As the translanguaging corriente forms an integrated whole, it allows bilingual students to combine social spaces with language codes that are usually practiced separately. For example, it is often said that Latinx students use Spanish at home and English in school. In reality, however, language use is more fluid. In Latinx homes, some families may speak Spanish; others may speak English; and most speak both. Spanish might be spoken or used while listening to the radio, while English might be used for reading or watching television.

Fluid Language Practices in the Classroom

We find the translanguaging corriente in every classroom that includes bilingual students; of course, the strength of the corriente varies depending on the sociopolitical corriente with which it interacts. The characteristics of the translanguaging corriente in any particular classroom reflect the language repertoires of the bilingual students and their teachers. Therefore, teachers like Carla, Stephanie, and Justin experience the translanguaging corriente differently because their linguistic repertoires and those of their students are diverse. Moreover, the implicit and explicit language policies in bilingual and English-medium classes are different. The corriente is stronger (and more visible) in the bilingual classroom, where the language other than English (LOTE) is also the language of instruction and the ability to use it is an explicit goal and expected student outcome.

Teachers also experience and respond to the translanguaging corriente differently. For example, Carla is bilingual and, like her students, has experienced what it means to suppress some of the features in her linguistic repertoire in academic contexts. She was trained in the traditional dual-language bilingual model, which rigidly separates the two languages used for instructional purposes. As explored in Chapter 1, when Carla learned about the translanguaging corriente, she at first questioned and resisted it. Only later, when she realized that students used their languages flexibly despite her "language policing," did she embrace the corriente and leverage it with great success. Stephanie, on the other hand, speaks a relatively standard variety of English, and the features of her language repertoire, with few exceptions, have rarely been called into question socially or academically. Stephanie does not consider herself bilingual, yet she responded to her students' bilingualism and translanguaging positively from the start. She saw that her students were already using all their linguistic resources to make meaning of the complex social studies content, so she began explicitly building this kind of translanguaging into her instruction. Despite their different experiences with languages and their different contexts, both Carla and Stephanie make use of the translanguaging corriente in instruction and assessment.

In school the lesson might be in English, but Latinx students often speak Spanish to each other, and language features that are considered Spanish may populate their inner speech as they write, read, talk, and think. Because it is always moving, the translanguaging corriente changes the static linguistic landscape that establishes limits on when one language or the other is used and transforms the traditional concept of "a language."

Creative Potential of the Translanguaging Corriente

The translanguaging corriente produces new language practices. For example, in Latin American countries, Spanish is constrained by governmental edicts and official discourses that reflect national histories, with Spanish used in monolingual and monocultural ways. (Although, of course, there are variations in the language features associated with Spanish in different countries.) But in the United States, bilingual Latinx experience the Spanish language in interaction with English and its histories. Thus, the Spanish used in different U.S. communities includes features of what are considered varieties of Spanish (e.g., Cuban, Mexican, Argentinian, Puerto Rican) used by the bilingual Latinx in those communities—interwoven with features of what are considered features of English. Because of the many different histories and ideologies of these bilingual Latinx, their use of language shifts as they mold it to their own intentions in a new context. Language is **semiotic** in nature; that is, it has meaning and is used to communicate meaning. Thus, the language of bilinguals will always be different from that of monolinguals because it is being used to communicate new messages. English in the United States, in the speech, minds, and hearts of bilingual Latinx, acquires the intentions of speakers with different histories and ideologies.

U.S. Latinx, as well as other bilinguals, experience language as an integrated system of linguistic and cultural practices. The translanguaging corriente generates creative energy and produces the speaker's way of interacting with others and other texts, rather than responding to restrictions imposed by the officially accepted way of using language monolingually. It involves, as Li Wei (2011) has said, going both *between* different linguistic structures, systems, and modalities and going *beyond* them. For Wei, translanguaging "creates a *social space* for the multilingual user by bringing together different dimensions of their personal history, experience, and environment; their attitude, belief, and ideology; [and] their cognitive and physical capacity into one coordinated and meaningful performance" (p. 1223). In short, the translanguaging corriente is generated by the students' bilingualism, and it sets in motion learning and teaching in the translanguaging classroom.

TRANSCENDING TRADITIONAL NOTIONS OF MONOLINGUAL AND BILINGUAL CLASSROOMS

What would it mean to use dynamic bilingualism and the translanguaging corriente to reimagine how bilingual students are educated? U.S. classrooms are said to be either monolingual or bilingual; there does not seem to be anything in between. But classrooms today are never just monolingual or bilingual. If we look closer, there is much more diversity, and much more dynamic language use in classrooms, than what we hear and see at the surface level.

Limitations of Traditional Models

In any "monolingual" classroom we find children who speak LOTEs, even if they also speak English. Students in English as a second language (ESL) classrooms are also highly multilingual, and yet little attention is paid to the use and development of their multilingualism, except for calling them "multilingual learners" (for exceptions, see, for example,

Tian et al., 2020). By ignoring linguistic practices other than those that are regarded as "legitimate school English," schools are ignoring the potential to build on a child's entire linguistic repertoire. Schools are, in effect, rendering other ways of speaking and making meaning invisible.

Furthermore, despite the existence of many bilingual classrooms, bilingual education often suffers from a **monoglossic ideology**. That is, bilingualism is often understood as simply "double monolingualism" (Grosjean 1982; Heller, 1999). Both major types of bilingual education classrooms—transitional bilingual and dual-language bilingual—conceptualize the two languages as separate. **Transitional bilingual education** classrooms transition children who are acquiring English (emergent bilinguals in this book, also called English language learners [ELLs] or limited English proficient) to English-only instruction. In **early-exit** programs, the transition is as soon as possible. In **late-exit** programs, students do not exit until they finish the program of instruction. The proportion of English used for instruction increases as the use of the other language decreases. English language development, then, never benefits from its interrelationship with the existing language features and practices of the student's language repertoire. And Spanish development is not supported over time.

Most **dual-language bilingual education** (DLBE) classrooms also suffer from the same monoglossic ideology (García, 2009; García & Kleifgen, 2018; Martínez et al., 2015; Palmer et al., 2019), that is, the idea that the two languages are to be used only in monolingual ways. Echoing this idea, Fitts (2006) demonstrates how language separation in DLBE programs is a mechanism that "authorizes the use of standard forms of English and Spanish in separate spaces, and illegitimizes the use of vernaculars" (p. 339). The prototypical dual-language model requires that English and the partner language always remain separate (for critiques of the language separation approach, see Gort, 2015; Gort & Sembiante, 2015; Palmer & Henderson, 2016; Palmer et al., 2014). Furthermore, **two-way dual language bilingual programs** (or two-way immersion, as they are sometimes called) insist on balanced numbers of English-speaking children and speakers of the other language. Recently, there has been much criticism of some dual-language bilingual programs because of the attention they are giving to White English monolingual children, as well as the ways they are being used to gentrify neighborhoods (see Delavan, 2024; Freire et al., 2022). Adopting a raciolinguistic ideology framework, Flores et al. (2020) and Chávez-Moreno (2024) have pointed to the ways in which dual-language programs often reinforce, rather than challenge, racial inequities.

In the case of English/Spanish DLBE classrooms, students are generally recognized as either "English dominant" or "Spanish dominant," but rarely both. Teachers in these programs teach in either English or Spanish, but never both. The language use in these classrooms seldom reflects the language use of the community, whose members speak English or Spanish, but mostly both. In many DLBE classrooms, the community's translanguaging is generally not overtly recognized, and teachers talk about students as either ELLs or ESL speakers, or Spanish language learners or Spanish as a second language speakers (Lee et al., 2008; Palmer & Martínez, 2013). This dichotomous conceptualization prevents bilingual identities from emerging. For example, an Anglophone child is socialized in the classroom as English speaking and a Hispanophone child as Spanish speaking, with little leveraging of their bilingualism and ways of knowing, which would strengthen their identities as U.S. bilinguals.

Imagining Translanguaging Classrooms

Translanguaging classrooms transcend traditional definitions of monolingual and bilingual education and build on the linguistic complexity of language practices used by multilingual speakers. Translanguaging classrooms could be either officially monolingual (like Stephanie's and Justin's classrooms) or bilingual (like Carla's classroom). The vision of translanguaging classrooms shifts us from the deficit view of "así no se dice" [this is not how it's said] or "no se dice aquí" [we don't say it here] that is so prevalent in both monolingual and bilingual classrooms to a more inclusive one of "también así se dice" [this is also how it's said] or "también aquí se dice" [it is also said here] and "¿qué más se dice?" [what else is said?].

If bilingual students constantly make meaning bilingually, how can we assess them solely in one language? If students' intrapersonal voices are bilingual, how can we tell them to "think in English"? If students' identities and ways of knowing are formed by deploying features from complex, multiple linguistic and cultural repertoires, how can we provide them with texts and academic experiences that present the world as static and monolingual? The answer to these questions is—we simply cannot. In order for bilingual students, and especially Latinx students, to be successful, participatory members of society, they must be provided with educational spaces—with translanguaging classrooms—where all the features of their language repertoires are valued and leveraged in ways that support and strengthen learning.

THE TWO DIMENSIONS OF THE TRANSLANGUAGING CLASSROOM

The direct participants in all education activities in school are the students and the educators. The translanguaging classroom framework focuses on both dimensions and pays attention to who the students are and what they can do with language, as well as to how teachers draw on the translanguaging corriente to teach and assess those students.

Translanguaging classrooms are not chaotic; students and teachers do not just do as they please. On the contrary, these classrooms are constructed based on planned and structured activities by the teacher in interaction with students, families, and communities, ensuring that students' entire linguistic repertoires are used. Regardless of whether the classroom is officially an English-medium classroom or a bilingual classroom, teachers in translanguaging classrooms design their instructional units and their assessment systems purposefully and strategically to mobilize all features of their bilingual students' linguistic repertoires; accelerate their content learning and language development; encourage their bilingualism and ways of knowing; strengthen their socioemotional development, bilingual identities, and critical consciousness; and advance social, racial, and cognitive justice.

A translanguaging classroom, then, is built by weaving together two dimensions: the students' translanguaging performances and the teacher's translanguaging pedagogy (see Figure 3.4). It is the translanguaging corriente that creates the dynamic flow, the movimiento, between these two dimensions. The students' translanguaging performances shift the instruction and assessment, and the teacher's instruction and assessment shift the students' translanguaging performances.

Students' Translanguaging Performances

The first dimension of a translanguaging classroom revolves around the students' translanguaging performances. The flow of the translanguaging corriente moves from the concept of linguistic *proficiency*, which is assumed to develop along a relatively linear path that is more or less the same for all bilingual learners, to one of linguistic *performance* in situated practice, that is, according to the task at hand.

Both Haugen (1953) and Weinreich (1979), pioneers in the study of bilingualism in the United States, considered even minimal proficiency in two languages as a sign of bilingualism. The range of bilingual performances of today's students, however, is broader and more complex. Bilinguals today acquire and use many different linguistic features because mobility and technology have given them more opportunities to interact with texts and speakers whose repertoires differ from their own. In bilingual communities and homes, speakers do not shy away from using all their linguistic features to communicate. In most schools, however, bilingual students are often required to suppress half of the features of their language repertoires to perform only in English or, in the case of bilingual programs or world language programs, in the other language of instruction.

Teachers in translanguaging classrooms view students' linguistic performances holistically. They look at the students' performances while taking into account what they (the teachers) know about the translanguaging corriente in their classes. Students' linguistic performances are valued not only when the features they use conform to the official language used for school purposes, but also when they leverage the full range of their linguistic repertoires to learn.

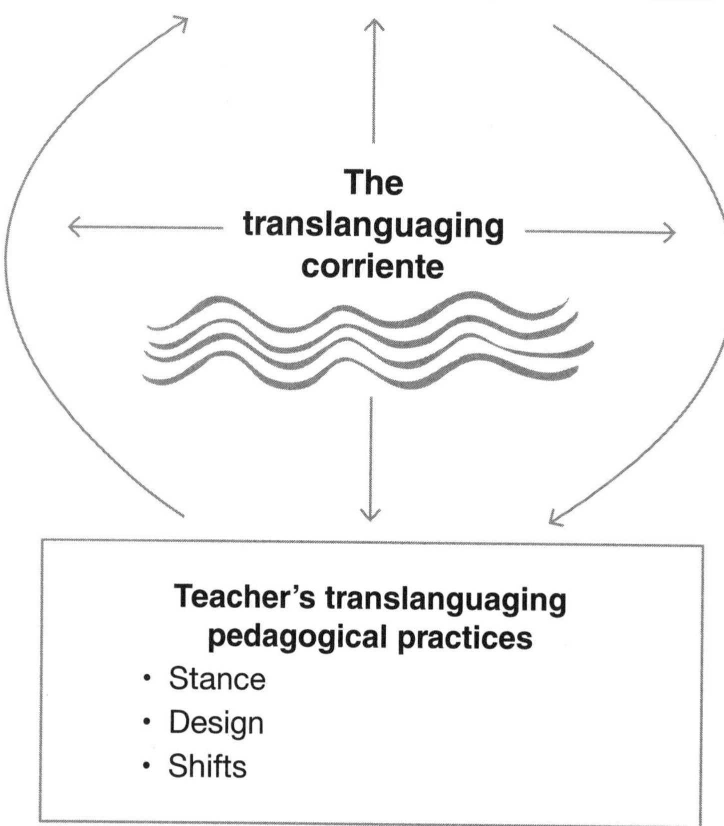

Figure 3.4 A diagram of the translanguaging classroom framework.

In contrast to the notion of language proficiency as demonstrated on a standardized test, the focus in translanguaging classrooms is on task-based performances in situated practice. It is possible for the performance level to be emergent on some tasks and more experienced on others. For example, in immigrant settings where not much attention is paid to bilingualism in schools, youth oracy performances in a home language may be more experienced. However, the same students may not have experience with literacy in their home language, and thus the literacy dimension might be more emergent. A Deaf bilingual child may have different degrees of signacy, literacy, and even oracy. All bilinguals are emergent bilinguals in some aspect or another, in certain situations and with different interlocutors. Students' linguistic performances shift in dynamic and creative ways depending on different contexts and factors and cannot simply be captured by a one-time proficiency score.

To understand students' translanguaging performances, teachers pay attention to two elements—the *dynamic* nature of students' bilingualism (which we have discussed) and the difference between their *general linguistic* and *language-specific performances* (bilingual student profiles will be discussed in detail in Chapter 4).

General linguistic performance refers to an oral, written, or signed performance that draws on a bilingual speaker's entire language repertoire to demonstrate what that speaker knows and can do with content and language (e.g., to explain, persuade, argue, compare and contrast, or evaluate). When bilingual speakers draw on the full features of their language repertoires, they are not required to suppress specific linguistic features (of what is perceived to be the LOTE, of the vernacular variety of a language, etc.).

Language-specific performance refers to an oral, written, or signed performance that only draws on those features associated with a specific named language; here the focus is on standard language features associated with school contexts. Bilingual speakers, to demonstrate what they know and can do, deploy only the features in their language repertoires that correspond to the language of the content-specific task and produce only what schools consider to be standard language features. Regardless of the specific language they may be using, a bilingual speaker always leverages their entire language repertoire to make meaning, even when only using features of one specific language.

The dynamism of students' translanguaging performances makes it clear that bilingualism is not static; it is not attainable; it is not something that one purely "has." On the contrary, one needs to "do" bilingualism—work with it, use it, perform it in different ways, whether through oracy, literacy, or signacy (for Deaf populations)—or any combination thereof. Bilingual students also need to understand the potential of their linguistic performances when they are allowed to use all the features of their language repertoires, that is, when schools also legitimize their translanguaging performances.

Teachers' Translanguaging Pedagogical Practices

The second dimension of the translanguaging classroom framework focuses attention on the teacher's instruction and assessment, which adapt to, and leverage, the students' translanguaging performances. The translanguaging pedagogy proposed in this book (which will be explored in Section II) includes the teacher's general stance toward the students' dynamic bilingualism, the intentional ways that teachers design curricular units of instruction and assessments to build on what students can do with the full features of their language repertoires, and the moment-to-moment shifts that teachers make in response to their observation of student participation in language-mediated classroom activities.

Although some teachers understand the power of translanguaging and are able to give students this flexibility so that they can translanguage moment-by-moment in their classes, it takes thoughtful, effective planning. That is, it is not enough to go with flow of the translanguaging corriente. A teacher needs to have a **translanguaging stance**, build a **translanguaging design**, and make **translanguaging shifts**—the three strands of a **translanguaging pedagogy**.

Methods to develop these strands in both instruction and assessment will be explored in later chapters. Here we simply introduce them.

> All teachers can take up a translanguaging pedagogy! See how researchers Sara Vogel, Christopher Hoadley, and other members of the PiLa-CS (Participating in Literacies and Computer Science) Project work with computer science/technology teachers to develop these three strands of a translanguaging pedagogy in "Episode 3: Translanguaging Pedagogy in Computer Science Education," which you can access via the Brookes Download Hub.

Stance A stance refers to the philosophical, ideological, or belief system that teachers draw from to develop their pedagogical framework. Teachers cannot leverage the translanguaging corriente without the firm belief that by bringing forth bilingual students' entire language repertoires they can transcend the language practices that schools traditionally have valued. Clearly, teachers with a translanguaging stance have a firm belief that their students' language practices are both a resource and a right (Ruiz, 1984). But beyond these orientations to language, teachers with a translanguaging stance believe that the many different language practices of bilingual students work **juntos**/together, not separately as if they belonged to different realms. Thus, the teacher believes that the classroom space must be used creatively to promote language collaboration. A translanguaging stance always sees the bilingual child's complex language repertoire as a resource, never as a deficit.

The influence of this translanguaging stance can be seen in educators' actions. Teachers' planned actions in translanguaging classrooms are what we term the translanguaging design.

Design Teachers in translanguaging classrooms must design units, lessons, and instruction and assessments that build connections between, as Flores and Schissel (2014) say, "[community] language practices and the language practices desired in formal school settings" (p. 462). The translanguaging instructional and assessment design does not simply direct the translanguaging corriente toward the school and away from the home or simply construct a bridge across the two banks (home and school) of the river. Instead, teachers purposefully design instruction and assessment opportunities that integrate home and school language and cultural practices. Learning is created by the translanguaging corriente that teachers and students jointly navigate to reduce the distance between home and school practices.

This translanguaging design is what prevents learners from being swept away by different currents—those created by school language practices that are beyond their reach or those of home language practices that, without blending with those of the school, do not lead to academic success. But the translanguaging design is not a simple scaffold for the kinds of languaging and understanding that the school deems valuable. Instead, students' bilingual practices and ways of knowing are seen as both informing and informed by classroom instruction.

Teachers' translanguaging design is based on their translanguaging stance, as they affirm the students' strengths that are drawn from their own community practices and knowledge systems. Teachers' trust in their students, their families, and their communities enables them then to open up *translanguaging spaces* in their instructional design. That is, teachers give their students the freedom to learn from what Walter Mignolo (2000) calls "their own locus of enunciation."

The design is the pedagogical core of the translanguaging classroom. But to open ourselves and our students to constructing this flexible design together, we need to make room for translanguaging shifts.

Shifts Because the translanguaging corriente is always present in classrooms, it is not enough to simply have a stance that recognizes translanguaging performances and a design that directs it. At times it is also important to follow el movimiento de la corriente. The translanguaging shifts refer to the many moment-by-moment decisions that teachers make in the classroom. They reflect the teacher's flexibility and willingness to change the course of the lesson, as well as the language use planned in instruction and assessment, to release and support students' voices. The translanguaging shifts are related to the translanguaging stance, for it takes a teacher willing to keep meaning-making and learning at the center of all instruction and assessment to go with the flow of the corriente.

Teachers can use the translanguaging pedagogy to leverage the translanguaging corriente that runs through their classes. A translanguaging pedagogy encompasses both instruction and assessment and can be used to mobilize students' bilingualism and accelerate their content and language learning. The strands of the translanguaging pedagogy are interrelated and form a sturdy but flexible rope that strengthens the learning and teaching of both language and content, as shown in Figure 3.5.

These interrelated strands enable the translanguaging corriente to flow through the daily life of the classroom—planning lessons, facilitating conversations about content, strengthening of students' general linguistic and language-specific performances, and assessing student growth. These strands also weave together the translanguaging purposes.

Together, the strands of this pedagogy not only secure instructional purposes, but also connect the educational project to a higher goal—constructing a more socially, racially, and cognitively just world, especially for minoritized students.

Figure 3.5 Depicts the three strands of a translanguaging pedagogy.

CONCLUSION

This chapter has encouraged reflections on language use through the movimiento of the translanguaging corriente, and especially the language use of bilingual students. Notions of additive bilingualism were called into question, and the concept of dynamic bilingualism was explored, along with the concepts of translanguaging and the translanguaging corriente. The two dimensions of the translanguaging classroom framework—the students' translanguaging performances and the teacher's translanguaging pedagogy—were introduced, and the three strands that make up the translanguaging pedagogy for instruction and assessment—the stance, design, and shifts—were identified. In Chapter 4, we explore a highly important element of translanguaging classrooms: documenting students' bilingual performances. It is through the careful documentation of these performances that teachers can shape their translanguaging pedagogies for instruction and assessment.

REFLECTION QUESTIONS AND ACTIVITIES

1. Have you ever experienced or felt the linguistic and sociopolitical elements of the translanguaging corriente? Where and why? How did it make you feel?
2. How does the concept of bilingual students' translanguaging performances differ from traditional concepts of language proficiency?
3. What are the challenges that translanguaging poses for you? Identify and talk through with other educators the challenges posed by each of the three strands—the stance, design, and shifts.

TAKING ACTION

1. Visit a bilingual community of your choice. Listen to the ways that language is used in the street, in the stores, and in the restaurants. What do you hear? Look for signs written by store owners and others. What can you conclude about the ways that bilingualism is used in this community? How does it adjust (or not) to the concept of dynamic bilingualism discussed in this chapter?
2. What evidence of the translanguaging corriente can you see and hear in your focal classroom? Pay attention to the corriente of students' dynamic bilingualism and take notes on the ways that your bilingual students draw on all of the features of their linguistic repertoire orally and in writing in different communicative activities at school. Pay attention, as well, to the sociopolitical flows of the corriente and note what arises (e.g., how persistent raciolinguistic ideologies often arise alongside students' translanguaging).

4

Observing, Documenting, and Understanding Students' Translanguaging Performances

LEARNING OBJECTIVES

After reading this chapter, you will be able to:

- Understand how to build a robust multilingual ecology in the classroom.
- Identify students who are bilingual and understand the complex nature of their language performances by using the Bilingual Student Identification Checklist and Profile tool.
- Develop a bilingual classroom profile that summarizes both the bilingual exposure that all students have and their different bilingual performances.
- Develop a translanguaging lens on observing bilingual students' linguistic performances, including separating their general linguistic performances from their language-specific performances.
- Understand how translanguaging builds on, and goes beyond, how states assess the performances of bilingual students, and especially emergent bilinguals.

To set learners in motion in the translanguaging classroom, educators must be able to first see and understand how students are using their dynamic bilingualism. To understand students' bilingualism holistically, teachers must be able to gather information on how students use language both in school and at home, in and across different situations and contexts. The tools offered in this chapter formalize ways in which teachers can see and hear bilingual students' complex language practices and adjust their pedagogical practices to ensure an engaging, fair, and productive educational context for these students.

When bilingual students are in motion, as they use language in different contexts, they become more than simply categories; they exhibit their full capacities and complexities. Carefully documenting students' bilingual performances in different classroom activities informs and shapes the translanguaging pedagogies for instruction and assessment that are developed in Sections II and III of this book.

In documenting the complex linguistic practices of bilingual students, we can effectively reframe our understandings of students' bilingualism. Documenting how students use their translanguaging facilitates a *coupled* movement. Traditional language progressions, adopted by many states, enable educators to place students across a progression in one or the other language. But acknowledging students' translanguaging performances means that those scores must always be interpreted in the context of the students' full use of their repertoire in performing academic tasks. Thus, a translanguaging classroom takes into account the student's translanguaging, and the teacher's pedagogical practices leverage their full linguistic repertoire.

Because translanguaging is relevant not just for those who are emergent bilinguals but for *all* bilingual learners, this chapter begins with how schools and teachers can identify the bilingual potential of all their students. Building a robust multilingual ecology is an integral step toward developing a translanguaging classroom.

BUILDING A ROBUST MULTILINGUAL ECOLOGY AT SCHOOL

Families who register their children in U.S. schools fill out a home language survey. It has been said, however, that many parents do not share their children's bilingualism for fear that this will be a stigma. Although every school is required to administer a home language survey to the families of every child in the school, the information gleaned from this survey is used mostly to identify students who could be classified as limited English proficient or English language learners (ELLs). When schools determine that students have command of English, not much else is done with the information on the home language survey. Thus, bilingual students are not properly identified, and their bilingualism is generally ignored.

The first step to appropriately identify bilingual students, especially when they are proficient in English, is to encourage parents and students to self-identify as bilingual. To do so, the school can build a **multilingual ecology**—or an interrelated environment that includes everything from the textual landscape of the school to the interactions of those within it—enabling every parent and student to feel that their languages are appreciated, are valued, and make an important contribution to learning in the school. There is a lot that can be done to develop a multilingual ecology that encourages the translanguaging corriente to flow. Schools can have multilingual welcome signs and multilingual resources for parents who are registering their students in school (for more ideas, see Espinosa & Ascenzi-Moreno, 2021, as well as the work of the CUNY-NYSIEB project at www.cuny-nysieb.org; see also chapters in CUNY-NYSIEB, 2020). Teachers can request that they be given access to the information on the home language survey or conduct their own inquiry. Teachers can also engage students early in sharing their bilingualism, especially through personal stories, language biographies or testimonios, and discussions.

The *Promoting an Ecology of Multilingualism Checklist* (Appendix 4.1) was developed to help school leaders and teachers identify the bilingual language practices of all of their students from a variety of perspectives. This checklist includes actions that school leaders and teachers can take to encourage families and students to share their bilingualism, thus allowing the translanguaging corriente to flow across the home and school environments. It provides a vehicle for educators to engage families and students in the promotion of multilingualism in the school.

When families and students are encouraged to share their bilingualism, it becomes clear that many classrooms today have bilingual students and that children's range of abilities with their bilingual repertoire differs greatly. In the United States, most bilingual students will be Spanish speaking, and most will also be categorized as English speakers. However, depending on where educators teach, the level they teach, and the type of classes they teach, their bilingual students will have very different characteristics. For instance, many of those U.S. Spanish-speaking students will also be speakers of Indigenous Latin American languages, something that goes unrecognized unless educators probe. The following section outlines some of the ways educators can ascertain bilingual students' performances and become more acquainted with their complexities.

DEVELOPING BILINGUAL PROFILES

Since schools are not required to recognize the bilingualism of their students, not even of those who are classified as ELLs, it is important for teachers to uncover this information. One way to do this is by using the *Bilingual Student Identification Checklist and Profile,* which appears as Appendix 4.2. The answers to the questions posed in this identification tool can help teachers begin to see and hear the translanguaging corriente in their classes and understand the students' bilingual performances.

Filling out the *Bilingual Student Identification Checklist and Profile* for each student helps ascertain not only who is bilingual, but also what bilingual and multilingual resources the students can draw on for learning. The form consists of two parts. Part 1, *Bilingual Student Identification Checklist*, includes topics teachers can use to start conversations with students about their bilingualism. In the case of very young students, teachers can use this part of the checklist with parents. If the student is identified as being potentially bilingual (that is, if they have received a score of more than 2 on Part 1), the teacher then proceeds to Part 2, *Bilingual Student Profile*.

Part 2 asks about variables that research has identified as important to bilingual acquisition and development—age, nativity and residency, socioeconomic status, and educational history (Wright, 2015). The *Bilingual Student Profile* also includes a place for teachers to note their observations about students' performances in English and the LOTE that help them make further sense of students' bilingualism, including their performances on standardized assessments (reading/language arts test scores, both formative and summative, students' ACCESS or other English language proficiency levels, LOTE proficiency levels, etc.). In sum, the *Bilingual Student Identification Checklist and Profile* tool allows teachers to collect preliminary information about their students' bilingualism across both home and school perspectives.

Why is this understanding of the student's bilingualism important? The sociolinguistic, socioeducational, and sociopolitical factors that influence the complex linguistic performances used by bilingual students are essential for teachers to consider. For instance, the language the student speaks can give teachers information about whether there is a long literacy tradition in that language or not, the language family to which it belongs, as well as the script in which it is written. For example, if a new student has been educated in their country of origin in a language that does not use the Latin script, attention will have to be paid to their development of the new script. If a student has studied English in their country of origin, their English language development could progress faster than that of those who are being exposed to English for the first time. A more affluent student who has been formally educated in their home language may also progress more quickly than students who have not had the same opportunities. Likewise, young students' language development at school will seem to advance faster than that of older students because they have simpler things to communicate, although, of course, older students can draw more from what they already know. Using the *Bilingual Student Identification Checklist and Profile* tool, teachers can obtain information from the parents, as well as students, and begin to unpack their linguistic reality, especially at home, in order to leverage their bilingualism at school.

In schools and classrooms today, attention also needs to be paid to bilingual students' language development in relationship to the standards used in their state. Thus, teachers can also adapt the *Bilingual Student Identification Checklist and Profile* to include relevant information from their specific state's assessment requirements and grade level. At the same time, teachers can use this powerful tool to look critically at the categories that they are expected to work with in traditional language development frameworks. The example in the next section, describing how Stephanie thought about the profiles of Luis and Mariana, two students in her class who are classified as English language learners, is a case in point.

Developing Bilingual Profiles in Stephanie's Class

When ***Stephanie*** filled out the *Bilingual Student Identification Checklist and Profile* for **Luis**, a new student from a rural area of El Salvador, it was clear that his home language was Spanish and his new language was English. When he initially entered school the year before, in the 10th grade, Luis had been classified as an English language learner because in the New York State Identification Test for English Language Learners (NYSITELL) he was identified as a Beginner. He had also been classified as a student with incomplete/interrupted education (SIFE) because he had stopped going to school in El Salvador in the sixth grade. Since then, he has made progress. He took the New York State English as a Second Language Assessment Test (NYSESLAT) in the spring of his 10th-grade year and placed in the Emerging category. When looking at the assessment results, Stephanie could see that Luis's scores in reading and writing were much lower than his scores in listening and speaking. Luis also took the English Regents exam at the end of the 10th grade. Not surprisingly, his score on this high-stakes standardized exam was also low.

Stephanie needs to understand what Luis can do with reading, writing, listening, and speaking in English (his new language) and Spanish (his home language). She has no trouble filling out the form for his English performance, but she has to rely on another resource—Luis's teacher in his "Spanish for Spanish speakers" class—to understand how he is using Spanish for academic tasks in school.

Performance indicators developed by state and other education agencies can provide ideas of what students can do with language. They are especially helpful to teachers who are new to the field of language development because they provide concrete descriptions of student performances using all of the languages in their linguistic repertoire. However, educators must remember that these performance indicators are intended to be understood as approximations of what students can do with oracy and literacy and not as fixed categories. This important point is explored later in the chapter.

When Stephanie began to fill out the *Bilingual Student Identification Checklist and Profile* for another student, ***Mariana***, she ran into a problem. Mariana was born in Puebla, Mexico, but speaks English better than she speaks Spanish. Mariana prefers English to Spanish for schoolwork, and she speaks mostly English at home. However, Mariana was classified as an ELL when she entered school and is now labeled a long-term English language learner (LTELL), as she has not been able to test out of ELL status. When Stephanie tried to complete the form for Mariana, she found herself asking: What is Mariana's home language? What is her new language? Stephanie realized that the categories didn't quite fit Mariana, although to complete the form she decided to indicate that English was the new language and Spanish was the home language. By filling out the form, Stephanie realized that the way in which bilingualism had been constructed by the state guidelines and by the school does not fit the complexity and fluidity of her bilingual students' language use. This added to Stephanie's criticality, a most important factor in teaching bilingual students. She made notes about her observations at the bottom of the form.

Documenting bilingual students' linguistic performances through the *Bilingual Student Identification Checklist and Profile* tool is a more holistic way of understanding students' bilingualism than simply looking at students' "language proficiency." Teachers can develop student profiles that combine different dimensions of assessment, such as performances in new and home languages, initial and subsequent performances, and their own critical reflections on the holistic profile. These student profiles help teachers recognize the potential and the needs of each student in their classroom, which can stimulate ideas for creating instructional opportunities that leverage each student's bilingualism in instruction. It is also a powerful way of initially assessing students' linguistic performances.

Developing a Classroom Bilingual Profile in Carla's Class

Teachers not only need to be mindful of individual bilingual students' profiles but also must find ways of making the *Classroom Bilingual Profile* visible as well. This section describes Appendix 4.3, which provides teachers with a way to summarize the bilingual performances of the whole classroom.

Recall that ***Carla*** teaches in a dual-language bilingual education (DLBE) classroom in New Mexico. She draws on different data sources to develop a classroom bilingual profile for the students in her class. In English, she differentiates students who have been classified as English language learners as a result of taking the test given by New Mexico, the WIDA ACCESS Placement Test, from those who are not. For those emergent bilinguals, she notes whether they have been classified as such for more than 6 years and are thus what the state calls "long-term English language learners." She also notes whether their formal schooling has been limited or interrupted and, if so, categorizes them as students with incomplete/interrupted formal education (SIFE). She then documents each student's performance according to the six WIDA language proficiency levels on ACCESS: (1) Entering, (2) Emerging, (3) Developing, (4) Expanding, (5) Bridging, or (6) Reaching.

Following New Mexico guidelines for DLBE classrooms, Carla also collects home language data for all her students by using the Language Assessment Scale (LAS) Links for Spanish, which rates the students' performance according to five levels. Her school district also requires that all students in dual-language bilingual programs be given a formative literacy assessment in English and Spanish—the Development Reading Assessment 2 (DRA2) and the *Evaluación del desarrollo de la lectura* 2 (EDL2). The DRA2 and EDL2 scores are arranged by Lexile scores—40 (fourth-grade level), 50 (fifth-grade level), and 60 (sixth-grade level).

Because there are so many pieces of information for Carla to keep track of, the *Classroom Bilingual Profile* provides an easy way for her to see at a glance what her students can do in Spanish and English according to the data sources she draws on in the DLBE program at her school. This inclusive approach transcends traditional categorizations of bilingual students in the United States that render the bilingualism of most bilingual students invisible. It also allows Carla to begin to see and hear the linguistic assets that her students bring with them to school and to perceive the translanguaging corriente that moves through her classroom in an integrated manner.

The Importance of Bilingual Profiles for the Translanguaging Classroom Instructional decision making in the translanguaging classroom requires teachers to develop a holistic profile of bilingual students' language practices that is based on empirical evidence. This requires long-term systematic observation of students' language performances and dialogue with students and their families, as well as evaluation of practices through formative assessments, a topic that will be further considered in Chapter 8. It is crucial to keep in mind that data are not static and should shape pedagogy fluidly. But preliminary information on students is important, and the *Bilingual Student Identification Checklist and Profile* and the *Classroom Bilingual Profile* are the first steps to understanding the translanguaging corriente of students and classrooms. Throughout her instruction, as we will see, Carla uses the profiles she created to remind her of the current bilingual status of her students, knowing that these scores change depending on the task they are performing and the translanguaging support she gives them. The movimiento of the translanguaging corriente of students' language practices informs Carla's instruction and adds movimiento to her own teaching, which in turn moves students' practices forward.

Most of the current work regarding standards and English language development has addressed only those emergent bilinguals officially classified as ELLs, that is, students like Luis and Mariana in Stephanie's class. However, it is important to capture the translanguaging performances of *all* bilingual students.

Besides being interested in students' performances in English and other languages, educators in translanguaging classrooms are especially interested in developing and assessing bilingual students' ways of performing academic tasks with language without regard to the external features that have been defined as belonging to one language or another. Teachers in translanguaging classrooms do not simply develop bilingual profiles that help inform instruction in *a* language (that is, *one* language, whether English or Spanish as defined in schools), although they do that also. Teachers in translanguaging classrooms start by ensuring that they develop and assess the *holistic linguistic performances* of children, which we refer to here as their *general linguistic performances*. As noted in Chapter 3, this encompasses the ability to express complex thoughts effectively, to explain things, to persuade, to argue, to compare and contrast, to give directions, to recount events, to tell jokes, and so forth, without regard to the language used to accomplish these linguistic tasks. Teachers in translanguaging classrooms are also interested in developing bilingual children's performance in the language(s) of school—their *language-specific performances*—since this is most important to be successful in many tasks. But because teachers in translanguaging classrooms understand dynamic bilingualism, they differentiate between the bilingual students' language-specific performances, which they execute using only certain features of the linguistic repertoire with English speakers or speakers of the other language, and their general linguistic performances. If children can express complex thoughts effectively through the use of their entire language repertoire, then they will be able to develop the specific linguistic features that they will have to draw on to perform academic tasks in English or in another language.

Giving bilingual students opportunities to use their entire linguistic repertoire in school leads to greater linguistic confidence because it lessens the fear of expression that is often the result of artificial linguistic boundaries in schools. For example, Susana, one of this book's authors, has been involved in evaluating a New Mexico high school's Seal of Bilingualism and Biliteracy portfolio presentations the past 5 years. To obtain the seal, students are required to present a portfolio about their academics, their personal accomplishments, a self-reflection, and a language reflection. The teachers at this high school have opened up a space for students to organize their presentations in a way that best suits them; students select a language-specific performance for each part of the presentation *and* understand that they can use both languages if needed or desired. For instance, one student began explaining his math coursework in English, ended up discussing what he learned in Spanish, and at times described his coursework in both. The evaluators are not concerned with how much time was spent in English or Spanish; rather, they want to assess the students' performances in English *and* Spanish. If we are interested in gauging what students do with language to accomplish content-specific tasks, and if we understand translanguaging as the experienced performances of bilinguals, then translanguaging has to be considered a valid way of demonstrating linguistic virtuosity, as well as content understandings.

To summarize, the development of student and classroom bilingual profiles is important in translanguaging classroom for three reasons: (1) it identifies *all* bilingual children, not just emergent bilinguals, (2) it promotes understanding of the linguistic performances of bilingual children as the use of *one language repertoire,* and not simply one named language or the other, and (3) it frames translanguaging not as simply a scaffold in beginning stages, but as *accomplished bilingual performance* capable of propelling students forward and leveraging their learning, creativity, and criticality.

ONGOING DOCUMENTATION OF STUDENTS' TRANSLANGUAGING PERFORMANCES

This chapter has been concerned mostly with the *early and holistic identification* of bilingual students and their performances. The rest of this chapter sets the foundation for *ongoing assessment practices,* which are developed further in Chapter 8. The discussion of these assessment practices is grounded in the following four ideas:

1. Language performances are not static but dynamic, depending on the task, the interlocutors, and the context in which the action occurs.
2. The identification and description of what a student can do may change depending on whether the evaluator is the teacher, the student, the family, students' peers, or the testing instrument itself.
3. There is a difference between evaluating students' general linguistic performances and evaluating those that are constrained by language-specific demands.
4. Standardized systems of assessments can be valuable in the identification and evaluation of students' language performances, but they must be considered in relationship to students' translanguaging performances.

1. Dynamic Performances of Bilingualism

The emphasis on the dynamic nature of bilingualism recognizes that bilingualism can ebb and flow with experience and opportunities. Bilingualism is thus not static, not attainable, or "had." Bilingualism has to be "done," performed.

Any identification or evaluation of students' bilingualism must be explicit about the task that the student is performing, when, where, and with what resources. While the early identification of students' bilingual performances is important, educators must remember that these performances will shift depending on the interaction between the students' cognitive and emotional state at that moment and the task that they are being asked to perform. Translanguaging recognizes that language performances are not flat; that is, they do not occur on neutral ground, on monolingual territory, but on territory that has peaks and valleys that are shaped by the interlocutors in an event and the task at hand. As such, bilingual students' language performances must be evaluated initially, and then re-evaluated often, in interaction with different interlocutors, tasks, and contexts. Furthermore, teachers must make an effort to imagine what other ways of using language take place in the community beyond the classroom.

Take ***Noemí***, the 11th grader in Stephanie's classroom who came to the United States from Ecuador 3 years ago with a strong education. At home, she has more experienced biliteracy performances than she is invited to demonstrate in school. For example, she reads, translates, and helps complete health insurance forms in English for her Spanish-speaking parents. She helps younger siblings write essays in English, as she speaks to them in both English and Spanish. She reads from the Spanish-language Bible at church, where the service is bilingual. She writes in a personal journal in both languages. Though Stephanie wouldn't necessarily have an opportunity to see these kinds of literacy practices, her translanguaging stance shapes her belief that the performances in English she is privy to at school are only part of Noemí's linguistic and literate story.

2. The Role of the Observer/Evaluator

Stephanie observes that although Noemí uses English, she struggles with writing in English. When Noemí's parents were asked about her bilingualism, her parents evaluated her performance as more experienced than Stephanie did. After all, her biliteracy was stronger than that of her parents, who relied on her for a variety of English tasks. As teachers develop bilingual profiles of their students and classrooms and engage in ongoing assessment of students' linguistic performances, it is important to remember that these evaluations are based on their own, singular viewpoint of the students' language performances. Although it is important for teachers to develop this ability to gauge and describe the students' bilingual performances, it is also important to remember that this will always be a partial view that is limited by the teacher's own perspective, positionality, and experience.

3. Separating General Linguistic Performances from Language-Specific Performances and also Seeing them as Interconnected

Language does not develop or progress linearly but has different dimensions that must be viewed both separately and in connection with one another. The two dimensions of language performance, as introduced in Chapter 3, are the following:

- *General linguistic performance:* Bilingual speakers deploy any of the features in their entire language repertoire to show what they can do to accomplish language and content-specific tasks.
- *Language-specific performance:* Bilingual speakers, to show what they can do, deploy only the features in their language repertoire that correspond to the language of the content-specific task, although they leverage their entire language repertoire in the process.

The general linguistic performance dimension acts on the understanding that bilingual speakers have one linguistic repertoire with full features; thus, the construct of "national languages" or "standard language" is not in any way addressed. It liberates bilingual students from always having to suppress or activate certain features of their repertoire. It not only is liberating for bilingual speakers, but also supports their creativity and enhances linguistic feats and accomplishments by encouraging linguistic experimentation. By focusing on general linguistic performances, bilingual students are put on par with monolingual students, who always have access to their full (or at least mostly full) linguistic repertoire. Thus, besides encouraging linguistic creativity and experimentation, this dimension recognizes the potential of translanguaging for social justice and for disrupting the linguistic hierarchies at work in most schools.

General linguistic performance helps students achieve many of the important skills outlined by state language standards. In reading, it means being able to provide text evidence of key ideas, making inferences and identifying main ideas and relationships in complex texts, recognizing the text's craft and structure (chronology, comparison, cause/effect), and associating knowledge and ideas from multiple sources and texts. In writing, general linguistic performance refers to producing text types for various purposes such as opinion, informative, explanatory, and narrative pieces. Finally, the standards in listening and speaking that refer to comprehending knowledge and ideas and presenting them collaboratively are also part of general linguistic proficiency.

Bilingual students' general linguistic performances enable them to make meaning for themselves by drawing from their own life experiences and epistemologies. The production of oral or written translingual texts allows bilingual students to locate themselves not in different cultural and linguistic communities, but in their own bilingual community. It allows them to "be," to live in a Nepantla entre medio that partakes of different practices and epistemologies that together create a whole (Anzaldúa, 1987; Kabuto, 2022).

Viewing translanguaging through linguistic theory and pointing out the inaccuracy of measuring a bilingual's language proficiency by forbidding translanguaging, Otheguy et al. (2015) point out the following:

> Accuracy of measurement is a bedrock value in the context of educational testing. Yet forbidding bilinguals to translanguage, or assessing it negatively, produces an inaccurate measure of their language proficiency. If proficiency assessment is to be accurate and informative, it must adopt the inside perspective that will reveal the linguistic condition of the individual student's idiolect, irrespective of the social rules that qualify or disqualify some or all of the idiolect as belonging to a particular named language (p. 299).

Of course, students in English-medium and bilingual classrooms must also learn to perform as fluent users of a named language. But this language-specific performance must be assessed *independently* of general linguistic performance.

The language-specific performance dimension relates to the ways in which schools have always expected language to be used by bilingual students, reflecting what is considered one national language or even two in bilingual instructions. This is different from developing and assessing students' general linguistic performance. It focuses on performance with language features that have been pre-approved for school use—so-called standard grammar, usage, and vocabulary. It also demands that any child whose language repertoire has features that are not sanctioned by schools—not only bilingual students, but also students who speak different varieties of the "same" language (e.g., forms of what is called African American or Chicano or Appalachian English, Hawaiian Creole)—learn to suppress those features and activate only those approved in academic contexts.

Educators in translanguaging classrooms understand that language-specific performance cannot be achieved without general linguistic performance. Students must be encouraged to perform linguistically, independent of the features they use, whether those belong to one or another language. For example, recall that ***Jennifer***—one of the featured students from Carla's classroom introduced in Chapter 3—uses the word "swings," which for her is not "English" or "Spanish" but merely her way of understanding the concept (although she has learned that in school it is considered English). If Carla, as the bilingual teacher, constantly told her not to use "swings" during the time the instruction is in Spanish, Jennifer would simply become silent or decide to speak English only. The more practice students gain through general linguistic performances, the more occasion they will have to appropriate and distinguish features when the occasion calls for some and not others. In this way, students' languaging is respected and leveraged, not simply punished in a constant "así no se dice." Viewing language performances in this way develops la voz of bilingual students.

As will become apparent when discussing a translanguaging pedagogy in Section II of this book, educators in translanguaging classrooms emphasize the development of bilingual students' ways of using language for a variety of purposes, including those referred to as "academic," regardless of the features they use. Viewing bilingual students through a translanguaging lens means that teachers evaluate differently and gain a much deeper understanding of students' linguistic capacities. They do not view bilingual students simply through state or other language development standards and progressions, but through translanguaging practices that push their performances forward and higher as they adjust to a more variable bilingual terrain of communication.

4. Viewing Standardized Systems Through a Translanguaging Lens

It is possible to work with any of the existing state and consortia systems for language development and assessment while also building an awareness of the difference that assessing general linguistic performance separately from language-specific performance makes for students. It is important to understand that for both the general linguistic performance and the language-specific performance, it is translanguaging that leverages and uplifts the linguistic performances of the bilingual students. In the former, translanguaging is the impetus for the sophisticated linguistic performance, bringing it to greater heights; in the latter, translanguaging underlies language performances that conform to standardized conventions used in schools.

For example, recall that Carla has designed an instructional unit, *Cuentos de la tierra y del barrio,* that focuses on how students, families, and the local community are tied to their land, and, by extension, to their traditions. Carla knew that state standards required her students at Grade 4 to read grade-level texts, explain what the text says explicitly, and draw inferences from the text. Carla differentiated the learning and language outcomes for each student based on their bilingual profile and allowed them to leverage translanguaging to meet the standards by the following:

- Providing Spanish, English, and bilingual texts to preview specific textual evidence of the local farming practices in New Mexico,
- Accessing YouTube and other media sites in Spanish and English to find specific textual evidence of local farming practices in New Mexico, and
- Making available community resources (e.g., bilingual guest speakers and local farming sites) to review specific textual evidence of local farming practices in New Mexico.

By taking up a translanguaging lens on her students' language performances, Carla was able to individualize and potentialize her bilingual students' engagement with texts and also see and assess their full linguistic performances. By looking at students' general linguistic performances, Carla could assess whether students could draw inferences using evidence from the text, independent of whether they were using one language or another. Carla was then able to adapt her teaching to ensure that those students who needed assistance in finding evidence and inferring were supported, without regard to whether they could perform this task in the language of instruction or not.

Carla also made sure to communicate to her students that they would have to speak and write only in English at times and only in Spanish at others. That is, Carla also valued and wanted to assess and support students' language-specific performances in one named language or another. But regardless of the language in which Carla expected the *product* (e.g., a piece of writing, a presentation), she ensured that students leveraged all their translanguaging resources in the *process* of creating those products and learning deeply. In sum, Carla expected all her students to perform and meet grade-level standards according to what they can do with language and literacy, leveraging their entire language repertoire.

Teachers in translanguaging classrooms can use whatever standard and assessment systems their state has adopted, but they always take into consideration the difference between general linguistic performance and language-specific performance. How to further gather the evidence to evaluate students appropriately and monitor their performances is considered in Chapter 8 in Section II of this book when assessments are discussed. More information about how teachers in translanguaging classrooms can understand and work with standards is available in Chapter 10 in Section III.

CONCLUSION

This chapter opened by emphasizing the importance of identifying every student's bilingualism from different perspectives, by different actors, in different contexts and tasks, over time. Three tools were introduced that teachers can use to:

- Build a robust multilingual ecology.
- Develop individual bilingual profiles.
- Develop classroom bilingual profiles using state, district, and program data.

In essence, the students' translanguaging performances enable the teachers to see, hear, and leverage the translanguaging corriente that is otherwise lost in many classrooms.

Four elements were then established that must be kept in mind when identifying and evaluating bilingual students' linguistic performances:

1. The dynamic nature of these performances
2. Their shifting nature, depending on an external observer
3. The complex interaction between what we call general linguistic performance and language-specific performance
4. How to both work within and go beyond standardized state assessment systems to further develop these performances.

Bilingual students, like monolingual students, must be given opportunities to draw on all the features of their linguistic repertoire to perform academic content-specific tasks. In inviting bilingual students to use all the features of their repertoire, translanguaging opens up the possibility for developing more expert performances in one or another language *and* across languages. Section II of this book turns to the *how,* that is, the development of the translanguaging pedagogy.

REFLECTION QUESTIONS AND ACTIVITIES

1. What are some steps you could take to encourage students and their families to share their bilingualism with you? How might you feature that bilingualism in your multilingual ecology?
2. Evaluate the standards and/or language development system used in your state. What do you think are its advantages or disadvantages? How, if at all, can you integrate a translanguaging lens into this system?
3. Select any standard you wish and three bilingual students in your classroom. Evaluate generally (more specific assessment instruments will be discussed in the chapter on assessment) their general linguistic proficiency and their language-specific proficiency. What can you say about the differences?

TAKING ACTION

1. Ask your school administrator and a teacher in your school to try out the *Promoting an Ecology of Multilingualism Checklist* (Appendix 4.1). Interview them afterward and find out what they learned about their students as a result.
2. Use the *Bilingual Student Identification Checklist and Profile* (Appendix 4.2) and/or the *Classroom Bilingual Profile* (Appendix 4.3) with 10 of your students. What did you learn about them? How were you able to gather the information? Is there something that doesn't fit neatly into the form?

Promoting an Ecology of Multilingualism Checklist

Instructions: Check off the actions you currently take to promote a multilingual ecology in your school. Identify areas that need attention, make plans to address them, and check them off as you do.

For School Administrators

- ❒ Ensure that your school has welcome signs and bulletin boards that include all of the languages of the community so that families and other visitors can see them when they enter the school.
- ❒ To accompany the home language survey, have a family member from each of the different language groups represented in the school translate a short welcome message into their home language that emphasizes the importance of bilingualism.
- ❒ Have students who speak languages other than English (LOTEs) prepare a multilingual presentation or short video about the school in the different LOTEs represented. Provide important information about the school that families and community members need to know and include a section that emphasizes the value of bilingualism.
- ❒ Adapt the home language survey for the needs of your school.
- ❒ Ensure that the information on the home language survey is given to teachers and entered into a database that all teachers and administrators can access.
- ❒ Ask family members whether they can volunteer to serve as interpreters or translators. Hire office staff members who speak the languages of the community.
- ❒ Purchase/utilize translation tools and/or software programs for the office staff.
- ❒ Put together a list of school personnel who are bilingual and the languages they can use.

For All Educators

- ❒ Insist on getting information from the home language survey.
- ❒ Engage students in an initial discussion of bilingualism in their families and communities.
- ❒ Have students create their autobiographical language portraits (see Chapter 8).
- ❒ Have students write a short journal entry about their use of oral and written English (and varieties thereof) and LOTEs (if applicable) at home and in other contexts.
- ❒ Engage students in a classroom activity in which different varieties of English and home languages are needed. Have a pair of students ask each other questions about their language and literacy use at home and in the community.
- ❒ Have students teach others how to sing songs or say a common phrase such as "good morning," "thank you," or "happy birthday" in their home languages.

APPENDIX 4.2

Bilingual Student Identification Checklist and Profile

PART 1: BILINGUAL STUDENT IDENTIFICATION CHECKLIST

Name of bilingual student: ______________________________

Give each of the following questions a score from 0 to 2 according to the number in parentheses after the student's answer.

1. Bilingual use at home	Does the student/parent say that household members
	❐ Speak English exclusively? (0)
	❐ Speak English and LOTE? (2)
	What languages?
	❐ Speak LOTE exclusively? (2)
2. Bilingual friends	Does student say their friends
	❐ Speak English exclusively? (0)
	❐ Speak LOTE exclusively? (2)
	❐ Speak English and LOTE? (2)
3. Bilingual exposure in the life of the student	Does student say they
	❐ Have never traveled to a country where the home LOTE is used? (0)
	❐ Have traveled to a country where the home LOTE is used, but less often than every 1 to 3 years? (1)
	❐ Travel to a country where the home LOTE is used every 1 to 3 years, or they have been in the United States less than 3 years? (2)
4. Education in the LOTE	If this student is entering a grade other than kindergarten (if they are entering kindergarten, skip to Question 5), were they
	❐ Educated mostly in the LOTE in another country? (2)
	❐ Educated mostly in any type of U.S. bilingual program where the LOTE was used as a medium of instruction? (2)
	❐ Taught the LOTE as a subject in a U.S. school or program? (1)
	❐ Never taught the LOTE in school? (0)
5. Literacy in the LOTE	Does this student say that they know how to read and write the LOTE?
	❐ Yes, well (2)
	❐ Yes, but not well (1)
	❐ No (0)
Add the scores for Questions 1–5. The higher the score, the more exposure to bilingualism. Maximum score = 10 (8 for kindergarten); minimum score = 0.	
Total score:	

PART 2: BILINGUAL STUDENT PROFILE

Name of bilingual student: ______________________________

1. LOTE spoken or heard consistently at home:
2. Country(ies) where the student has lived since birth:
3. Country(ies) where the student has gone to school since birth:
4. Nativity or residence: Was/did this bilingual student ❐ Born in the United States of U.S.-born parents? ❐ Born in the United States of immigrant parents? ❐ Arrive before first grade? ❐ Arrive during middle school? ❐ Arrive during high school?
5. Education in English: Has this bilingual student been taught English ❐ In their country of origin? ❐ In their country of origin and in the United States? ❐ Only in the United States?
6. Education in the LOTE: Has this bilingual student been taught the LOTE ❐ In their country of origin? ❐ In their country of origin and in the United States? ❐ Only in the United States (indicate where)?
Teacher observations and notes on student's performances in English and the LOTE:

Classroom Bilingual Profile

Students
Languages Used at Home
English Language Learner Status (Yes/No)
Proficiency and Performance in English*
Student Can**
Proficiency and Performance in Language Other Than English (LOTE)*
Student Can**

* Teachers should adapt these language proficiency and performance columns in ways that accommodate all of the data collected in their program, district, and state in English and the language other than English (LOTE). For example, for state-mandated English language proficiency, we find the following categorizations: reading, writing, listening, and speaking in the WIDA system; interactional, interpretive, and productive in the California system; and receptive and productive in the New York system. Some systems number their levels and others name their levels. Some bilingual elementary schools collect DRA2 and EDL2 as evidence of students' reading development in English and Spanish.

** Teachers can make observations about what students can do with language relative to the language demands of state standards and to the goals of the language education program.

II

Translanguaging Pedagogy

5

Translanguaging Stance

LEARNING OBJECTIVES

After reading this chapter, you will be able to:

- Describe the importance of the first strand of the translanguaging pedagogy—the stance.
- Identify the three core beliefs of the translanguaging stance.
- Explain how the stance is reflected at the classroom and societal levels in English-medium and bilingual programs.
- Describe how a teacher's stance is enacted in practice.
- Articulate your own stance toward your students' dynamic bilingualism.

Creating a translanguaging classroom is not easy. It runs contrary to what has traditionally been taught in teacher education and what some may consider common sense. General education teachers are usually taught that their role is to teach content in English only and that all students should know how to use English to learn. English as a second language (ESL) teachers are often told that the emergent bilinguals they teach in **push-in**, **pull-out**, or **structured English immersion** programs are "limited" or just "English learners." **Transitional bilingual education** teachers are frequently encouraged to transition students to English as quickly as possible, often without providing students with opportunities to learn to use Spanish or English for complex academic purposes. Dual-language bilingual teachers are usually taught to keep the two languages separate for instructional purposes and to protect Spanish (or the other language) from the encroachment of English. All teachers are taught to emphasize English to prepare students for what is often seen as most important—mandated, standardized assessments.

In this chapter, these beliefs about educating bilingual students are challenged in order to open existing pedagogy to other perspectives that are brought into classrooms by the translanguaging corriente, or the constant flow of students' dynamic bilingualism. The translanguaging stance is the first strand of the translanguaging pedagogy. The **translanguaging stance** refers to a teacher's belief that bilingual students have one holistic language repertoire that they draw on at school as teachers address the four social purposes of translanguaging:

1. Supporting students as they engage with and comprehend complex content and texts
2. Providing opportunities for students to develop their linguistic practices for a variety of purposes and contexts, including those deemed academic
3. Supporting students' bilingual identities, socioemotional development, and critical consciousness and disrupting ideologies that render bilingual students as deficient
4. Making space for all students' language practices and ways of knowing, and in so doing building a classroom and society that is inclusive of linguistic, racial, gender, and ability differences

Teachers with a translanguaging stance have a strong social justice orientation; they understand the political nature of seeing and hearing students differently, through assets-oriented lenses. They know that effective, equitable instruction and assessment for bilingual students requires drawing on or leveraging students' bilingualism for learning.

JUNTOS/TOGETHER

We all remember a teacher who strongly influenced our learning or the trajectory of our lives. Many of us have been saved, inspired, changed, or given renewed hope by educators who took the time to help us become the best versions of ourselves. These kinds of memorable teachers bring with them more than just good teaching strategies or a deep understanding of content (though they bring those, too!). They also act on the belief that who their students are, what they know, and where they come from matters and that they have the potential to do great things with their lives. While all students deserve teachers like these, they are especially important for those young people who have been historically marginalized and underserved by schools. Though teachers alone cannot solve the difficult economic, political, and social realities faced by many students and their families, they can make a powerful, *local* impact by putting their students' languages, cultures, interests, and ways of knowing at the center of their classrooms.

The translanguaging stance refers to the philosophical and political orientation that teachers draw on to construct a translanguaging classroom. It is a necessary mindset or framework for educating bilingual students that informs everything from the way educators view students and their dynamic bilingual performances and cultural practices to the way they plan instruction and assessment. The term juntos, the Spanish word for together, is used in this book to describe this stance. The juntos stance is informed by three beliefs of joint collaboration:

1. Students' language practices and cultural understanding encompass those they bring from home and communities, as well as those they take up in schools. These practices and understanding work juntos and enrich each other.
2. Students' families and communities are valuable sources of knowledge and must be involved in the education process juntos.
3. The classroom is a democratic space where teachers and students juntos co-create knowledge, challenge traditional hierarchies, and work toward a more just society.

This is the stance that our teachers—***Carla***, ***Stephanie***, and ***Justin***—hold and that many of us share. Of course, how the translanguaging classroom framework is implemented will differ for educators in different contexts.

ENACTING A TRANSLANGUAGING STANCE IN BILINGUAL AND ENGLISH-MEDIUM PROGRAMS

Though the translanguaging stance is mostly explored in this book at the classroom level, it is important to emphasize that at the larger societal level, taking up a translanguaging stance supports social, racial, and cognitive justice. The discourse around many bilingual students, especially Latinx bilinguals, is often that of deficiency and failure. The increasingly large number of Latinx students in U.S. schools is not reflected in the mostly White, English-speaking teaching force. We see deficit thinking and prejudice even among the most well-meaning educators, and sometimes even among teachers who share linguistic and cultural characteristics with students.

Furthermore, in response to increasing numbers of Latinx and other minoritized groups, harsh, draconian immigration policies have been enacted across the country as well as anti-bilingual education legislation in states like California, Massachusetts, and Arizona in the early 2000s that were only overturned almost two decades later. Legislators and school boards across the country have attempted to erase Latinx and other minoritized characters and their stories through book bans and other efforts to combat **critical race theory (CRT)**[1] and exert "parents' rights." Such past and present measures make the lives of Latinx and other immigrant students and their families difficult and, at times, dangerous. Thus, teachers of bilinguals, and especially Latinx bilinguals, can understand their translanguaging stance as influential beyond the local, classroom level. In a very real way, the kind of philosophically informed pedagogy advocated here has the power to make changes on a larger societal level.

For this reason, taking up a translanguaging stance cannot be limited to bilingual teachers. In reality, *every* teacher of bilingual youth can take up a translanguaging stance, no matter their language background or program type. To explain this further, we look at how our three very different teachers, Carla, Stephanie, and Justin, enact a translanguaging stance through their practices.

Carla: A Spanish–English Bilingual Teacher in a Dual-Language Bilingual Education Program

Carla, born in Puebla, Mexico, immigrated to New Mexico when she was a young girl. Like her students, Carla understands and lives a borderlands existence, both culturally and linguistically. She and her family and friends speak with features of both Spanish and English that are specific to their New Mexican context. The translanguaging corriente is strong and ever-present, and strict separation of languages is uncommon. Keeping her own language practices in mind, Carla teaches her **dual-language bilingual education (DLBE)** class in ways that push the boundaries of the program. Traditionally in these classrooms, students' languages are rigidly separated. There is time set aside for English and time set aside for Spanish, and students are discouraged from using the other language during those designated times. Though at first Carla's practice was philosophically aligned with this more traditional approach, learning about translanguaging shifted her stance and helped her make space *within* that program for students' bilingual, bicultural voices.

Though she adheres to the macro-level language policy of her school, which sets out specific times and spaces for each language, Carla enacts her stance by creating translanguaging spaces in a variety of creative ways. Carla created in her class what she calls a Cuéntame Algo space, where students actively bring together their language practices by reading translanguaged texts, engaging in activities and discussions that hone their metalinguistic awareness, and creating their own texts that include both English and Spanish. She also plans translanguaging instructional units that draw on students' experiences with their families and in their communities. Learning within these units is active and hands-on, and brings together/juntos students' languages, cultural understanding, family and community, and the school. In this way, as described in Chapter 1, the Cuéntame Algo space is a space of transformation, wherein students' translanguaging subjectivities are recognized and leveraged and critical consciousness is fostered (Sánchez et. al., 2017; Sánchez & García, 2022).

[1]Critical race theory (CRT) is an academic framework that emerged primarily from within legal studies, aiming to understand and challenge the intersection of race, law, and power structures. CRT has come under attack and been politicized, which has led to widespread misconceptions of it and attempts to stamp out any talk of race and racism from K-12 public school curricula.

For example, part of Carla's *Cuentos de la tierra y del barrio* unit involved working in a garden run by members of the local community. Carla planned a series of lessons on preparing a jardín and invited ***Sonia***, a bilingual herbalist in the community, to deepen students' understanding. She also invited some students' padres y abuelitos to accompany the class on a field trip to the reclaimed plot of land where they would garden. Here is one small dialogue that ensued between Sonia and a student, ***Erica***:

Sonia (S): ¿Qué pasa con nuestro jardín durante el invierno?
[What happens to our garden during the winter?]

Erica (E): El jardín se comienza a dormir. . . . Well, it falls asleep, but not all of it.
[The garden starts to fall asleep. . . .]

S: ¿Por qué no todo el jardín falls asleep?
[Why doesn't the entire garden fall asleep?]

E: Es que los perennials que son herbs, flowers, and shrubs, no todos se van a morir.
[It's because of the perennials that are herbs, flowers, and shrubs, not all will die.]

S: Claro, muchos perennials regresan año tras año, y es por eso que tenemos que cortarlos once they completely go to seed.
[Of course, many perennials will come back year after year and this is why we have to cut them.]

Carla believes that the linguistic and cultural practices that students bring from home and community must work juntos with those used in school to encourage deep understanding. That is why she never stops the dialogue and tells Sonia or the students, "Así no se dice," "English only, please," or "Spanish only, please." Carla's stance enables her to reject the notion that Sonia and the students speak "Spanglish," a stigmatized version of Spanish. And she also rejects the notion that these students have incomplete acquisition of English. Carla's stance encourages students to value their dynamic bilingualism, the way they speak with all the features of their language repertoires, and to continue developing language practices for academic purposes. This also makes it possible for Carla's students to develop strong bilingual identities. Carla's stance contributes to the students' socioemotional growth and academic learning.

In the case of multilingual speakers, language instruction has largely been focused on English-only practices that stunt bilingual development and fail to develop positive student multilingual identities. By deeply understanding translanguaging theory, teachers in our district are better equipped to meet the needs of multilingual students. The practical application of translanguaging has helped teachers to figure out HOW to implement it in lessons.

—Natalia Benjamin, Director of Multilingual Learning, Rochester Public Schools

Carla also involves students' families and communities to work juntos with the children to teach and learn from the close relationship that she establishes among all of them. For Carla, teaching is also about co-learning (Wei, 2014) with her students and with the community and families. In the jardín, we often find Carla and her students, as well as community members like Sonia, planting juntos. According to Carla's stance, and echoing our third and fourth translanguaging purposes, school learning can only occur if students are able to leverage their ways of knowing and using language that they learn from those at home and in their communities and if they are secure, socioemotionally, in their bilingual identities. Carla's stance enables her to make specific pedagogical choices to respond to students' bilingual practices and thus shift the ways in which bilingual students see themselves relative to the White monolingual students in their schools and in society.

In summary, Carla enacts her translanguaging stance in her DLBE classroom by:

- Creating translanguaging spaces within the macro-level language policies of her school, which separate students' languages

- Planning units and activities and reading texts that connect with students' local understanding and their families' and communities' funds of knowledge (Moll et al., 1992)
- Partnering with students' families and community members to co-educate and nurture students so that they can see their community reflected in school work
- Pursuing a holistic understanding of what bilingual students know and can do with content and language by assessing their general linguistic performances (e.g., using the full features of their linguistic repertoires to learn about and demonstrate their understanding of perennials and annuals) and their language-specific performances (using either Spanish or English appropriately to express their content learning)
- Leveraging students' general linguistic performances in ways that deepen content-area understanding (e.g., to explain the difference between perennials and annuals without concern for specific language features) and then to further oracy and literacy development in language-specific performances.

Stephanie: An English-Speaking Teacher in an English-Medium Content-Area Classroom

Unlike Carla, Stephanie does not speak her students' home languages, nor does she teach in a bilingual program. Furthermore, though most of her students are Latinx, they have a wide range of experiences with Spanish. Some speak Spanish at home with their families and friends and feel comfortable using it for many purposes. Others hear Spanish from an abuela or a parent, but do not feel comfortable using it themselves. Still others use Spanish outside of school, but do not have experience using it for academic purposes. Adding another layer of complexity, some of Stephanie's students are African American and Caribbean, with language practices and varieties of English that are also marginalized in school. Informed by this complex linguistic and cultural landscape, as well as her own language background, Stephanie's translanguaging stance is enacted differently from Carla's.

Stephanie believes that all students must have access to all their linguistic resources at all times to make meaning of the complex, grade-level content they encounter in her social studies class. As a monolingual English speaker, however, Stephanie must enact her stance through the use of other people and other resources, such as bilingual dictionaries, online translation tools and other technologies, bilingual staff members, and, most importantly, the students themselves. Entering Stephanie's classroom, one can see how she utilizes the resources at her disposal to leverage the translanguaging corriente and enact her stance through her practice.

For example, during her interdisciplinary unit "Environmentalism: Then and Now," Stephanie asked students to use their textbooks and several short, supplemental readings in English to construct a timeline that illustrated the major events of the environmentalist movement. Students had access to the textbook in both English and Spanish and sat in heterogeneous groups of students with diverse linguistic profiles. Because Stephanie could not find appropriate supplemental readings in Spanish, the readings she provided were in English, but at different levels of text complexity. The following vignette illustrates how Stephanie's planning and design, informed by her stance, created a translanguaging space and made room for the corriente to flow:

Stephanie circulates through the classroom, listening to her students' conversations and checking their progress. One group, which includes ***Teresita*** and ***Luis***, is speaking Spanish but writing its timeline in English. Luis has recently arrived from El Salvador and is just beginning to learn English, while Teresita is a strong reader and writer in both languages. The group uses Spanish to ensure that Luis can participate. Stephanie listens to their Spanish conversation for a moment, and then asks Teresita to tell her, in English, what they're talking about. Teresita fills her in; Stephanie contributes a few ideas that Teresita translates for Luis, and Stephanie moves on.

Next to this table, there is another group working together. In this group, ***Noemí***, who emigrated from Ecuador and whose literacy performances are more experienced in Spanish than in English, and ***James***, an African American student, are working together. James summarizes a piece of the reading in English, while Noemí listens and nods in understanding. Noemí asks a question in Spanish, and ***Eddy***, who is a more experienced bilingual, translates it for her. James consults the English version of the textbook, Noemí consults the Spanish version, and they collaboratively reach an agreement that answers Noemí's question. In the exchange, James learns the word "estereotipo," which he loves to repeat out loud, while Noemí adds the word "stereotype" to her repertoire. They return to their timeline.

Meanwhile, Luis and ***Carlos***, another recently arrived emergent bilingual are using an online translation tool on the classroom computers to find words in English to contribute to the timeline. As they find each new word in English, they write it above the Spanish word they had initially written on their timelines.

Several aspects of Stephanie's stance are visible in this snapshot from the daily life of her classroom. First, we see her comfort with linguistic flexibility. She does not police students' language, nor does she push them to use "English only." Rather, she allows students to pool their linguistic resources to make meaning. We also see the many resources at work in Stephanie's classroom. Because she does not speak Spanish, Stephanie knows that she cannot be the only source of knowledge in the room. Instead, she has made available to students a whole host of resources—including their bilingual peers—that not only help them carry out an academic task, but also increase students' participation in, and responsibility for, their own learning. Lastly, the organization of her students into heterogeneous groups helps all students engage with complex content and texts and eliminates the marginalization faced by so many emergent bilinguals in English-medium classrooms. Thus, to summarize, Stephanie enacts her translanguaging stance in her English-medium content-area classroom by

- Ceding control and being comfortable with students' linguistic flexibility
- Providing students with access to other resources, such as bilingual dictionaries, online translation tools, a variety of written texts in both English and Spanish, and fellow bilingual students
- Organizing students into heterogeneous groups so that they can pool their linguistic resources and avoid marginalizing those who speak less English than others.

Justin: A Seventh-Grade ESL Teacher in a Multilingual, Multiethnic English-Medium Classroom

Like Stephanie, Justin does not speak all of his students' home languages. Though he is bilingual, speaking English and some Mandarin, the diverse students in his classes speak a variety of languages, such as Fula, Tagalog, and Cantonese. Some of his students' languages do not share any cognates or even a script with English, so drawing connections to English can be challenging. He also has one student who is the *only* Korean speaker in the classroom, which makes it difficult for her to consult with others to make meaning of new content. Because Justin often "pushes in" to his students' content-area classrooms, he is also charged with ensuring that students are academically *and* linguistically supported, without being "marked" among English speakers as less intelligent or competent because they have less experience with the new language.

Despite the numerous challenges present in Justin's context, he is resolute in his translanguaging stance. Like Stephanie, he believes that students must have access to all their linguistic resources at all times, even if he does not understand those languages himself. Also like Stephanie, Justin uses a variety of resources, such as online translation tools and more experienced bilinguals, to ensure that his translanguaging stance is enacted in practice. He also works with his co-teachers to ensure that lesson content is adapted to meet the linguistic needs of emergent bilinguals and bring their unique experiences to the surface. This last point is especially important. Because Justin is the ESL teacher in "mainstream" content-area classrooms, he thinks of himself as not only an educator, but also an advocate and an ally. The following vignette of Justin co-planning with the seventh-grade science teacher illustrates this aspect of his stance:

As Justin and his co-teacher sat down to plan out the week's lessons, Justin intentionally created a translanguaging space so that emergent bilinguals could participate meaningfully in the instruction. The focus of the week was genetics, and the culminating design of the week was for students to carry out and write up a report of a lab experiment. Originally, the science teacher had planned for the experiment to be carried out by students individually, but Justin suggested partnering students who spoke the same home languages so that they could work together using all their linguistic resources. Justin also suggested that students build their background knowledge by pre-writing and brainstorming on the topic of genetics in any language. He explained how the teacher could use translanguaging with a traditional KWL chart, which asks students what they *know*, what they *want* to know, and what they have *learned* about a topic. Students could write what they know and what they wanted to know about genetics using all their linguistic resources, and then share what they learned in English, with translanguaging rings such as home language supports and scaffolds. Later in the week, when they wrote up their findings, Justin and his co-teacher planned out lessons so that all students had sufficient academic and linguistic support and the flexibility and space to use all their linguistic resources to make meaning of content in English.

Taking up the role of advocate and ally for his emergent bilingual students meant that Justin often had to help his colleagues sense and understand the translanguaging corriente. Rather than being relegated to the sidelines, as some ESL teachers are, Justin positions himself as an instructional leader. He has gained the respect of his colleagues, which makes it easier to introduce new ideas that help emergent bilinguals learn. Justin's work with his co-teacher to create a translanguaging space ensured that students would be provided with access to content and would be invited to share their prior knowledge and experiences with the topic. It also enabled all students—even the student who did not have a partner or group of peers who spoke her home language—to tap into their inner, intrapersonal translanguaging voice so that they could participate meaningfully. When his co-teacher worried that she would not know how to assess her students if they spoke their home languages, Justin assured her that their translanguaging design would also serve as an opportunity for documentation, bringing students' knowledge and understanding to the surface. This, Justin assured his co-teacher, would *help*, rather than hinder, their ability to assess their students.

THREE CORE BELIEFS

Although Carla, Stephanie, and Justin enacted their translanguaging stances differently because of their diverse backgrounds, experiences, and contexts, each of their stances was informed by the three core beliefs introduced earlier in the chapter.

1. Students' language practices and cultural understanding encompass those they bring from home and communities, as well as those they take up in schools. These practices and understanding work juntos and enrich each other.

Traditionally, schools have separated students' "home languages" from their "school language" ("standard" or "academic" English). This separation, based on false dichotomies and harmful raciolinguistic ideologies, essentially takes from students their most vital tools for communicating effectively, forming relationships, and fully engaging in the educational experience. Teachers in translanguaging classrooms embrace a flexible stance toward students' dynamic bilingualism. This does not mean that they do away with objectives and goals for students' language practices. On the contrary, teachers of bilingual students always think strategically about how they use language and how students can expand and enrich their linguistic repertoires.

By embracing the translanguaging corriente, teachers make space for students to use their language practices in ways that lead to increased understanding and engagement. The metaphor of interlocking gears can explain the necessity of this kind of flexible language use. Without students' existing language practices, new language practices and features have nothing to lock into and, as such, cannot gain purchase. Recall the first and second social purposes for translanguaging: *supporting students as they engage with and comprehend complex content and texts* and *providing opportunities for students to develop their linguistic practices for a variety of purposes and contexts, including those deemed academic.* Encouraging students to use all their language practices in conversation facilitates the process of content and language learning juntos.

In addition to strengthening academic understanding and increasing classroom engagement, being open to the co-existence of English and other language practices can ease the tension that often occurs when one language is considered more valuable than another. When students are told to speak only English and not Spanish, for example, the implication is that Spanish—the language of their families, friends, and communities—is unwelcome in the classroom. When we, this book's authors, think about times in our own lives when those we love or the places we are from have been denigrated or left out, we feel anger, frustration, shame, discouragement, and sadness. As Kate remembers the humiliation she felt when a classmate made fun of "how Jewish people talk," by making up words that sounded like Yiddish. Susana remembers growing up in the borderlands of Mexico and the United States, where her relatives on the Mexican side of the border called her a "pochita" and the Texas side called her a "pobrecita" because she spoke "ni inglés ni español bien" [neither English nor Spanish well]. And Ofelia has been told numerous times to "go back to her country," even though she considers the United States her country, as much as the Cuba she left for New York at the age of 11.

The emotions we feel when our lives, experiences, and understanding are not recognized or respected are not conducive to learning or to building a classroom community. When students feel they must choose between school and home, English and another language, being American or something else, academic success or being true to themselves, they are put in an impossible bind. Choosing the former in these dichotomies may feel like treachery. Choosing the latter may lead to abandoning school and discarding a chance at academic and economic success. Taking up a translanguaging stance means making a commitment to teaching students that these one-or-the-other choices are untrue and unnecessary, that, in fact, students can be successful in school *and* feel like authentic versions of themselves. Instead of asking students to be simply one or the other, we can emphasize places in our instruction that enable students to make connections from their own language practices and knowledge to those of the school. This can help ease students out from between the proverbial rock and hard place, situations of antagonism, resistance, or failure, and toward opportunities that support their socioemotional development and bilingual identities. For example, in Justin's situation, working as the students' advocate and ally by putting their needs and experiences at the center of the "mainstream" classroom ensured that their voices would be heard and that their bilingual and bicultural identities would be valued. Justin's stance was clearly one of affirming a sense of social justice in education.

Embracing a translanguaging stance aligns with a social justice-oriented perspective, promoting linguistic equity. For bilingual students, this approach fosters pride in their linguistic identity and helps protect their heritage language, empowering them academically and personally. It transforms language from a barrier to a dynamic resource, enriching their learning experience and cultivating a more inclusive educational environment. As educators, we must stand up for our students with a stance that supports and elevates them through the learning process. Our students deserve this from us.

—Angelica Wortham, professional learning consultant and PhD candidate, Dallas, Texas

2. Students' families and communities are valuable sources of knowledge and must be involved in the education process juntos.

Taking up a translanguaging stance means first recognizing and rejecting negative discourses about minority students in mainstream schools and society. When we turn on the news, look at social media, stream our favorite shows and movies, or read popular magazines, we can see how minoritized people, especially Latinx, are viewed by our society. Popular media generally portray Latinx people in a variety of crude stereotypes; we are much more likely to meet the gangster, the undocumented immigrant, or the teen mother than we are to find authentic, nuanced Latinx stories. News programs report ad nauseam on poverty, crime, drugs, and school failure in the Latinx community but leave out its long history of activism and legacy of fighting for social justice. Worse yet are the xenophobic and racist policies and discourses that have pervaded the political and social landscape over the past few decades—harsh immigration laws, anti-bilingual education acts, and bans on ethnic studies. These discourses and policies limit educational opportunities for Latinx and other youth to learn their own histories and use their own language practices. Though we cannot change these realities, we can ensure that students walk away from our classrooms knowing that their families and communities are integral to—rather than a mark against—their success.

Taking up a translanguaging stance means countering these negative discourses and making space for students' families and communities to participate in their education. This is precisely what Carla did in her lesson on the jardín when she invited a community gardener, as well as the padres and abuelitos, to plantar with their children. The following vignettes from other translanguaging classrooms further demonstrate how adopting this kind of stance extends engagement with students' families and community members in ways that go beyond token gestures:

A monolingual, English-speaking ESL teacher in Port Chester, New York, noticed that few parents and families attended the first conference of the year. She spoke with a few of her students, who told her that their parents did not speak English and did not think that they could interact with her. The teacher spoke with her assistant principal about finding an innovative way of addressing the problem. They decided to purchase headsets that allowed for simultaneous translation, which meant that, with the help of the assistant principal, the teacher and parents could communicate without a delay so that more authentic and open conversations could occur.

Rather than take up the all-too-common tactic of blaming families for not attending school meetings, this teacher tapped into her translanguaging stance to make a positive change. This powerful scenario illustrates that taking up a translanguaging stance means challenging and talking back to the negative discourse around Latinx families and communities by actively engaging them in the educational process. Here translanguaging itself becomes an act of social justice, uniting the school with families.

Taking up a translanguaging stance might also involve using culturally relevant, local examples from the community to teach academic content:

When she was an ethnic studies teacher, Cati de los Ríos, now a researcher and faculty member at the University of California, Berkeley, knew that many of her students and their families listened to corridos, Spanish-language ballads that tell stories of romance, oppression, revolution, and daily life. She used corridos as a vehicle for teaching poetic elements like rhyme and metaphor and had students compare them with genres like hip-hop and political speeches. She brought in several members of the community to sing corridos and discuss their history and importance to the Chicano community.

Cati, and many of the ethnic studies teachers she worked with in California, tapped into a translanguaging stance to validate and leverage the resources present in her students' families and communities. With them, juntos, she was able to help her students better understand academic content, build their Spanish language literacy, and see their culture represented in the classroom. This kind of instructional design, directly influenced by her stance, allowed the translanguaging corriente to flow freely and powerfully through both the classroom and students' communities. It also enabled students and their families to draw on their bilingualism and bilingual ways of knowing to better connect with classroom learning.

3. The classroom is a democratic space where teachers and students juntos co-create knowledge, challenge traditional hierarchies, and work toward a more just society.

Teachers who take up a translanguaging stance open themselves up to the idea that "traditional" classrooms do not always benefit, and may even harm, Latinx and other bilingual students. Transforming a classroom into a translanguaging space means thinking differently about traditional notions of what it looks like to teach, assess, and learn. It means thinking about whose voices and stories are represented and heard and whose are silenced. It means reviewing textbooks and curricular resources with a critical eye. It means opening up opportunities for students to use all of their language practices in every lesson and assessment. It means planning culturally and linguistically sustaining units (Paris & Alim, 2017) that culminate not just in an exam, but in meaningful, action-oriented projects that challenge students to engage with the world outside the classroom walls. In sum, it means making the familiar classroom strange and taking steps to redesign it.

Creating a more democratic classroom involves inviting students to actively participate and take a leading role in their own learning. This requires moving away from a banking model of education, where teachers deposit knowledge into passive students' empty heads, and embracing a dialogic, problem-posing model in which both students and teachers are actively engaged in the learning process (Freire, 1970). For bilingual students to engage in this way, they must be encouraged to use all their language practices to help them question, critique, and participate in important dialogue. Without access to their complete linguistic and cultural repertoires, students will not be able to participate in the kinds of conversations that lead to increased engagement and academic success. When bilingual students are forced to learn content in ways removed from their daily realities using only some of their language practices, they are also limited in their ability to develop the critical consciousness, what Freire (1970) calls conscientização, that we introduced in Part I of this book. A monolingual or bilingual monoglossic curriculum cannot engage Latinx and other students in the kind of thinking and imagining that will make them the social actors and critical activists that they can be.

The adoption of a translanguaging stance is a necessary ingredient for the transformation of the traditional classroom into what Gutiérrez (2008) calls a "third space." Gutiérrez defines a third space as "a transformative space where the potential for an expanded form of learning and the development of new knowledge are heightened" (p. 152). This necessarily calls for teachers to relinquish their traditionally hierarchical roles and embrace the idea that students bring with them knowledge and experiences that enrich and enhance learning. Thus, as we saw in Stephanie's classroom, teachers in a translanguaging third space are no longer the sole knowledge keepers, the only classroom experts, or the ideal language speakers. To help students engage in an "expanded form of learning," they need access to the language practices that help them *release* that knowledge. Without the ability to translanguage, students cannot tap into (and then expand) what they know.

NEGOTIATING A TRANSLANGUAGING STANCE

Valenzuela (1999) and others have written that Latinx students are often subjected to a *subtractive* education that leads to the loss of home languages and cultural practices because bilingual students are pushed to learn English as quickly as possible so that they can achieve academically at school. In light of this fact, and coupled with particularly Latinx students' experiences of racism and discrimination in the United States, taking up a translanguaging stance can be challenging. Though we firmly believe that most educators want the best for their students, taking up a translanguaging stance may require us to confront those who do not value or refuse to perceive the translanguaging corriente in classrooms.

In our own experiences talking about the translanguaging corriente with teachers, administrators, and policy makers around the country, we are sometimes met with skepticism, if not outright resistance. Some of these constituents hold tight to traditional notions of language acquisition and worry that students will never learn English if they continue to use what is considered "mixing," or **code-switching**. Others compare their own or their family's immigrant narratives to those of our students, unable to understand why *these* students shouldn't just learn English like they or their families did. Still others stigmatize translanguaging, comparing it unfavorably to "Spanglish" and viewing it as inappropriate for academic contexts. Some are skeptical that translanguaging can actually sustain and develop minority languages, fearful that Spanish is not being protected from the encroachment of English. Adopting a translanguaging stance in the face of resistance like this is never easy. Translanguaging, as Nelson Flores (2014) reminds us, is a political act. It requires knowledge, confidence, and even *bravery*.

We cannot tell you exactly how to develop a translanguaging stance of your own when facing monoglossic, raciolinguistic ideologies and policies that reinforce the monolingual status quo or even the traditional bilingual status quo. However, we recommend that you equip yourself with knowledge about the translanguaging corriente, learn to use tools and strategies that constitute the translanguaging pedagogy, and document your bilingual students' growth and success in your translanguaging classroom. Such knowledge, tools, and evidence will allow you to defend your stance and pedagogical choices.

Teaching for social, racial, and cognitive justice means joining our students as they challenge deep-seated ideologies and power structures and working collaboratively toward changing the colonial hierarchies that legitimize national, "standard" languages instead of the languaging of people. We believe that taking up a translanguaging stance is a powerful way of letting our bilingual students know that, like Carla, Stephanie, and Justin, we are their advocates and their allies, and that we will do everything in our power to give them the education they deserve.

CONCLUSION

This chapter has explored the first of the three interrelated strands of the translanguaging pedagogy, the translanguaging stance. We use the term juntos, the Spanish word for together, to describe the philosophical and political orientation that teachers who translanguage embrace and that informs everything from the way they view students and their language and cultural practices to the way they plan instruction and assessment. We have seen that bilingual education teachers (like Carla), English-medium content-area teachers (like Stephanie), and ESL teachers (like Justin) can all enact a translanguaging stance in their classes, although the particulars vary. This stance is what allows the translanguaging corriente, which is the basis for translanguaging for instruction and assessment, to flow openly and freely in our classrooms.

REFLECTION QUESTIONS AND ACTIVITIES

1. What elements in the translanguaging stance do you see as easy to take up and which do you find difficult? Why?
2. Why is the translanguaging stance linked to the idea of juntos?
3. What sociopolitical and socioeducational factors affect some teachers' negative reactions toward translanguaging? How could you counteract such negativity?

TAKING ACTION

1. What elements make up *your* translanguaging stance? Write down three to five beliefs that inform who you are and what you do as a teacher of bilingual students.
2. What evidence of a translanguaging stance can you find in your practice? Provide examples to illustrate your points.
3. Where, in your own context, might you draw on your translanguaging stance to critique manifestations and enactments of raciolinguistic ideologies?

6

Translanguaging Design for Instruction: The Classroom Space and Instructional Framework

LEARNING OBJECTIVES

After reading this chapter, you will be able to:

- Explain how teachers can design classroom spaces to encourage the translanguaging corriente to flow.
- Describe two major components of translanguaging instructional design: the translanguaging unit plan and the translanguaging instructional design cycle.
- Describe how Justin purposefully plans and implements a translanguaging unit with his co-teaching partner.
- Start crafting a translanguaging unit of instruction for your own teaching context.

Teachers in translanguaging classrooms must design instruction so that it responds to the translanguaging corriente, sets the right course for learning, and simultaneously leverages students' language practices and expands their repertoire to include new practices. Recall that the translanguaging pedagogy consists of three interrelated strands: stance, design, and shifts. This chapter focuses on translanguaging in instruction, specifically the "big picture," macro planning that teachers can do when it comes to purposeful instructional *designs*. Chapter 7 will discuss the more micro pedagogical practices and moment-to-moment *shifts* teachers can make that fill in the details of this big picture and leverage students' bilingualism for learning.

Translanguaging design in instruction refers to how teachers strategically plan instruction to work within the translanguaging corriente. A strong design allows teachers to address the four social purposes of translanguaging: to support students as they engage with complex content and texts; develop linguistic practices for a variety of purposes and contexts, including those deemed academic; support students' bilingual identities, socioemotional development, and critical consciousness; and make space for all students' language practices and ways of knowing and being.

The design is purposeful but flexible; it intentionally validates bilingual students' home and community language practices as they are leveraged for academic purposes while working to transform the subjectivities of inferiority often held by emergent bilingual students and address social justice. Consider the following teachers' instructional designs in their translanguaging classrooms:

- ***Carla***, our bilingual teacher, creates a Cuéntame Algo space where she and her students collaboratively explore bilingual language use.
- ***Stephanie***, our social studies teacher, encourages groups of students to use the Internet to research information on the Clean Air Act in English and in Spanish.
- ***Justin***, our ESL teacher, creates collaborative groups that have common home languages so that students can discuss texts using their own language resources and look up translations and other support texts in their home languages.
- An English language arts teacher organizes a unit around authors and poets who use multiple languages in their writing.
- A bilingual teacher gives out a Spanish text and its English translation and asks students to compare and contrast the lexicon (words), syntax (word order), morphology (word formation), and discourse structure of the text.

The ways these teachers designed different aspects of their instruction reflect their stance about teaching and learning. They believe that a classroom's design—its physical design and the process of designing units, lessons, pedagogical practices, and assessments—must emerge "from the students up." Thus, when designing instruction in a translanguaging classroom, it is important to take stock of what students know and can do, how they learn, and what their needs are. That is, teachers must design instruction that responds to where students are and plans out where they are going.

This chapter begins with the classroom space and focuses on how teachers can encourage the translanguaging corriente to flow as they structure the learning environment for collaboration and create a **multilingual ecology**. The majority of the chapter presents the translanguaging design for instruction that is at the core of the translanguaging pedagogy. One of our focal teachers, Justin, co-designs a *translanguaging unit plan* with his co-teacher and uses the *translanguaging instructional design cycle* to implement that unit plan. Chapter 6 concludes with thoughts on how all teachers can implement elements of this big picture, macro instructional planning, no matter what designated program or curriculum they use.

DESIGNING THE CLASSROOM SPACE

Though we cannot always choose the physical locations of our classrooms, we can usually make decisions about how we organize them. Whether we have our own classroom, share a classroom, or teach in multiple locations, we can all make design choices that reflect our translanguaging juntos stance. Though there are many different things that can be done with classroom or other learning spaces to help students succeed, two are described here: designing space for collaboration and designing a multilingual ecology.

Fostering Collaboration

Vygotsky (1978) argues that learning is inherently social. By organizing opportunities for collaboration among students of different abilities, teachers create optimal scenarios for learning. Vygotsky calls the space between what students can do alone and what they can do with a "more knowledgeable other" the **zone of proximal development**. In this zone, students can learn and do *more* than they can on their own because of the "boost" they receive from their peers, some of whom know and can do more. When this collaboration includes the use of students' full **language repertoires**, students' performances are enhanced. Moll (2013), building on Vygotsky, refers to the space between what students can do alone and what they can do bilingually as the **bilingual zone of proximal development**. The ideas proposed by Vygotsky and Moll are important for emergent bilingual students, who benefit from opportunities to learn from, and interact with, students who have more experience with the language the emergent bilinguals are newly learning (Celic, 2009; Kibler et al., 2021; Walqui, 2006).

To maximize these learning opportunities, it is helpful to organize your classroom in ways that encourage effective group work, communication, and idea-sharing. This can be accomplished in a number of ways:

- Switch out individual desks in rows for tables or flexible desk clusters.
- Organize tables or desk clusters so that students can see and communicate with other group members.
- Create strategic groupings so that students are seated with peers who have different general linguistic and language-specific performances and different knowledge of content, but who share a home language.
- Plan activities and task-based projects that require communication and use different kinds of language and skills.

While there will be times when homogenous groupings are necessary, it is also beneficial for students to sit with, and learn from, peers at different levels of language performance and content knowledge. This also helps build classroom community and eliminates the stigma that can be attached to emergent bilinguals, who are often isolated in their own groups and kept apart from the movimiento of the classroom.

Creating a Multilingual Ecology

Developing a robust multilingual ecology helps all students and their families feel that their languages are welcome in school. This in turn brings the translanguaging corriente closer to the surface, making students' dynamic bilingualism more palpable and thus easier to leverage. The word *ecology* in this section is used to refer to how teachers shape the linguistic space of a classroom to interact with students, families, and communities.

To create a multilingual ecology at the classroom level, we must ensure that all students' language practices are present and visible in their learning environment. For example, teachers can:

- Hang bilingual posters and signs.
- Put up students' work in English and in the students' home languages.
- Create multilingual word walls or cognate charts.
- Project or give out notes in English and in the students' home languages.
- Include books/magazines/newspapers in all students' languages in the class library.
- Use versions of a textbook in English and in the students' home languages.
- Give students access to bilingual dictionaries, bilingual picture dictionaries, and iPads or laptops.
- Encourage students to use both English and their home languages in conversation and in writing.
- Set up a listening center where students can hear the content in all languages.
- Encourage family and community members to come in to class to tell a story in their home languages.
- Use video clips with subtitles in English and in the students' home languages.

Actively bringing students' languages into the ecology of the classroom sends a clear message that those languages are valued and important to learning. However, it is not enough simply to hang posters or put bilingual dictionaries on bookshelves. Creating a multilingual ecology means *utilizing* these resources to help students tap into their entire linguistic repertoires for learning. In short, making the most out of a collaborative multilingual space means designing rigorous and responsive instruction.

TRANSLANGUAGING DESIGN FOR INSTRUCTION

When teachers learn about translanguaging, many say that they have been doing it for years but have not had a name for it, and that, in fact, they had been operating under the assumption that they were "cheating" or "breaking the rules" by allowing students to use both English and their home languages in the classroom at the same time. These teachers knew that the English-only rules they were being asked to follow did not fully serve them or their students, and they often transgressed these rules by using students' bilingualism quietly, behind closed doors. We hope that naming a design for instruction will enable educators and their students to translanguage en voz alta, with the doors wide open, in ways that lead to increased engagement, improved academic results, stronger relationships, more secure identities, and more social equality.

Taking up a translanguaging stance and developing a translanguaging design means crafting instruction by listening to the perspectives that matter most—our own and those of our students. The translanguaging design for instruction pushes teachers to put imagination and action into teaching bilingual students. Every unit of instruction is driven by students' specific, local knowledge and language practices, and each encourages students to take learning out into the real world and make it *do something*. We also see each step of this process coming alive through students' fluid language practices, which enable them to learn about and access a topic or theme in critical and creative ways.

To dig into the big picture of planning translanguaging instructional designs, we turn now to several short vignettes of Justin's unit planning with his colleague, a seventh-grade math teacher. Remember that Justin provides push-in ESL services in middle school math and science classes and that the emergent bilinguals he works with come from a wide range of linguistic and cultural backgrounds. Together, Justin and his co-teacher designed a math unit entitled "Geometry in Our World." In addition to teaching student grade-level math content, the unit builds students' literacies and taps into the translanguaging corriente by inviting them to write bilingual children's books that communicate understandings of geometry in linguistically and culturally sustaining ways. The vignettes from Justin and his co-teacher's planning demonstrate how teachers can implement two macro components of instructional design for the translanguaging classroom: the translanguaging unit plan and the translanguaging instructional design cycle. A third macro element of instructional design—assessment—is explained in Chapter 8. And, as noted earlier, the micro components of instructional design—daily pedagogical practices—and translanguaging shifts are explored next, in Chapter 7.

Translanguaging Unit Plan

Most of the planning elements of a translanguaging unit of instruction are the same as those necessary in any instruction; some of them (e.g., content and language objectives) are especially important in bilingual classrooms and for teaching emergent bilinguals in English-medium classrooms. But there are also elements that are specific to the translanguaging classroom (e.g., translanguaging objectives). The six elements in the translanguaging unit plan are essential questions, content standards, content and language objectives, translanguaging objectives, culminating projects and assessments, and texts.

Each element of the plan and its importance to the translanguaging classroom is described in the following sections. Each element is also illustrated in action through excerpts from Justin and his co-teacher's planning, and you are encouraged to think about how you might plan a translanguaging unit of instruction that leverages students' bilingualism for learning in your context. After all elements of the unit plan have been introduced, Justin's translanguaging unit plan is provided in its entirety (Table 6.1). A blank *Translanguaging Unit Planning Template* is also provided in Appendix 6.1.

Essential Questions The translanguaging unit plan begins with essential questions, which are used to stimulate thought, provoke inquiry, and spark more questions. They are provocative and generative. By tackling such questions, learners are engaged in *uncovering* the depth and richness of a topic that might otherwise be obscured by simply *covering* it (McTighe & Wiggins, 2013, p. 3).

Table 6.1. Justin's Translanguage Unit Plan: Geometry in our World

Essential Questions	• Where do we see geometry at work in our lives? • How do we know how to measure? • Why is it important to understand the geometry of our world?	
Content and Language Standards	• CA CCSS.MATH.CONTENT.7.G.B.4: Know the formulas for the area and circumference of a circle and use them to solve problems; give an informal derivation of the relationship between the circumference and area of a circle. • CA CCSS.MATH.CONTENT.7.G.B.6: Solve real-world and mathematical problems involving area, volume, and surface area of two- and three-dimensional objects composed of triangles, quadrilaterals, polygons, cubes, and right prisms. • ELD.Part I.C.Productive: Writing literary and informational texts to present, describe, and explain ideas and information, using appropriate technology. • ELD.Part II.Connecting and Condensing Ideas: Condensing ideas.	
Content and Language Objectives	*Content Objectives* Students will be able to: • Use formulas for measuring area, volume, and surface area for different geometric objects. • Accurately draw geometric shapes. • Connect their mathematical understandings to real-world situations and problems.	*Language Performance Objectives* *General linguistic* Students will be able to: • Summarize solutions to real-world math problems both orally and in writing. • Synthesize their understanding of geometry into stories that are developmentally appropriate for elementary school students. • Interact orally with peers in ways that advance the group's math knowledge. *Language-specific* Students will be able to: • Explain their choices of measurement using appropriate content-area vocabulary in English. • Use nominalization in their summaries and stories in English.
Translanguaging Objective(s)	Students will be able to: • Work in groups to solve math problems using both English and their home languages. • Use both English and their home languages to write children's books about geometry. • Rationalize their language choices in oral presentations (e.g., why certain words or problems were given in one language or the other; why a certain character used one language and not another). • Read their books to bilingual children, expanding on their ideas and asking younger students questions in both languages. • Recognize and track math vocabulary cognates.	
Culminating Project and Assessments	*Culminating Project* In groups, students create bilingual children's books that explain a geometric concept using both English and an additional language, as well as culturally relevant examples and connections. Students present their books to elementary school teachers and later read them to groups of elementary school students with whom they share a home language. Students are assessed on their understanding of math content as well as their creativity and strategic use of both languages.	*Other Assessments* *Teachers' translanguaging assessment:* Students are assessed on content understanding, intellectual curiosity, and language practices. Focus on whether the student can perform tasks, independently or with assistance, using the full features of their repertoires (general linguistic performance) as well as language-specific features. *Reading math:* Students engage with a variety of readings from newspapers, magazines, and websites that connect geometry to the real world. Readings are in English and, when possible, the students' home languages. Students discuss the readings in home language groups and work together to ask questions, make connections, summarize, and answer comprehension questions. *Writing math:* Students create new geometry word problems using culturally relevant situations and translanguaging. Students are assessed on their creativity, use of language, and understanding of math content. Students are also assessed on why they made the linguistic and content choices they made via short process papers. *Student translanguaging self-assessment:* Throughout the unit, students provide feedback and self-assessment via questions about their own learning, language development, and content understanding.
Texts	*In the home language(s)* • Readings about geometry from websites, newspapers, and magazines • Children's books	*In English* • Math textbook • Readings about geometry from websites, newspapers, and magazines • Children's books

Let's look at the essential questions that Justin and his seventh-grade math co-teacher develop for a geometry unit of instruction.

Justin and his co-teacher wanted students to make connections between the content and their own diverse experiences with that content. Drawing on what Justin knew about the students' bilingual profiles and cultural backgrounds, he and his co-teacher came up with the following essential questions:

- Where do we see geometry at work in our lives?
- How do we know how to measure?
- Why is it important to understand the geometry of our world?

In the translanguaging classroom, essential questions help students make connections between their own lived experiences, including their language and cultural practices, and academic content.

Content Standards Standards are guidelines for language development and content knowledge that help organize instruction and promote student learning. When standards are *expanded* and *localized*—meaning that they *expand* past monolingual, monocultural understanding so that they connect with students' own *local* language practices, funds of knowledge, communities, families, and interests—they help bilingual students learn more and learn more successfully (more on this idea in Chapter 10).

Translanguaging classrooms reimagine the use of standards. Rather than starting with standards themselves, educators are encouraged to start with students' language practices. Teachers help bilingual students develop the language practices demanded by the standards using the full features of their linguistic repertoires. The following vignette shows how Justin and his co-teacher plan to expand and localize standards in their geometry unit of instruction:

Before introducing the unit to their students, Justin and his co-teacher looked at the standards required by their state: the seventh-grade California Common Core math standards. In doing so, they found two they could use:

CCSS.MATH.CONTENT.7.G.B.4: Know the formulas for the area and circumference of a circle and use them to solve problems; give an informal derivation of the relationship between the circumference and area of a circle.

CCSS.MATH.CONTENT.7.G.B.6: Solve real-world and mathematical problems involving area, volume, and surface area of two- and three-dimensional objects composed of triangles, quadrilaterals, polygons, cubes, and right prisms.

They then revisited California's seventh-grade English language development standards and chose two that aligned with their chosen Common Core standards:

ELD.Part I.C.Productive: Writing literary and informational texts to present, describe, and explain ideas and information, using appropriate technology.

ELD.Part II.Connecting and Condensing Ideas: Condensing ideas.

Using these language and content standards helped Justin and his co-teacher ensure that they were engaging students with rigorous content, helping them add English practices to their repertoires, and helping them prepare for necessary standardized exams. These standards also fit into their plan for helping their students create authentic, culturally relevant children's books that use local scenarios and real-world problems to demonstrate an understanding of geometry. In these ways, the translanguaging unit design is both aligned with required content and language standards *and* connected with and built on bilingual students' local knowledge and strengths. Overall, no matter what content and language development standards you use in your context—be they state standards, ACTFL, WIDA, CEFR (Common European Framework of Reference for Languages), or another—the important takeaway is to make them work for you and your students, and not the other way around.

Content and Language Objectives Content and language objectives align with standards and help organize units and individual lessons. Reflecting the holistic view of language, language objectives in translanguaging classrooms are informed by students' general linguistic and language-specific performances. The translanguaging unit plan therefore distinguishes between general linguistic performance objectives (which encourage students to use their entire language repertoires to make meaning and express complex thoughts, interact with texts and people in engaging ways, and make inferences from multiple sources and with multiple resources) and language-specific performance objectives (which focus on meeting the objectives using standard grammar, usage, and vocabulary in a national language). While content objectives are more or less the same for all students, language objectives must be differentiated according to students' bilingual profiles and levels of language development in English and/or the additional classroom language. Here are Justin's content and language objectives:

Content Objectives

- Students will be able to use formulas for measuring area, volume, and surface area for different geometric objects.
- Students will be able to accurately draw geometric shapes.
- Students will connect their mathematical understanding to real-world situations and problems.

Once they developed their *content objectives*, which aligned with their chosen Common Core state standards, Justin helped his co-teacher come up with *language objectives* that aligned with their chosen English language development standards and that would help students access the content.

For example, Justin knew that to "give an informal derivation of the relationship between the circumference and the area of a circle" would require students to use content-area vocabulary as well as abstract language structures like nominalization that are used in academic contexts. Solving real-world and mathematical problems would require students to break down linguistically difficult word problems and explain their solutions both mathematically and in their own words. Justin made sure that there were language objectives that relied on students' general linguistic performances, as well as objectives that focused on language-specific performances and new features of their linguistic repertoires.

Because Justin works in an English-medium classroom, he only includes language-specific performance objectives in English on his translanguaging unit plan.[1]

Language Performance Objectives

General linguistic

- Students will summarize solutions to real-world math problems both orally and in writing.
- Students will synthesize their understanding of geometry into stories that are developmentally appropriate for elementary school students.

[1]Teachers who work in bilingual classrooms develop language-specific performance objectives for both languages used for instructional purposes.

- Students will interact orally with peers in ways that advance the group's math knowledge.

Language-specific (English)

- Students will explain their choices of measurement using appropriate content-area vocabulary in English.
- Students will use nominalization in their summaries and stories in English.

Justin differentiates the language objectives for his students based on their performances in English and the other languages in their linguistic repertoires.

For example, one of Justin's Chinese students, ***Yi-Sheng***, has recently arrived from Taiwan, speaks little English, and needs practice with the Latin script that English uses. Justin uses his state's ELD evaluation tool and evaluates Yi-Sheng's performance in English as *emerging*. However, according to her Chinese language teacher, her performance in Mandarin is at grade level, meaning that her general linguistic performances are probably *expanding*. Another student in class, ***Pablo***, came from Argentina 2 months ago. Pablo had taken private English lessons in Argentina, and his performance in English is *expanding*. Furthermore, his academic performance in Spanish in the Spanish language arts class is quite high. Pablo can leverage his understanding of how texts work in Spanish to read and write texts in English.

Fatoumata's case is different. She is from Guinea and speaks Pular (Fula) and French, which she learned because it was used as a medium of instruction in school. However, her school attendance was sporadic because she was from a rural area. Justin considers Fatoumata's oral English to be at about the same stage as Pablo's (*expanding*). However, her written English is at the *emerging* stage. With the help of a French-speaking paraprofessional, Justin determines that Fatoumata's French literacy is not at grade level. When Fatoumata reads, she comprehends little, and she has a lot of trouble expressing herself in writing. Justin cannot assess Fatoumata's performance in Pular, but he always sees her engaged in conversation with students who say they speak Pular. Because Pular is not used as a medium of instruction, the other students from Guinea have told Justin that they cannot write it. So Justin's best guess is that Fatoumata's performances in Pular would be *emergent* in academic contexts. Fatoumata cannot leverage her understanding of Pular or French texts in the same way that Pablo can draw on his Spanish to comprehend English texts. Based on his students' language performances in both English and their other languages, Justin differentiated the language objectives to meet his students where they were and help propel their language performances forward.

Regarding the general linguistic performance objectives, Justin noted the following:

- Yi-Sheng would summarize the solution and generate the story in Mandarin, but she would summarize her work orally in English, with the help of her Chinese-speaking peers.
- Pablo would prewrite both tasks in Spanish but then produce them in English while supported by iPad resources and his Spanish-speaking peers in the class.
- Fatoumata would summarize the solution and generate stories only orally, using Pular and French. Justin also provided her with some sentence starters in written English so that, using Google Translate and the help of other French-speaking peers, she could write responses.

Regarding the language-specific performance objectives, Justin distributed a vocabulary sheet with the content-area words in English that the students would need to summarize and write their stories.

- Pablo would use the vocabulary sheet only for guidance.

- Yi-Sheng and Fatoumata would write 10 of the words down in their notebooks.
- Because nominalization is a specific structure that students would need, Justin used the Internet to look up the different ways English, Spanish, Chinese, and French constructed nominalizations. He showed the students the following:
  - English often adds "people." Justin gave the example "Rich people are lucky."
  - Spanish and French usually add an article. Justin asked Pablo to give an example, and he shared "los ricos." Fatoumata added in French "les riches."
  - Chinese adds a particle. Justin called on Yi-Sheng to show students how to add the particle 的.

Justin then told the students to use nominalizations in their stories in English, French, Spanish, and Chinese.

- Pablo was to identify nominalizations in Spanish and write them in English.
- For Yi-Sheng and Fatoumata, he supplied a paragraph in English and asked them to look for "one" and "people" and try out how it was said in Chinese and French.

Translanguaging Objectives While content objectives set the course for what students will learn, and language objectives outline the *general* and *specific* language practices they will need to meet the content standards, **translanguaging objectives** are planned ways of leveraging bilingualism and ways of knowing so that students can better access both content and language practices valued in school and interact with their peers. Justin's translanguaging objectives are as follows:

Translanguaging Objectives

- Students will work in groups to solve math problems using both English and their home languages.
- Students will use both English and their home languages to write children's books about geometry.
- Students will rationalize their language choices in oral presentations (e.g., why certain words or problems were given in one language or the other; why a certain character used one language and not another).
- Students will read their books to bilingual children, expanding on their ideas and asking younger students questions in both languages.
- Students will recognize and track math vocabulary cognates.

These objectives allow students to appropriate content and language in ways that they could not have done in English (or any other language) alone. Translanguaging objectives reframe students' existing language practices and local understanding as important to classroom learning.

Building translanguaging into the unit's final project enabled *all* students to express their understanding in complex ways. Through one translanguaging objective, "Students will use both English and their home languages to write children's books about geometry," Justin and his co-teacher expected students to meet and *exceed* the standards, as well as create something that they could not have produced using only one language. For example:

While creating their bilingual children's books, Yi-Sheng excitedly spoke to her partner in Mandarin. Her partner, a more experienced bilingual, added a short line of dialogue in Mandarin to their book. Justin went over to the two students and asked the student who was more comfortable with English to explain to him what the character was saying in

Mandarin. Yi-Sheng's partner did so, and Justin learned that not only did Yi-Sheng contribute an excellent explanation of the geometric concept, but she also had a great sense of humor! He told both students to do their best to translate the line into English and include it in the book.

Culminating Project and Assessments The culminating project is the authentic, action-oriented product that students create and implement throughout the course of the unit. The culminating project pushes students toward taking meaningful action, and it offers an opportunity to evaluate students' understanding of content and their development of language and literacy practices for academic purposes. An action-oriented culminating project is especially important to the translanguaging classroom because it provides students with the opportunity to use their bilingualism and ways of knowing to create something new and innovative.

The culminating project also functions as a differentiated assessment that allows students to demonstrate what they know and can do with content and language. We will take a deep dive into assessment in Chapter 8, but included here are descriptions of Justin's culminating project and other assessments used in this unit plan:

Culminating Project

In groups, students will create bilingual children's books that explain a geometric concept using both English and an additional language, as well as culturally relevant examples and connections. Students will present their books to elementary school teachers and later read them to groups of elementary school students with whom they share a home language. Students will be assessed on their understanding of math content as well as their creativity and strategic use of both languages.

Throughout this unit of instruction, teachers assess students' content understanding, intellectual curiosity, and language practices, with attention to whether students can perform tasks independently or with assistance, using all the features of their linguistic repertoires (general linguistic performance) as well as language-specific features. Specifically, Justin and his co-teacher focus on the following areas:

- *Reading math*: Students will engage with a variety of readings from newspapers, magazines, and websites that connect geometry to the real world. Readings will be in English and, when possible, the students' home languages. Students will discuss the readings in home language groups and work together to ask questions, make connections, summarize, and answer comprehension questions.
- *Writing math*: Students will create new geometry word problems using culturally relevant situations and translanguaging. Students will be assessed on their creativity, use of language, and understanding of math content. Students will also be assessed on why they made the linguistic and content choices they made via short process papers.

The translanguaging unit plan also includes a *student translanguaging self-assessment* in which students provide feedback and self-assessment by responding to questions about their own learning, language development, and content understanding (more on this and other ongoing assessments in Chapter 8).

The following vignette demonstrates Justin's students' active engagement in the authentic culminating project:

Students worked in shared home language groups to create bilingual children's books that used culturally relevant examples to teach children about geometry. Students took pictures of objects in their homes and neighborhoods and created stories that taught younger students about the mathematical properties of the shapes using recognizable language and cultural objects. Students' contributions to the culminating project varied depending on their comfort with English and their literacy in their home languages. For example, Danilo demonstrates literacy performances that are experienced in Tagalog. However, his language-specific performances in English were just emerging. His strong general linguistic performance allowed him to be an active participant in the collaborative writing process, and he planned to read the parts of the book written in Tagalog when his group presented to the elementary school students.

Before reading the books to the elementary students, Justin and his co-teacher brought elementary school teachers to listen to the students' presentations of their books. Students shared their stories, using both English and their home languages. Fatoumata read her story in French, and Yi-Sheng read her story in Mandarin. These students explained the choices they had made regarding both language and math content and discussed how they planned to present the books to younger students. The elementary school teachers gave constructive feedback to the students and to Justin, and Justin's co-teacher assessed students on both their understanding of the math content and their strategic language choices. Students took the feedback they received, refined their projects, and later, in groups, read their bilingual math books in several elementary school classrooms.

Texts The texts that students read, watch, listen to, and engage with are very important to the success of an instructional unit. In the translanguaging unit design, texts refer to the multilingual and multimodal resources that supplement content and language learning. Choosing texts also involves looking for relevance to students' daily lives so that meaning can be made more easily. As España and Herrera (2020) remind us, it is important to always be mindful of including the three Ts: temas, textos, and translanguaging. Texts that are diverse in language, point of view, and modality provide students in English-medium and bilingual classrooms multiple ways to understand and connect with new content and language.

For example, in classrooms like Carla's that work to develop students' bilingualism and biliteracy, this means choosing texts in both languages and allowing students to use their full linguistic repertoires to understand them. In English-medium classrooms like Justin's and Stephanie's, choosing texts includes differentiating for students according to their language-specific performances in English and considering how to leverage their general linguistic performances to strengthen what they can do in English.

In several of my class sessions across ethnic studies, critical pedagogy, and Spanish-language courses, we analyze current curricula. This book provides a lens to approach that analysis and return to our schools with a critical, translanguaging stance. We place deficit-oriented instruction from published curricula side-by-side with ideas from The Translanguaging Classroom and notice how the former focuses on developing "academic vocabulary" with no awareness of what bilingual and multilingual speakers can already do with their language practices, while the latter creates learning opportunities that leverage translanguaging.

—Carla España, Ph.D., bilingual teacher educator, co-author, En Comunidad, New York, New York

Justin and his co-teacher worked hard to supplement the required standards-aligned textbook with other diverse texts. Their unit plan included excerpts from additional math books, readings about geometry from websites, newspapers, and magazines, and children's books in the students' home languages and English. As they worked through the unit plan, the teachers and students realized that there simply weren't enough books about geometry in other languages:

Justin and his co-teacher utilized the required textbook, which they had in English and Spanish, short readings from the Internet in a variety of languages, and video clips in English that students discussed in groups using their home languages. In addition to reading about math content, students also read math-focused children's books but quickly realized that there were not enough bilingual books about geometry—especially not in languages like Mandarin and Tagalog. This realization pushed them toward the unit's culminating project. Justin and his co-teacher's work on expanding and localizing the standards in this geometry unit of instruction allowed students to meet and exceed the standards.

Translanguaging Instructional Design Cycle

While a translanguaging unit plan can help when envisioning the big instructional picture, it is also important to envision a cycle of instructional goals that sequence and structure the learning within that unit. The **translanguaging instructional design cycle** is a framework that can be used to plan scaffolded, integrated instruction that enables students to demonstrate their learning in differentiated, authentic ways. This design cycle framework can be used to envision the arc of *all* learning within a multi-week unit, a week of instruction within a unit, or even, with some modification, a single instructional lesson. This section of the chapter describes the five stages of this translanguaging instructional design cycle: *explorar, evaluar, imaginar, presentar,* and *implementar* and illustrates how Justin and his co-teacher used it within their planning (see Figure 6.1).

Though much instruction is designed in this cyclical, integrated fashion, most is not planned specifically with bilingual students in mind. The translanguaging instructional design cycle, which teachers can use in English-medium and bilingual programs, is meant to leverage the translanguaging corriente by bringing students' complex bilingual language practices to the surface.

Explorar When we encourage students to explore a new topic or theme, we are inspiring them to follow their natural interests or questions. This process helps them understand new content and uncover new ideas on their own terms. As students explore and build their fields of knowledge, they become invested in their learning, and they connect new content and language to their own lives and local bilingual contexts. Justin facilitated this by setting up opportunities for his students to explore various examples of new geometric concepts,

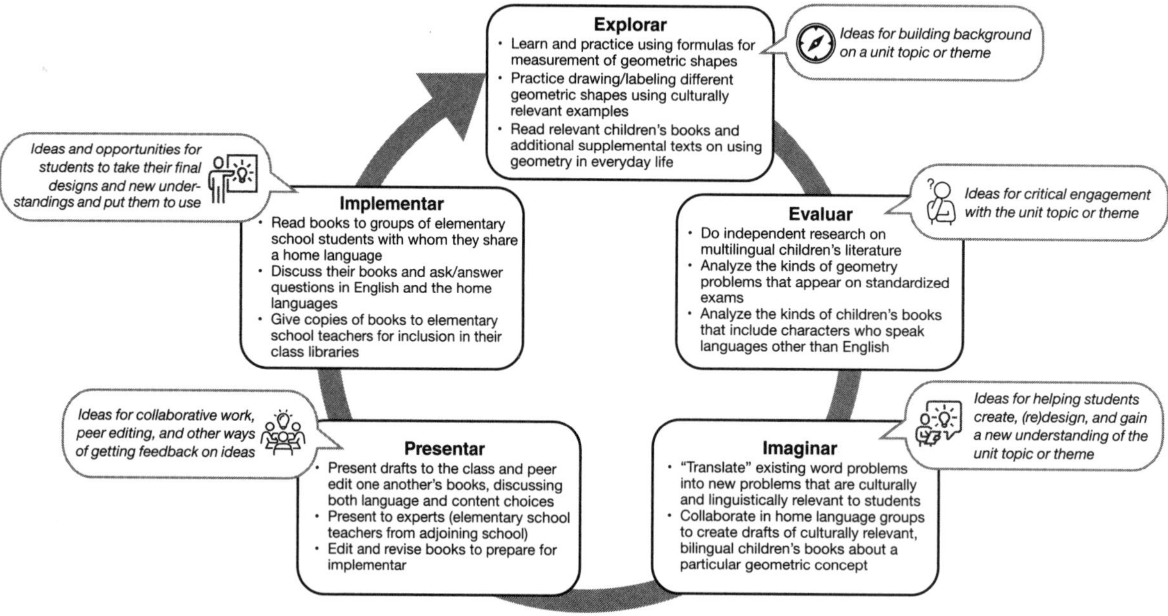

Figure 6.1 Illustrates Justin's translanguaging design cycle.

solve different problems, and research children's literature on the Internet in both English and their home languages.

Gaining a multifaceted, complex, *bilingual* understanding of a topic enables students to reimagine, transform, and, in fact, *redesign* that topic in ways that improve their lives and those of their communities. In many ways, the explorar stage can be compared to the building background stage in many traditional learning cycles. What makes the explorar stage different from simply building background is that students are specifically expanding their understanding of a topic from a variety of viewpoints in both their home and new languages, and with multimodal texts.

Evaluar Just as the process of explorar is ongoing, so is the process of evaluar—assessing what we learn. As students learn more about a topic, they should be encouraged to put forth opinions, raise questions, and think critically about what they're exploring, using their entire linguistic repertoires. Thus, this stage is very much connected to a translanguaging stance. Rather than asking students to passively consume information, teachers taking a translanguaging stance use this stage of the design cycle to push students to be active, critical, and creative thinkers. For example, they set up opportunities for them to ask questions:

- Whose voices do we hear in our research on the topic?
- Are the bilingual groups represented by students in class under- or overrepresented in the discourse?
- Are the examples we see representative of our experiences? Of bilingual practices?
- Are there opportunities to add our local knowledge, including our bilingual voices, to the conversation?

Because of their unique position on borders and margins and their experiences in two linguistic and cultural worlds, Justin's bilingual students saw that there were not many books about geometry for children, let alone in different languages. It is this kind of criticality that opens the doors to the next stage—imagining new ways of viewing a topic or using different language practices for understanding it.

Imaginar Equipped with the strong understanding developed in the first two stages, students use what they have learned to support and stimulate new thinking and new ways of using language to learn. This third stage can involve group and individual brainstorming, planning, drafting, hypothesis testing, and, as always, researching further, using the full features of their linguistic repertoires. It is in this stage that students shift their focus from what already exists in the field in English and other languages to imagining what could exist, or what is possible. For example, Justin and the math teacher engaged their students in imagining how translanguaging in math texts could change math comprehension and transform the conversations and levels of access that students have in math classrooms.

Presentar In the presentar stage, students engage in peer editing, conferencing, rewriting, and, finally, presenting their work—always mindful of the language practices that they are selecting and the reasons for those choices. This opens up space for all students to participate and share their work, think about the ways they use language, and remain engaged in completing their task. This stage offers opportunities for students to receive authentic feedback before putting their work into action and to be assessed on their authentic performances. Students can present their work to teachers and peers, members of the school community, their families, or other relevant constituents with language practices that meet the different communication needs of the interlocutors. Students' general linguistic and language-specific performances in different communicative activities can be assessed, documented, and monitored. As we saw in Justin's translanguaging unit plan, students made presentations to local elementary school teachers before sharing their books with the children. They then read their reimagined bilingual math books with the children.

Implementar The implementar stage pushes students to demonstrate their content and language learning as they show what they know and can do using the full features of their linguistic repertoires. This stage also encourages bilingual students to use language for authentic purposes to take meaningful action. Instead of decontextualized language learning, students learn new ways of using language to carry out a task and communicate with different people who have various language resources and practices. As students put their learning to work, they leverage their bilingualism to find academic success, contribute meaningfully to their communities, and grow as active, engaged citizens. This was indeed the case for the students involved in the math lesson that Justin supported. Figure 6.1 shows the translanguaging design cycle template filled out for Justin's geometry unit. A blank template is included in Appendix 6.2.

It is important to remember that each stage of the design cycle has its own linguistic demands. For example, the explorar stage, which requires students to ask questions, build background, and understand multiple facets of a topic, should draw on students' *general linguistic performances,* as they learn and make meaning using their full linguistic repertoires. The presentar and implementar stages, which demand some kind of display, presentation, and authentic use of students' work, require more *language-specific performances,* as they make intentional, metalinguistic choices about the task, genre, audience, and context. Taking a translanguaging stance and implementing a translanguaging design require teachers to evaluate the linguistic demands of *all* instructional tasks in the classroom and to determine what kind of scaffolding and supports students need based on their understanding of students' bilingual profiles and performances.

CONCLUSION

Translanguaging in instruction means *purposefully and strategically* designing classroom space and teaching with the translanguaging corriente and students' general linguistic and language-specific performances at the center. Though teachers' translanguaging designs will vary across different instructional contexts, we always find intentionality, purposefulness, and mindful flexibility in translanguaging classrooms.

This chapter has discussed the "big picture" of instructional planning, offering both a tool for planning macro instructional designs (the translanguaging unit plan) and a framework for sequencing and structuring all instruction (the translanguaging instructional design cycle). However, many teachers today are working within programmatic and curricular bounds. Some may work with scripted curricula with strict pacing guides that do not allow for much deviation. Others may feel that post-COVID-19 pandemic "learning acceleration" plans have them moving too quickly to attend to yet another element of instructional design. For those in these and many other situations, the prospect of using a full unit plan or organizing instruction along a five-stage design cycle may seem unrealistic.

With this said, all readers are encouraged to look for what they can do. Where might there be space in a scripted curriculum to ask different questions, provide a supplemental text in students' home languages, or adapt a project so that it more explicitly leverages students' translanguaging? How might you tweak an existing lesson plan so that it differentiates between general linguistic and language-specific performances, thus enabling students both to access content and expand their linguistic repertoires? If you do not have the time and space to implement "big picture" instructional designs, elements of these designs may work for you and your context and, in small ways, open up your instructional designs to the translanguaging corriente.

REFLECTION QUESTIONS AND ACTIVITIES

1. Are English and students' other languages present in the ecology of your classroom? Does the ecology encourage students to use their full linguistic repertoires when learning? If not, what changes could you make?
2. Does the way you plan instruction make room for students' use of their home languages and cultural understanding? If not, what changes could you make?

3. Look at an instructional design you currently use in your context (e.g., a lesson, a unit, a project). Where is there room in this instructional design to implement elements of the translanguaging unit plan or (re)organize it according to the translanguaging instructional design cycle?

TAKING ACTION

1. Review Justin's translanguaging unit planning template in Table 6.1 and his translanguaging design cycle in Figure 6.1. Using the blank templates provided in Appendices 6.1 and 6.2, plan a translanguaging unit of instruction for your class. Explain how your unit plan leverages the translanguaging corriente and is informed by your students' general linguistic and language-specific performances. Share your thinking with a planning partner, coach, or administrator.
2. Implement the unit plan you developed. Videotape or take pictures of your unit in action and share it with your colleagues. How does your unit plan reflect your translanguaging stance? What stands out? What works well? What questions do you have?

APPENDIX 6.1

Translanguaging Unit Planning Template

Essential Questions	
Content Standards	
Content and Language Objectives	
Content Objectives	
Language Performance Objectives	
General Linguistic	
Language-Specific	
Translanguaging Objectives	
Culminating Project and Assessments	
Culminating Project	
Other Assessments	
Texts	
In the home language(s)	
In English	

APPENDIX 6.2

Translanguaging Instructional Design Cycle Template

Explorar
Ideas for building background on a unit topic or theme
Evaluar
Ideas for critical engagement with the unit topic or theme
Imaginar
Ideas for helping students create, (re)design, and gain a new understanding of the unit topic or theme
Presentar
Ideas for collaborative work, peer editing, and other ways of getting feedback on ideas
Implementar
Ideas and opportunities for students to take their final designs and new understandings and put them to use

7

Translanguaging Design for Instruction: Pedagogical Practices That Make Space for and Leverage Translanguaging

LEARNING OBJECTIVES

After reading this chapter, you will be able to:

- Explain how teachers can open up translanguaging spaces through the use of pedagogical practices that support emergent bilingual students and encourage the translanguaging corriente to flow.
- Describe how Justin and his co-teacher utilize pedagogical practices within their unit plan that align with the five stages of the translanguaging instructional design cycle.
- Connect pedagogical practices that make space for and leverage the translanguaging corriente for learning to unplanned, moment-to-moment translanguaging shifts.
- Begin to add new practices to your own instructional "toolkit" that encourage students' translanguaging and support their learning.

In Chapter 6, two "macro" structures were introduced that can help you plan translanguaging instructional designs—the translanguaging unit plan and the translanguaging instructional design cycle. These two structures were framed as "big picture" approaches to designing instruction that could enable you to strategically leverage and celebrate the translanguaging corriente. The next chapter, Chapter 8, will be a discussion on assessment, which is an integral part of the big picture of designing successful instruction. This chapter delves into the "micro"—the pedagogical strategies, approaches, and translanguaging shifts that can structure the daily life of classrooms. These practices, both planned and unplanned, align with the translanguaging instructional design cycle and support the four purposes of a translanguaging pedagogy. Overall, this chapter will explore how these pedagogical practices can be integrated into instruction to scaffold, deepen understandings, and overall support and affirm students as they draw on all of their linguistic and other meaning-making resources to learn.

Teachers use *translanguaging pedagogical practices* every day to make content and language more comprehensible to bilingual students and to make space for all students to use all of their language resources for learning. Teachers use these flexible teaching approaches to integrate students' existing knowledge and language practices and those that are expected of them in school. For the purposes of this book, **translanguaging pedagogical practices** can be understood as ways that teachers:

- Scaffold students' engagement with content and language, enabling them to do more than they could in one named language or another, or with only the spoken/written mode;
- Engage students and deepen their understandings of content in ways that connect to their uniquely bilingual ways of knowing; and
- Enact their translanguaging stances through daily design choices that make space for and leverage la corriente and put bilingual students at the center of the classroom.

It is important to reiterate here that translanguaging must be thought of as *more* than just a series of strategies. In fact, surface-level, strategy-based interpretations of translanguaging often result in framing it merely as a scaffold to English-only instruction. Because translanguaging is what *all* language users do *all* the time, translanguaging is not merely a removable scaffold; the communicative norm of bilingual people and communities can never be removed. However, it is also incumbent upon teachers to help students expand their linguistic repertoires to include those language practices expected of them in schools, a task that often requires support and scaffolding. One way to do this is by opening up **translanguaging spaces** that explicitly invite the language practices of bilingual communities, enabling students to language flexibly and creatively as they learn and make meaning of new content and language.

TRANSLANGUAGING PEDAGOGICAL PRACTICES

Sánchez et al. (2017) put forth a framework that enables teachers to open up such translanguaging spaces, even within language allocation policies that separate English and languages other than English such as are found in most dual-language bilingual education (DLBE) programs. They describe how separate linguistic spaces can be "strategically accompanied by spaces in which translanguaging is used intentionally for three purposes: (a) to have a more holistic understanding of the child as learner (translanguaging documentation), (b) to scaffold instruction for individual students (translanguaging rings), and (c) to transform the normalizing effects of standardized language in school and the hegemony of English (translanguaging transformation)" (p. 7). Though Sánchez et al. developed this framework for DLBE programs, it is applicable to *all* programs, as nearly all bilingual students' learning is organized by the separation of their language practices into false dichotomies like "home language/school language" or "English/language other than English (LOTE)," to name only two.

The discussion of translanguaging pedagogical practices in this chapter is aligned with Sánchez et al.'s (2017) discussion of *translanguaging rings*. If, as they write, translanguaging documentation helps teachers "understand how each student negotiates and uses their linguistic resources in different language spaces," teachers can use what they learn through assessments to "differentiate the design of instruction, learning experiences, and find instructional material and strategies that support each individual student" (p. 9). In this way, teachers make available a variety of **translanguaging rings**, providing students with scaffolding, differentiation, and various ways of connecting what they already know and can do with both language and content to what is expected of them in the classroom.

Translanguaging rings can be planned or unplanned, intentional translanguaging designs or moment-to-moment translanguaging shifts, but they always provide students with affordances that enable them to leverage their own translanguaging for learning. More than simply supporting students academically, translanguaging rings can also destigmatize students' translanguaging. By building these strategies, options, and supports into *all* instruction for *all* students, teachers can use translanguaging rings to communicate to students that their ways of languaging and being are integral to their academic success *and* to their development of a critical consciousness and proud, empowered identities. Nelson Flores, in his introduction to Sánchez and García's (2022) book, *Transforming Translanguaging Espacios*, connects translanguaging rings and pedagogical approaches to a broader political purpose: "centering the cultural and linguistic practices of Latinx children through the incorporation of translanguaging pedagogy must occur in conjunction with the transformation of the broader society that has deficitized the language practices of those communities to begin with" (p. xx).

Just as the "macro" instructional designs introduced in Chapter 6 align with the four central purposes of translanguaging, so too do these "micro" instructional practices and shifts. Recall that these purposes work juntos to mobilize and accelerate bilingual students' opportunities to learn and advance social, racial, and cognitive justice. Here, we revisit those purposes and demonstrate how different translanguaging pedagogical practices align with each one.

Purpose 1: Supporting Students as They Engage with and Comprehend Complex Content and Texts

Translanguaging pedagogical practices help students engage with, and make meaning of, complex content and texts by providing more points of entry and more opportunities for students to be active participants in their own learning. The following practices can open up space for translanguaging and serve as helpful scaffolds and ways of engaging students meaningfully with complex, grade-level content and texts:

- Teach students to use the Internet to build background on a topic or concept in both their home and new languages.
- Assign bilingual reading and writing partners who share the same home language for mutual support and discussion.
- Encourage students to annotate texts they are reading with translations of vocabulary and other important textual information, including interesting structures and phrases.
- Encourage the use of dictionaries, glossaries, and iPads with translation apps to make meaning.
- Provide multilingual books/translations of books and materials whenever possible.
- Encourage students to "read the room" to find phrases, sentence starters, vocabulary, and transition words in multiple languages that are important for their writing.
- Create a multilingual listening center composed of fiction and nonfiction texts, narratives of community members, and books recorded by students or their families (a favorite book or students' own writing).
- Allow students to explain things to each other using all their language resources, including drawing and role playing.

Purpose 2: Providing Opportunities for Students to Develop Linguistic Practices for a Variety of Purposes and Contexts, Including those Deemed Academic

All students must have the opportunity to expand their linguistic repertoires to include the language practices that are associated with academic contexts. This means opening up space to invite what students are *already* doing with language and expanding their repertoires to include new features and practices—what Nelson Flores (2020) calls language architecture. In this way, rather than starting from the premise that students lack so-called **academic language**, teachers tap into their stance, which includes the belief that students and their communities already language in rich, sophisticated, highly "academic" ways. They then make space for students to use their translanguaging in ways that both affirm their existing linguistic gifts *and* expand their repertoire to include new features and practices. The following pedagogical practices can be used to further develop students' linguistic practices for academic contexts:

- Allow students to audio record ideas using all their language resources before writing.
- Have students brainstorm and prewrite using all their linguistic and other resources; then select one language/voice in which to publish it.

- Have students discuss the different ways in which language is used at home by the adults and others in their families during dinner time and when they are participating in activities in institutions such as school or their church, mosque, synagogue, or temple. Have them role-play both interactions.
- Provide students with opportunities to write translations of portions of a text.
- Assign language partners in class who share home languages and differentiate language objectives (general linguistic and language-specific).
- Group students so they can use the same home language resources in collaborative work.
- Allow pairs to "turn and talk" using all their language resources.
- Allow students to raise questions, answer them, and participate in class discussion using the full features of their linguistic repertoires.
- Have students record a short interaction of family members at home and record a short interaction in the classroom between teacher and students. Write out both interactions. Role-play them. Which purposes did each interaction serve? Why?
- Have students compare and contrast specific language features across languages to help them develop greater metalinguistic awareness.

Purpose 3: Supporting Students' Bilingual Identities, Socioemotional Development, and Critical Consciousness and Disrupting Ideologies that Render Bilingual Students as Deficient

Students who are secure in the importance of their bilingual practices benefit socioemotionally as they transform the subjectivities of inferiority that schools have assigned to them and acquire control over their education and lives. Students must be invited to use their bilingualism and bilingual ways of knowing to think critically about content, as well as how language and race have been co-constructed in ways that have taken power from certain racialized populations. To do this, space must be made for students to engage the full features of their linguistic repertoires and their own epistemologies, rather than asking them to "think in English (or another language) only." Translanguaging pedagogical practices do not support students solely academically; they support their development of proud, empowered bilingual identities and support them as they forge their critical consciousness. Here are some additional pedagogical practices that make space for students' bilingualism and bilingual ways of knowing to support their identities and socioemotional development, as well as their critical consciousness:

- Provide books/stories where authors use translanguaging and that have culturally relevant meaning.
- Encourage students to do research using multilingual reading material, especially on the Internet.
- Urge students to share their own stories of language and schooling. These stories can be performed orally, visualized through pictures and images, or written.
- Have students identify moments in U.S. history when language was used to racialize populations.
- Have students write stories with bilingual characters or situations where other language practices have to be used.
- Encourage students to write performance pieces, for example, plays that include translanguaging for voices of bilingual characters.
- Share with students newspaper clippings of moments of linguistic discrimination in U.S. society and other national contexts.
- Show video clips of language activism around the world and reflect on what is different or the same in the United States.

- Have students use translanguaging in writing for bilingual audiences, including their families and communities, besides writing for monolingual audiences.
- Engage students in language inquiry tasks, comparing and contrasting different features of spoken language, and coming up with wordplays.
- Invite family and community members into the classroom to enrich instruction.
- Provide students with texts that highlight two or more sides of a complex issue, especially those issues that relate directly to their lives.

Purpose 4: Making Space for all Students' Language Practices and Ways of Knowing, and in so doing Building a Classroom and Society that is Inclusive of Linguistic, Racial, Gender, and Ability Differences

Translanguaging classrooms center bilingual students' language practices and ways of knowing, but not all bilingual students are the same. Besides speaking different national languages, all placed in a power hierarchy depending on the status of the country from which they come, students have different racial, gender, and ability differences. Translanguaging classrooms are inclusive of differences and make efforts to make these differences visible.

For example, many countries have one official or national language, but many emergent bilinguals coming from those countries speak other regional or local languages and have their own local practices. In addition, students vary in ways of performing language and work having to do with a range of abilities. Students also perform their genders differently. In a translanguaging classroom, students' different racial and gender identities are acknowledged. Translanguaging classrooms center student interactions, as they encourage students to mediate the work for other peers. At the same time that it is inclusive, the translanguaging classroom makes visible privilege, Whiteness, ability, and heteropatriarchy and invites students to reflect on how power gets constructed and how privilege can be dismantled. The following are pedagogical practices that can address this important purpose:

- Discuss what would have happened in a story if the characters were bilingual or if they exhibited different racial or gender characteristics.
- Have students perform their life stories using different modes and language practices.
- Extend research projects and other culminating designs out of the classroom and into the community, where students can use their bilingualism for authentic purposes as they adapt their performances to their individual and community identities.
- Engage students in bilingual writing assignments that have a social justice focus, such as letter writing, blogging, grant writing, or editorial or newspaper article writing.
- Choose topics and texts in multiple languages that give voice to groups that are commonly silenced or left out of the traditional curriculum.
- Assess general linguistic performance, as well as language-specific performance, while encouraging students to leverage their entire language repertoire.[1]

I use this book in my pedagogical methods courses to give teacher candidates the "how" of engaging their translanguaging stance in instructional planning and assessment. As a result, they are more able to take action on their social justice beliefs and extend their estudiantes' many skills and talents into new learning and languaging—and share their practice with others they work with too!

—Anel V. Rivera Guerrero, Ph.D. candidate, teacher educator,
and dual-language instructional coach, New Jersey

[1]See Celic and Seltzer (2012), García and Kleyn (2017), and García and Wei (2014) for more pedagogical practices that open up space for translanguaging.

IN CONTEXT: TRANSLANGUAGING PEDAGOGICAL PRACTICES WITHIN A UNIT PLAN

We now return to ***Justin***'s translanguaging unit plan and his use of the translanguaging instructional design cycle. We show how different translanguaging pedagogical practices align with each stage of that design cycle, enabling Justin and his co-teacher to create daily opportunities to leverage la corriente and make learning more engaging and supportive for their bilingual students. Recall that Justin and his co-teacher planned a translanguaging unit entitled "Geometry in Our World." The multi-week unit was aligned with California's Common Core state standards as well as the state's English language development standards, but it went *beyond* those standards through the development of a culminating project that required students to use their bilingualism and uniquely bilingual ways of knowing to create children's books that explained geometric concepts (see Chapter 6 for Justin's full unit plan).

As they taught their unit, Justin and his co-teacher organized the arc of their instruction according to the translanguaging instructional design cycle. Within each stage of this cycle, Justin worked with his co-teacher to plan daily opportunities to make space for and leverage the corriente of translanguaging for their students' learning. These opportunities came in the form of strategies, scaffolds, and differentiated approaches that enabled different students to engage with the content meaningfully. Here are just a few examples of how Justin and his co-teacher incorporated these pedagogical practices—planned-out daily lesson designs and unplanned translanguaging shifts alike—throughout the design cycle:

- In the **explorar** stage, students worked in shared home language groups to discuss ideas and negotiate new math content through their home languages and English. They also built background on the topic of geometry through Internet research, reading, and writing in both languages.
- In the **evaluar** stage, Justin and his co-teacher provided students with children's books that related to math in both English and their home languages. One of those books was *Grandfather Tang's Story*, which features tangrams, Chinese puzzles made up of different shapes. One group of Mandarin speakers immediately grabbed the book and read through it together, having side conversations in both English and Mandarin about both the story and its math-related content. Though the book was written in English, it had cultural relevance to the students, which not only helped them make connections to the content but also provided them with an opportunity to share their own stories with one another and in their own children's book.
- In the **imaginar** stage, ***Danilo***, one of Justin's Tagalog speakers, was struggling to write down his ideas in either English or Tagalog during a group brainstorm about the students' future children's books. Justin knew that this student had creative ideas that he wanted to contribute to his group, so he used his phone to record him talking through his ideas in both languages. After he had explained his ideas orally, Justin sat him with a more experienced bilingual in his group and the two students transcribed his ideas, many of which were included in the final draft of their children's book. Rather than render this student voiceless, Justin met him where he was and helped him see connections between his own oral language and the written forms expected of him in school.
- In the **presentar** stage, Justin created "presentation roles" for each member of the student groups. Using what he knew about each student, including their English language development (ELD) levels and their general linguistic performances, he set up differentiated ways for students to present their children's books to the elementary school classrooms. For example, some students read from their books in English and/or the additional language, others created the presentation slides, and others wrote up the required reflection piece about the geometry content they included in the book and how they used their bilingualism to write it. Each of these roles was laid out clearly and contained language-specific supports for the students who took on the roles.
- In the **implementar** stage, Justin had his students revisit something they had realized in the evaluar stage—that they could find very few children's books that related to math and were written bilingually. Justin and his co-teacher agreed with the students and

explained that, for this reason, students' books had to include both English and their home languages—they were the ones who could fill the gaps in the literature. After the students' positive experiences reading these books to the elementary school students, Justin and his co-teacher provided them with a "choice board" for ways of advocating for more bilingual representation in children's literature. Students had the option to write letters, create posters, record a "commercial," or act out a role play.

Teachers can plan a variety of ways to open up translanguaging spaces during different stages of the translanguaging instructional design cycle to help students use *all* of their language practices and ways of knowing to learn. Here are some ideas:

Translanguaging to Explorar

- Build background knowledge by engaging students in meaningful collaborative dialogue that includes translanguaging and the use of all students' language resources.
- Show short video clips with subtitles in English and students' home languages.
- Post content-related pictures around the classroom and do a gallery walk and discussion in any language.
- Have student groups brainstorm their prior knowledge on a topic in any language.
- Provide an engaging discussion question in one language and ask students to discuss it in any language.
- Provide content-related readings and have students make connections to the text and analyze the text in any language.
- Create a multilingual listening center composed of fiction and nonfiction texts, narratives of community members, podcasts, interviews, and music that are relevant to the topic being explored.
- Use graphic organizers to help students track their learning on a topic (e.g., KWL charts, semantic maps, word walls) and provide opportunities to do so in all languages.
- Invite community leaders to talk about local issues or topics using their own language practices.

Translanguaging to Evaluar

- Have students compare different texts on one topic. Focus students' comparison on what perspectives are included and excluded, what linguistic and stylistic choices are being made, and what readers take away from each text.
- Whenever possible, provide students with multilingual versions of reading texts to use as needed or to use for textual contrastive analysis.
- Have students do outside research on a topic. Provide relevant, bilingual websites or have students find their own. Have students present on how new research supports, refutes, or adds to what is covered in a textbook or set of readings.
- Provide students with "counter-stories," or alternative points of view on a topic. This can be done in English and the students' home languages through readings, guest speakers, and/or multimedia such as podcasts, video clips, film, and so forth.
- Come up with a set of questions that can help students think critically about a text of any kind. Make the use of these questions a routine when encountering a text or the overall topic.

Translanguaging to Imaginar

- Plan activities that can be differentiated for students according to what they can do with content and language. Make sure that there are ways for all students to participate meaningfully in any activity.

- Have students work in groups or partnerships to brainstorm, plan, draft, and revise an assignment, project, piece of writing, and so forth. No matter the language in which the final product is presented, students can use all of the languages in their linguistic repertoires to create that product.
- Provide students with models of what you want them to create for their performances. This could be a mentor text, a teacher-created resource, a sample poster, or anything that provides an example of what students should be working toward.
- Have students write stories with bilingual characters or situations where other language practices have to be used.
- Encourage students to write performance pieces, for example, plays or readers' theater, that include translanguaging to give voice to bilingual characters.
- Have peers review the translanguaging used in written texts to verify meaning.

Translanguaging to Presentar

- Provide time for students to engage in peer editing, revision, and rewriting using all their language practices, and then redesign based on feedback from you and their peers.
- Have students present collaboratively, with different students taking on different roles. These roles should be appropriately differentiated according to their oracy, literacy, and content knowledge.
- Make linguistic and stylistic choices part of students' presentation grade, which can enhance students' metalinguistic awareness.
- Provide students with a presentation outline, format, or set of appropriate sentence starters in English and their home languages.
- Have students create PowerPoint or other presentations for their multilingual families, using translanguaging for meaning making and images and multimodal texts for support.
- Encourage students to do their best to present in one language (English), but allow them to expand on, clarify, or further explain their ideas in the other language (Spanish).

Translanguaging to Implementar

- Attach some kind of action to students' learning. For example, lessons can be expanded by asking students to:
    - Interview family members about an instructional topic using appropriate language practices and report findings back to the class.
    - Share their writing on different public websites, blogs, Facebook pages, or other social media sites, being mindful of choice of language practices for different audiences.
    - Write emails or use social media to communicate with both teacher and peers about their learning, using appropriate language practices.
- Expand students' learning to the school community by:
    - Posting student work with translanguaged texts around the school.
    - Encouraging students to submit translanguaged work to a school newspaper, magazine, or website.
    - Creating opportunities for students to discuss their translanguaged work in other classrooms or with teachers and administrators.
    - Compiling translanguaged student work into bound books that can be accessible in a school library or resource center.

- Expand students' learning to the larger community by:
  - Partnering with local organizations whose work is relevant to the classroom topic/project/subject area and using relevant language practices.
  - Planning bilingual events that feature student work and are open to students' families and other community members.
  - Helping students submit their work to local newspapers, websites, radio stations, TV stations, and funding organizations, using appropriate language resources.

These practices promote the connections among teachers, students, families, and communities, as well as across language and cultural practices, that translanguaging classrooms require.

TRANSLANGUAGING SHIFTS IN INSTRUCTION

Translanguaging shifts refer to those unplanned moment-by-moment decisions that teachers make in response to the flow of the translanguaging corriente in their classrooms. The flexible shifts are an integral part of creating the translanguaging classroom—they enable teachers to engage with the flow of the translanguaging corriente whose movements cannot always be predicted. These shifts respond to content and language needs and interests that are not built directly into the translanguaging unit plan but that students need to be successful in the classroom. They emerge directly out of our stance and our flexible design. Our stance enables us to see and hear the translanguaging corriente, and our design makes space for the kind of performance-based learning that illustrates what bilingual students know and can do on different tasks. Going with the flow, rather than fighting and pulling away from it, is key to the success of bilingual students and translanguaging classrooms.

Flexible translanguaging shifts are important because, like planned instructional designs, they open space for students to language on their own terms and for teachers to leverage that languaging for learning. When teachers go with the flow of the translanguaging corriente, they meet bilingual learners where they are in terms of their general linguistic and language-specific performances, and they tap into the corriente to move student learning forward.

Flexibility is a key element of the translanguaging classroom. Educators must be flexible not only in terms of language use but also with students' understanding of new content. This means that the way *we* think they will learn something isn't necessarily the way they *actually* learn it. Each group of students brings a unique set of experiences, personalities, biases, and challenges. As teachers, we must open ourselves and our classrooms to students' own interpretations and perceptions of content and language. Translanguaging shifts allow for this flexibility in language practices, conversations, activities, and plans because the teacher is responding to an unanticipated aspect of the translanguaging corriente. And these shifts, like planned translanguaging designs, serve as supports and scaffolds and deepen students' understandings. Some shifts that we have seen teachers make in translanguaging classrooms include the following:

- Helping individual students understand difficult new vocabulary or phrases by providing translation, rephrasing, and using synonyms or cognates
- Helping students make sense of new content by using culturally meaningful metaphors and/or stories
- In moments of difficulty or misunderstanding, encouraging students to talk to one another about a new concept or vocabulary word using their own language practices
- Looking up words and phrases using online translation tools or having students do so on their own
- Encouraging students to relate new content to their own worlds through stories and other text/world connections

To demonstrate the unplanned shifts that can support and advance student learning, a vignette from another of Justin's teaching contexts is provided. Though earlier in the chapter Justin was working with his math co-teacher, here Justin is working with a small group of emergent bilinguals during a science class:

Justin was going over students' homework for their science class. As he discussed the topic—heredity—he got the sense that his students, especially Fatoumata and Yi-Sheng, who had recently arrived, did not understand what he was explaining. There were blank looks and some off-task behaviors, and there was very little participation. Rather than plow forward, Justin stopped and asked students to talk to one another in Spanish, Mandarin, French, Vietnamese, Tagalog, or any of their languages about whether they looked like people in their families or not. Though he did not speak most of these languages, Justin could tell from the shift in energy in the room and the excited conversations that students were engaged in the discussion. After they had spoken to one another, Justin asked them to share some of their ideas in English. Danilo, with the help of his Tagalog-speaking classmates, said that he had dark skin but that his sister was fair and even had freckles. A student translated for Fatoumata that though both her parents had brown eyes, she had green eyes, but no one knew why. Some students shifted the conversation to the many names for different skin colors in Spanish. Jumping off from these comments, Justin connected the idea of looking like (or not looking like) a family member to the work students had done that day with Punnett squares. Suddenly students started to make connections to concepts like dominant and recessive alleles, phenotype, and genotype that they had not tapped into before.

Rather than limiting the conversation, Justin's shifts—using students' connections and translanguaging to deepen their understanding of and engagement with the difficult new content—enabled him to go with the flow of the corriente and meet his students' needs. If Justin had not paid close attention to his students and applied flexibility and willingness to tap into the corriente, his lesson might have ended in frustration instead of excitement and learning. In this way, Justin's masterful translanguaging shifts served as improvised translanguaging rings, buoying his students and enabling them to draw on all their language practices and on what they already know to engage with complex, grade-level content.

CONCLUSION

"Translanguaging is not merely a series of strategies. It is not a scaffold to be removed when students become more experienced users of English or another named language. And it is certainly not a simple instructional approach or "best practice" that can be implemented neutrally. Translanguaging is the communicative norm in bilingual homes and communities. Teachers who foster a strong translanguaging stance recognize, value, and celebrate this communicative norm in their classrooms and have tangible ways to enact that stance in practice. For this reason, this chapter has put forth ideas for daily pedagogical practices—both planned and unplanned—that can help teachers open up translanguaging spaces, leveraging the translanguaging corriente for learning while simultaneously affirming bilingual students' language practices and identities. These pedagogical practices can enable all teachers to utilize translanguaging to scaffold and deepen understandings, making the translanguaging classroom engaging, rigorous, and oriented toward meaningful student learning. These pedagogical practices are organized according to the "macro" instruction framework put forth in Chapter 6, namely, the translanguaging instructional design cycle; they are tools in your ever-growing pedagogical toolkit. They are also closely tied to the assessment practices introduced next, in Chapter 8. As we document and get a grasp of what our students know and can do—as well as where they need support—we can supply them with the rings that affirm them and buoy them toward academic success.

QUESTIONS AND ACTIVITIES

1. How do you understand translanguaging pedagogical practices in relation to your translanguaging stance? How might you explain your use of these practices to someone whose stance differs from your own?
2. In the chapter, you saw how Justin and his co-teacher invited and leveraged students' translanguaging in both planned and unplanned ways. Reflect on a time in your own practice when you have done the same. What were the effects on students? On yourself as a teacher?
3. Which pedagogical ideas from this chapter resonated with you? How might you incorporate some of these ideas into your own practice in the near future?

TAKING ACTION

1. In Chapter 6, you had the opportunity to start designing your own translanguaging unit plan and use of the translanguaging instructional design cycle. Now that you have learned about a variety of ways to open up space for translanguaging within these macro structures, add those designs. If you are using the design cycle, you might choose one or two pedagogical approaches to try out in each stage. If you are adapting an existing piece of curriculum to include translanguaging designs, you might see where the translanguaging pedagogical practices offered in this chapter align with and expand or supplement the curricular materials you are working with.
2. Document your own use of the translanguaging pedagogical practices offered in this chapter. What, if any, changes do you observe in student learning when you use them? What, if any, changes do you feel within yourself as you begin the daily practice of opening up translanguaging space?

8

Translanguaging Design for Assessment

LEARNING OBJECTIVES

After reading this chapter, you will be able to:

- Identify principles of translanguaging in assessment.
- Describe the key initial steps of the translanguaging design for assessment, which include creating student profiles, talking with parents/guardians, carrying out observations, and having students create autobiographical translanguaging portraits.
- Understand how to adapt state standardized assessments to take into account students' translanguaging corriente by looking at Carla's integration of instruction and assessment in her unit design.
- Learn how to use the Teacher's Assessment Tool, which not only distinguishes between general linguistic and language-specific performances, but also documents whether students can perform tasks independently or with assistance.
- Understand how to assess from many angles and through many actors, including self, peers, and family, and how to use this information to assess students fairly and accurately.

Since the No Child Left Behind Act of 2001, assessment and accountability have focused largely on students' performance on high-stakes standardized tests in English. Likewise, college and career-readiness standards rely on academic benchmarks in English to measure students' knowledge and skills relative to those standards. It is important to take these summative assessments in English into account because they are used in most states to make decisions about student performance and teacher effectiveness. However, to better understand bilingual students and create more equitable learning opportunities, teachers in translanguaging classrooms document and assess what students know and can do on classroom tasks using the full features of their linguistic repertoires.

Translanguaging in assessment is part of the translanguaging pedagogy and is intimately tied to translanguaging in instruction. *The translanguaging design for assessment* covers how teachers strategically plan evaluations of bilingual students' performances to document a holistic understanding of what students can do relative to the content, language, and **translanguaging objectives** of the translanguaging design for instruction. The translanguaging shifts in assessment reflect the moment-to-moment adjustments that teachers make in their assessment practices to go with the flow of the translanguaging corriente.

The **translanguaging design** for assessment relies on authentic, performance-based instruments that allow teachers to monitor students' general linguistic and language-specific performances. Recall that general linguistic performance refers to speakers' use of oral and written language to express complex thoughts (e.g., to explain, persuade, argue, compare and contrast, find text-based evidence, give directions, or recount events) drawing on the full features of their linguistic repertoires. Language-specific performance refers to speakers' exclusive use of features from a named language (e.g., Spanish, Mandarin, English) to perform classroom tasks.

Using a translanguaging design for assessment allows teachers to better evaluate students' content and language learning by ensuring that general linguistic and language-specific performances are never conflated. By distinguishing between these types of performances, a translanguaging design for assessment encourages bilingual children to display their entire language repertoires when their general linguistic performances are being assessed. Otheguy et al. (2015) discuss the differences between school assessment of bilinguals and monolinguals:

> In schools in general, but especially during testing, bilingual students, to their great disadvantage, are kept from using their entire language repertoires, are compelled to suppress a big part of their idiolect, are not allowed to translanguage. In contrast, monolingual students, to their great advantage, are forced to suppress only a small fraction of their idiolect (the part that is interpersonally inappropriate), are regularly allowed to translanguage. Both types of students are asked to be part of a teaching and testing game that each ends up playing under different rules. It is small wonder that the monolingual side usually comes out on top. (pp. 300–301)

A translanguaging design for assessment allows for a more accurate reading of bilingual children's performance by assessing students' general linguistic performance, not only their use of features of standard languages. Of course, being able to perform language-specific tasks is important, and so the translanguaging design for assessment also evaluates the bilingual child's use of English, Spanish, or any other language for a variety of purposes, including those deemed academic. However, this specific measure is never considered in isolation or as an accurate picture of what the child can do. Holistic assessment is always used by documenting both general linguistic and language-specific performances to better assess bilingual students' ways of knowing and doing language.

This chapter provides a step-by-step demonstration of how teachers can design a holistic, ongoing assessment plan that yields authentic evidence of students' performances relative to the school's content and language demands over time, with attention to how teachers can use this evidence to differentiate instruction and accelerate student learning. First, principles and dimensions that guide translanguaging in assessment are introduced. Then one translanguaging unit of instruction that ***Carla*** developed for her fourth-grade dual-language bilingual education (DLBE) class is highlighted to demonstrate translanguaging assessment in action. Carla uses the bilingual student profiles introduced in Chapter 4, helps students develop *autobiographical translanguaging portraits*, has conversations with family, and closely observes the children. This chapter also demonstrates how assessments can be used to take stock of the perceptions of different actors and their different perspectives/angles. For that, four assessment tools are introduced: the *Student Self-Assessment Tool*, the *Family and Peer Group Assessment Tools*, and the *Teacher's Assessment Tool*. Examples from ***Stephanie's*** and ***Justin's*** English-medium classrooms are also included to illustrate how they use the Teacher's Assessment Tool, given that they do not speak their students' home languages. At the end of the chapter, the focus turns to translanguaging shifts in assessment. As you read, think about how you can collect evidence of your students' dynamic performances on different tasks, at different times, from different angles.

"I use the book to introduce the concept of content assessment versus language-specific assessment to in-service teachers, many of whom had not considered these as separate skills. This notion helped these teachers consider new ways to assess multilinguals (e.g., via self, community/parent, and peer

assessments) that would more accurately demonstrate their knowledge of a particular content area or linguistic skill. It really hits home for teachers to look at it that way."

—Michele Back, Ph.D., Associate Professor, World Languages Education, Neag School of Education, University of Connecticut

PRINCIPLES FOR TRANSLANGUAGING DESIGN IN ASSESSMENT

Teachers need to continuously monitor what students are learning throughout the unit and give feedback for formative purposes (Popham, 2008). To do that, they must identify the purpose for assessment and how it is to be used and then select or develop the appropriate instruments (Mahoney, 2017). A translanguaging design in assessment must be clear about why, when, or how to give bilingual students the opportunity to draw from their entire linguistic repertoire or not. In addition, it must also activate students' **critical multilingual awareness**, enabling students to draw from their full repertoire of understandings and practices to render a linguistic performance appropriate for the task. In Chapter 4, four elements were identified that must be considered when identifying and evaluating bilingual students' performances from a translanguaging perspective:

1. The dynamic nature of language performances
2. The dependence of the assessment on who/what is the evaluator
3. The differences between and interactions across students' general linguistic performances and language-specific performances
4. The importance of going beyond a given state/other standardized assessment system

Though each of these four elements are described in detail in Chapter 4, they are brought together here as *two general principles* that form the theoretical foundation for the design of translanguaging assessments:

1. Assessment of what bilingual students know and can do must be based on authentic, performance-based tasks and must be considered from many angles and by many observers.
2. Assessment of what bilingual students know and can do must enable students to use all their resources, identify any assistance they may need, and distinguish between assessment of general and language-specific performances.

1. Assessment of what bilingual students know and can do must be based on authentic, performance-based tasks and consider many angles and observers.

Content must always be evaluated as students perform genuine tasks. The culminating project of a translanguaging unit plan must always be an authentic, action-oriented product that students create and implement throughout the course of the unit. Teachers can use students' performance on the culminating project, and on the activities leading up to it, as the basis for authentic performance-based assessment relative to the content and language demands of the instructional unit (Herrera, 2022). In addition, a translanguaging design for assessment always attempts to integrate the home and the school juntos. Thus, assessment in translanguaging classrooms always considers how students' families, the students themselves, their peers, and their teachers evaluate what students know and can do with content and language on school-based tasks.

2. Assessment of what bilingual students know and can do enables students to use all their resources, identify any assistance that they may need, and distinguish between assessment of general and language-specific performances.

A translanguaging design for assessment provides students with opportunities to use all the resources they have at their disposal in order to make sense of, and mediate, their own learning. When teachers make space for bilingual students to draw on their entire linguistic repertoires, these students can fully demonstrate their content learning without being limited to one specific language or another and they can use translanguaging for deeper understanding of texts (Ascenzi-Moreno, 2018; Ascenzi-Moreno et al., 2023; Pearson et al., 2020).

The **zone of proximal development** (ZOPD) is where a teacher and student participate together, advancing the student's knowledge and development (Vygotsky, 1978). Díaz and Flores (2021) describe the importance of organizing learning in the ZOPD so that it both includes the student's current level of development and moves the student to their full potential of knowledge acquisition and cognitive development. As Díaz and Flores (2021) describe, if instruction is organized to develop a student's full potential, then it is organized in a *positive ZOPD*. Drawing on Moll (2013), a translanguaging design for assessment ensures that the students are working in the **bilingual zone of proximal development** (BZOPD), further maximizing their learning in a positive ZOPD. Sometimes the resources students have at their disposal are the people around them (their peers and teachers) who can mediate the task. Other times the resources are the material tools of learning—glossaries, dictionaries, iPads, texts in other languages, images, videos, and so forth. Students can then be evaluated as performing independently or with moderate assistance (Bodrova & Leong, 2019). Furthermore, a student must always be given opportunities to use their inner voice—the intrapersonal voice that considers the entire language repertoire—to solve problems and show what they know.

A translanguaging design for assessment also differentiates how students use language to show what they know and can do using the full features of their linguistic repertoires from their ability to do so using only language-specific features. This distinction corrects a serious flaw in contemporary assessment of linguistically diverse students. According to the American Educational Research Association, American Psychological Association, and National Council on Measurement in Education (2014), every assessment is an assessment of language. Restricting emergent bilinguals' opportunities to demonstrate content understanding to what they can do with a language that is just emerging is denying these students equal access to educational equity and opportunity. However, when teachers make space for bilingual students to draw on their entire linguistic repertoires, these students can fully demonstrate their content learning without being limited to one specific language or another. How to design translanguaging assessments that take into account the two general principles described is the topic of the rest of the chapter.

"Thanks to this book, I now engage in discussions with my peers and students about the benefits of a translanguaging approach to formal and informal assessments. These conversations have had a remarkable impact on my building by fostering an environment where the teacher maintains fidelity to the language of instruction while letting the students use their entire linguistic repertoire. My peers have become more open to embracing bilingualism in their assessments and lessons, and my students have felt empowered to use their full linguistic repertoires throughout the day. This has led to richer, more nuanced evaluations and a more supportive and inclusive learning environment."

—Jesabel Centeno, Elementary Literacy Specialist,
Spanish Two-Way Immersion Program, Tigard, Oregon

TRANSLANGUAGING DESIGN FOR ASSESSMENT: CARLA AND HER STUDENTS

To illustrate translanguaging assessment in practice, we turn to Carla's fourth-grade DLBE classroom. Because students are at the center of the translanguaging pedagogy, Carla starts by using the information initially gathered from the *Bilingual Student Identification Checklist and Profile* introduced in Chapter 4 (also available in Appendix 4.2). She complements this information with what she has learned in conversations with students' families. She also adds all she has learned from observing her students deeply, in motion, as Patricia Carini (2000) has said. That is, Carla pays close attention to the children as they are using language while engaged in activities meaningful to them. Because she also wants to learn about her students' bilingual use from the students themselves, she asks the students to identify the languages and means of expression and communication that play a role in their lives by completing their own *autobiographical translanguaging portraits,* based on the work of Neville and Johnson (2022) and extending Busch (2010).[1]

Autobiographical translanguaging portraits invite students to map not their languages as such, but their language *use.* These portraits then provide students with the opportunity to take a critical perspective on their languaging and subsequently reflect on the meanings of their language practices. These portraits are meant to activate both students' critical multilingual awareness and their translanguaging as well as to develop the teacher's ability to understand students' dynamic language use. Information from Carla's holistic narratives on Erica, Jennifer, Moisés, and Ricardo—which she gained through the initial steps described previously—are included, as well as her analysis of their individual autobiographical translanguaging portraits.

To get her students to produce these autobiographical translanguaging portraits, Carla asked them to represent their language practices, thinking holistically of their lives at home, in the community, and at school. She asked them to think about how these language practices made them feel and what motivated those feelings. Carla told her students that they were to capture not their external language use—that is, not the named languages that others said they spoke—but their internal language use: how they motivated their entire language repertoire; when they did so, why they did so, and for what purposes; and how this made them feel. Carla asked them to reflect on what happened when they were free to engage in translanguaging. How did they feel? What colors represented those feelings and the ways the translanguaging corriente flowed through their bodies?

Erica began the DLBE program in first grade. Her parents are Puerto Rican but came to the mainland as children, so they spoke mostly English at home, although Spanish was also spoken. As a young child Erica grew up speaking English at home, although she understood Spanish and spoke it some. Because Erica was not officially designated as an English language learner (ELL) when she entered school, she was simply seen as an English speaker, and the Spanish she brought with her to school went unnoticed. After attending an English-medium kindergarten, her parents asked that she be put in the DLBE program so that she would develop her bilingualism and biliteracy. In the DLBE program, Erica was, and is still, considered an English-dominant student.[2] Erica is now in fourth grade, and her reading is at grade level in English (40 on the Developmental Reading Assessment [DRA2]) and almost up to par in Spanish (30 on the Evaluación del desarrollo de la lectura [EDL2]). Erica prefers to speak with her friends in class and during recess in English. At home, Erica's parents speak Spanish to her when they help Erica with her homework. In class, Carla notices that Erica is hesitant to speak in Spanish. Carla has also noticed that, since she allowed Erica to use both languages in class, Erica has further developed her comfort with using Spanish.

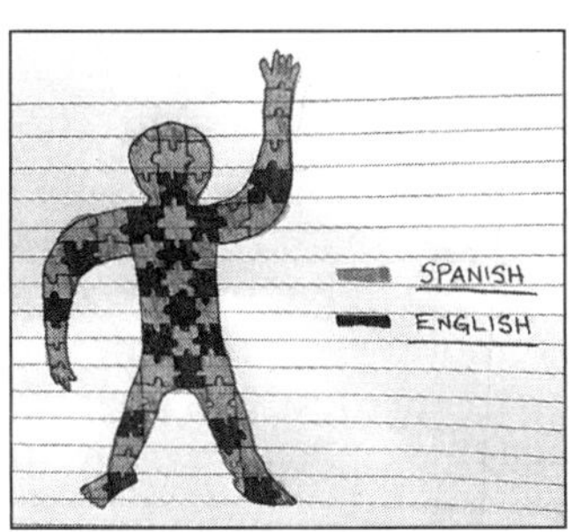

Figure 8.1. Shows Erica's autobiographical translanguaging portrait.

Erica's autobiographical translanguaging portrait (Figure 8.1) is designed like a puzzle with each of the pieces representing the named languages within her that make up who she is and how she uses language. It is interesting that there are more green pieces (which she has designated as Spanish) than blue pieces (English), given that, following Carla's narrative, Erica speaks more English than Spanish. But in Erica's own autobiographical translanguaging portrait, Spanish plays an important part as

[1]Brigitta Busch proposed *language portraits* as a way of having young people represent their multilingualism with different colors in a body silhouette. These language portraits are an important first step to make multilingualism visible. Although Busch (2012) argued that this multimodal biographical approach helps deconstruct preestablished categories, her intention has been misunderstood by many who use these language portraits. Thus, multilingual students often portray their languages as separate, located in different parts of the body.

[2]Some educators in the world-language education or **bilingual education** fields might have identified Erica as a heritage Spanish speaker when she entered first grade. However, Erica is described here as an emergent bilingual who is strengthening her Spanish as she continues to develop English for academic purposes at school. The term English dominant is not used here because the goal of this section is to emphasize the bilingualism that Erica brings to school and its potential for full emergence as she becomes bilingual and biliterate.

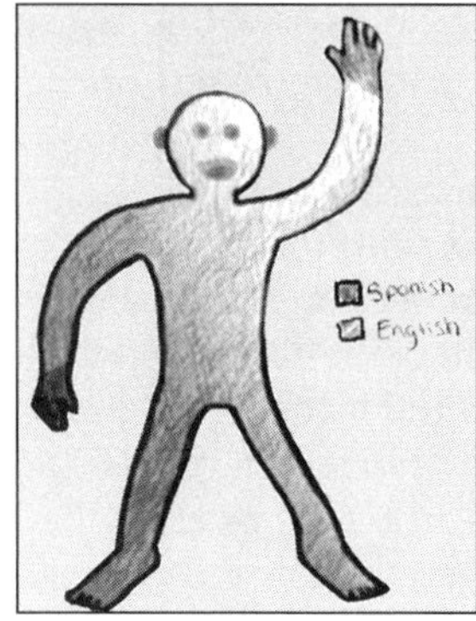

Figure 8.2. Shows Jennifer's autobiographical translanguaging portrait.

the language of Puerto Rico, her family, and her home. Eventually, once she started first grade, Erica started to learn in Spanish as well as in English. She writes, "Just like that I became bilingual, and I started to add new pieces onto myself."

Jennifer was born in the United States and began elementary school in the DLBE program. Jennifer's mother was also born in the United States to parents who emigrated from different regions of Mexico. Like Erica, Jennifer is officially designated as an English speaker, and traditional bilingual programs refer to her as English dominant. (Jennifer is referred to here as an emergent bilingual who is learning Spanish and developing English at school.) Although Jennifer has been diagnosed as having a learning disability and has an Individualized Education Program (IEP), she is a year ahead in English reading (50 on the DRA2) and on grade level in Spanish reading (EDL2), according to the district assessment. At home, Jennifer speaks English to her mother and siblings but Spanish to her grandmother, who lives with them and who has always been Jennifer's main caretaker while her mother worked. Her teacher, Carla, has recognized Jennifer's translanguaging practices with classmates and in lessons. For example, in mathematics (taught in Spanish), Carla realizes that Jennifer can explain the Pythagorean theorem better when using words and phrases that some may identify as English and Spanish but that, to Jennifer, are simply *her* words.

Jennifer's autobiographical translanguaging portrait (Figure 8.2) represents her bilingualism as purple for Spanish and blue for English. Jennifer mentioned that she was disappointed that her portrait mainly had blue for English when her peers' portraits were more colorful, representing more languages they spoke in class or home. She does not consider herself a monolingual English speaker since she understands Spanish. As shown in the drawing, her eyes, ears, and hands are purple because she can observe people speaking in Spanish and understand it, and she can also write in Spanish in school. Jennifer says that she wants to be a more experienced bilingual because when she travels to Mexico she wants to be able to communicate with her family and better understand their traditions, beliefs, and celebrations.

Moisés is a student who emigrated from Mexico to the United States 2 years ago and is thus considered a newcomer who was officially designated as an ELL when he entered school. Moisés learned to read and write in Spanish in Mexico, where he went to school until second grade. (Moisés is described here as an emergent bilingual who is learning English as he continues to develop Spanish.) He scores as a Level 3, *developing,* on WIDA's Assessing Comprehension and Communication in English State-to-State (ACCESS) for ELLs test. Moisés is at grade level in reading in Spanish (40 on the EDL2), and his English reading score is one grade level behind (30 on the DRA2). Moisés continues to develop both English and Spanish in Carla's DLBE classroom, although he still prefers Spanish at times. For example, when Moisés is beginning a reading or writing task in any content area in English, he verifies the task at hand with his friend *Diego,* who is comfortable using both languages. At home, Moisés communicates with his parents mostly in Spanish because they do not speak much English; with his siblings, however, he most often uses both languages to interact and play.

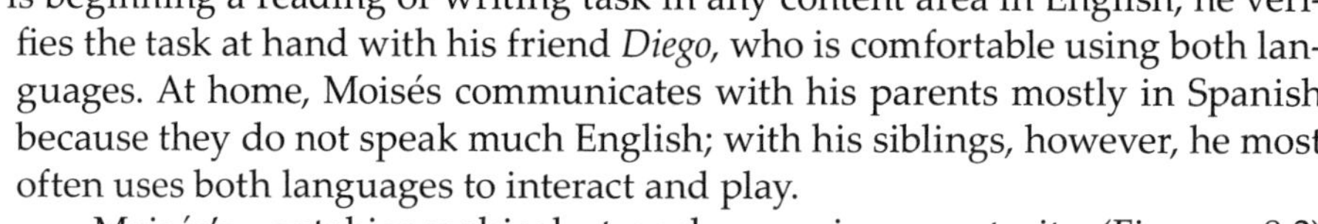

Figure 8.3. Shows Moisés's autobiographical translanguaging portrait.

Moisés's autobiographical translanguaging portrait (Figure 8.3) includes blue for Spanish and red for English, although he divides the two colors with a zigzag line across his body. He says that the zigzag symbolizes the corriente that flows through his body that is at the core of what he does with language, depending on the purpose, audience, and outcome. He also uses purple on his feet to symbolize that he has to navigate two worlds in ways that can only be understood by bringing forth his entire language repertoire. He also colors his hands purple to indicate that for him gestures are also language and that the multimodality of his performances goes beyond one named language or another. Finally, his mouth also is colored purple, for in Carla's classroom Moisés has learned that translanguaging is an important means of sharing ideas, thoughts, and feelings with his family and classmates.

Figure 8.4. Shows Ricardo's autobiographical translanguaging portrait.

Ricardo was born in Tlaxiaco, Oaxaca, and came to the United States at the start of fourth grade. Like Moisés, he is considered a newcomer and is officially designated as an ELL. (Ricardo is described here as an emergent bilingual who is learning English, developing Spanish, and drawing on Mixteco at school.) Ricardo's schooling in Oaxaca was in a local bilingual school that taught in Spanish and in Mixteco, his other home language. On the ACCESS for ELLs test, Moisés scores as Level 3, *developing*. He scores 1 year below grade level in reading on the Spanish EDL2 test (30) and 2 years below grade level in reading in English on the DRA2 (20).

Carla knows that Ricardo communicates in Mixteco and Spanish with his family but uses some English with his younger siblings. Carla therefore encourages him to use all his language resources (Spanish, English, and Mixteco) orally and in writing. For example, Ricardo chooses to write in his daily dialogue journal in Spanish and some Mixteco. Although Carla does not speak Mixteco, she meets with him once a week so that he can explain the content of his writing to her. Many times, her written comments in the journals use English and Spanish as a way of ensuring that Ricardo understands what she writes.

Ricardo's autobiographical translanguaging portrait (Figure 8.4) represents the many languages he feels he knows: green for Spanish, blue for English, and red for sign language, which he is learning in school. He drew his portrait with stripes across his body to signify the dynamic translanguaging corriente that runs through his body to make sense of his surroundings, learnings, and friendships that he is developing. Interesting enough, however, Mixteco is not represented with a color. Instead, Ricardo draws a heart and explains, "My heart is my Mixteco raíz, beliefs, and thoughts." It is the heart that makes his thoughts and actions meaningful, and so he brings his Mixteco/heart into school to better understand content, literacy, and language. The translanguaging current that flows through his body and fuels his brain emanates from a Mixteco heart.

Engaging students in this DLBE classroom in designing their own autobiographical translanguaging portraits gave Carla a lot of information that could not be simply identified through the *Student Identification and Profile* or through conversations with parents, and not even through her own close observations of students' actions. The autobiographical translanguaging portraits gave Carla a sense of how her students *felt* about their bilingualism. Sometimes their representations did not quite match what the standardized assessments indicated, but they gave Carla a better idea of her students' understandings of their own bilingualism and the ways they used language. Notice that in all cases these students acknowledged the dynamic nature of their bilingualism. With zigzag lines, puzzle pieces, purple, and the specific drawing of a heart, these students saw their bodies as representing a translanguaging corriente that energized them and moved them physically, intellectually, and especially emotionally. This is all important to consider in Carla's design of translanguaging assessment for her DLBE classroom.

Assessing Student Holistically vis-à-vis State Standards

Teachers in translanguaging classrooms need to go beyond the information they gather and are given that does not take account of how students themselves relate to and feel about their bilingualism. This section explores how Carla records her students' performances relative to the fourth-grade reading literature standard in New Mexico, which asks students to refer to details and examples in a text when explaining what the text says explicitly and when drawing inferences from it. Because New Mexico is a WIDA state, it evaluates students' oracy and literacy and organizes students' language performances along a progression: entering, emerging, developing, expanding, bridging and reaching.

Focus on how Carla evaluates Ricardo on this standard, following the principles of translanguaging assessment and, in particular, the difference between general linguistic performances and language-specific performances. Recall that Ricardo's scores on the two mandated measures for emergent bilinguals in New Mexico—DRA2 and EDL2—are a bit behind the scores of Erica, Jennifer, and Moisés. But Carla's consideration of the difference between general linguistic and language-specific performance gives her a completely different picture of Ricardo.

Ricardo's general linguistic performance relative to this reading standard is *expanding* in oracy and literacy. When he uses *only Spanish* to perform this type of task, Ricardo's oracy performances are *expanding* and his literacy performances are *developing*. Furthermore, Ricardo's language-specific performances in English relative to this standard are *emerging* in literacy and *developing* in oracy. Carla now knows that she can draw on Ricardo's strong general linguistic performance, as well as his stronger performances in Spanish, to accelerate his reading in English relative to this standard. Looking more closely at how Carla rated Ricardo's general linguistic and language-specific performances in literacy relative to this standardized reading standard, it becomes apparent that Ricardo's educational history provides insight as to why his general linguistic performances in literacy (*expanding*) are more experienced than his Spanish performances in literacy (*developing*).

Ricardo started to learn to read in Mexico in ways that are different from the ways he is learning to read in U.S. schools. Thus, his reading performances relative to the reading standards in Spanish only are conditioned by his reading experiences in school in Mexico. For example, Ricardo was never asked to find text-based evidence when he read at his Mexican school. Ricardo is now developing new reading practices through his experiences at his U.S. school, including referring to details and examples, as the reading standard demands. When Ricardo is told that he can use his complete repertoire of meaning-making resources, including his new understanding of what it means to read, which he has acquired through his English language arts curriculum, his general linguistic performance is more experienced than his Spanish literacy performance.

Integrating Instruction and Assessment

Equipped with information about her students' bilingualism, Carla is prepared to plan her translanguaging design for assessment. The translanguaging unit plan that Carla developed for her 4th-grade DLBE classroom, *Cuentos de la tierra y del barrio*, is reproduced in Table 8.1. It shows the instructional planning that shapes her design and provides important context for our discussion of Carla's culminating project and translanguaging assessment practices.

Carla's culminating project asks students to write an argumentative essay about local farming practices that includes text-based evidence, local sources, and human resources to support their positions. Students first present their argument orally to their peers and then to the school community during an open house. Carla will use the culminating project for assessment purposes. She also assesses her students formatively throughout the stages of explorar, evaluar, imaginar, presenter, and implementar that make up the translanguaging design cycle.

Teacher's Assessment Tool

Teachers need to assess what students know and can do with content and language relative to standards, objectives, and the culminating project of a translanguaging instructional unit. To do this, teachers must observe students as they perform different instructional tasks leading up to and including the culminating project. (It is interesting that the word assessment comes from the Latin assidere, which means to sit beside.)

A translanguaging design for assessment directs teachers to observe two aspects of student performance based on these two questions:

1. Is the student using all the features of their language repertoire and/or using language-specific features?
2. Is the student performing *independently*, with *moderate assistance* from other people and/or other resources, or is the performance *emergent*?

Table 8.1. Carla's Translanguage Unit Plan: Cuentos de la Tierra y del Barrio

<table>
<tr><td>Essential Questions</td><td colspan="2">• How are students, families, and the local community tied to their land, and by extension to their traditions?
• How do communities interact with one another and their environments?
• How does local farming differ from global farming?
• Why is it important to sustain local farming practices?
• How can students cultivate their local jardín del barrio?</td></tr>
<tr><td>Content Standards</td><td colspan="2">• NMCCSS.ELA-Literacy.W.4.1: Write opinion pieces on topics or texts, supporting point of view with reasons and information.
• NMCCSS.ELA-Literacy.W.4.3: Gather relevant information from multiple sources, including oral knowledge.
• NMCCSS.ELA-Literacy.RL.4.1: Refer to details and examples in a text when explaining what the text says explicitly and when drawing inferences from it.
• New Mexico Standards in Social Studies/History (fourth grade): Research historical events and people from a variety of perspectives.</td></tr>
<tr><td>Content and Language Objective(s)</td><td>Content Objectives
Students will be able to:
• Gather information from community leaders about their neighborhoods' agricultural, social, and historical landscape
• Summarize oral and written text-based evidence to support their position about why it is important to sustain local farming practices
• Compose an argumentative essay to support their opinion piece</td><td>General Linguistic Objectives
Students will be able to:
• Review information supporting a point of view
• Give specific details about point of view using a line of reasoning
• Know the language differences between a logical conclusion and an emotional point of view

Language-Specific Objectives
Students will be able to:
• Use the following structures to argue a point:
o In English: The advantages outweigh the disadvantages because ___; From my point of view ___; The benefits are obvious, for example, ___.
o In Spanish: Hay más ventajas que desventajas porque ___ ; Mi punto de vista es que ___; Los beneficios son obvios, un ejemplo es que, ___.
• Use the following signal words to argue a point:
o In English: defend, support, claim, believe, perceive
o In Spanish: defender, apoyar, reclamar, estar convencido de, percibir
• Use the first- and third-person singular pronouns and verb endings (morphology)
o The third person singular "s" in English and the obligatory use of the personal pronoun vs. the change of ending in verbs in Spanish and the variable use of the pronoun (not obligatory)
• In English: I defend vs. s/he defends
• In Spanish: (Yo) defiendo vs. (el/ella) defiende</td></tr>
<tr><td>Translanguaging Objective(s)</td><td colspan="2">Students will be able to:
• Gather information by interviewing community leaders/parents and using other local/global resources (technology) in English, in Spanish, and bilingually
• Complete a language analysis of bilingual texts during the Cuéntame Algo activity to better understand the meaning of the bilingual texto/contexto
• Collaborate in a small group to generate a list of ideas to answer a question: How do you think we can darle vida o más vida a nuestro jardín del barrio?
• Select a language to write and read essay to peers
• Integrate translanguaging (where appropriate) by choosing certain phrases, expressions, or words to better convey point of view</td></tr>
<tr><td>Translanguaging Assessments</td><td>Culminating Design
Individually, students write an argumentative essay about local farming practices with text-based evidence, local sources, and human resources to support their positions. Students first present their essays to their peers and then to the school community during the annual open house.</td><td>Other Translanguaging Assessments*
Teacher's Assessment: This instructive tool provides guidance about what the student can or will do in listening, speaking, reading, and writing tasks to demonstrate content knowledge using general linguistic and language-specific performances. In addition, it provides teachers with an opportunity to note whether students can perform a task independently or with assistance from other people or resources.
Student Self-Assessment: This reflective tool gives students an opportunity to express how and what they have learned throughout the project, which will better inform the teacher about their instruction.</td></tr>
</table>

(continued)

Table 8.1. *(continued)*

		Peer Group Assessment: This tool offers a reflective space to explain the role of the group and the performance within it. **Family Assessment:** La conexión: This tool gives the student an opportunity to share what they learned with a family member. Also, it provides a space for a family member to share their opinions, expertise, knowledge, experiences, and thoughts about the topic being learned at school.
Texts	*In Spanish*	*In English*
	• Rudolfo Anaya's *The Santero's Miracle*	• Fourth-grade social studies textbook
	• Literature about gardening written by the local community leader	• Fourth-grade science textbook
	• Readings about local/global farming practices from websites and magazines	• Readings about local/global farming practices from websites and magazines
	• Videos about local and global farming practices	• Videos about local and global farming practices

* See Appendices 8.1–8.4, respectively, for blank templates.

Up to this point, the discussion in this book has focused on only the first question as we considered how students are positioned differently and the degree to which they can use their entire repertoire or not to perform different tasks, with different interlocutors, for different purposes. Here, the second important dimension to the translanguaging design for assessment—whether the performance is undertaken independently, with assistance, or not at all—is explored.

The *Teacher's Assessment Tool for Translanguaging Classrooms* (Appendix 8.1) was developed to help teachers look more closely at students' performances within the context of their translanguaging designs in instruction. This tool is organized around the linguistic and academic demands of the Common Core State Standards (CCSS) Language Arts Standards for reading, writing, listening, speaking, and language. This tool also provides space for teachers to observe students' performances for evidence of their understanding, creativity, and curiosity relative to the essential ideas of the unit, both when they are using the full features of their linguistic repertoires and when they are exclusively using features of one named language or another. Teachers of different subject areas can adapt this template to address the standards of their disciplines with attention to specific content and language demands of a particular curricular unit of instruction.

The Teacher's Assessment Tool can be used in several different ways. First, teachers can use it to document how a student uses language to perform a specific task and with what assistance. Second, this tool can help teachers organize and document their holistic assessment of student performance within and across tasks relative to the standards addressed in any given unit. Teachers can see at a glance which tasks students can perform independently (IP), which they can perform with moderate assistance (PMA), and at which tasks they are still novices (NP). Third, teachers can use this template to reflect on their instruction by evaluating the types and range of performances that they are requiring of students. Teachers can use the evidence they collect with the Teacher's Assessment Tool to guide instruction and improve their translanguaging practice.

Next, Carla's methods of using the Teacher's Assessment Tool to assess Ricardo's reading performance within the context of her unit of instruction are demonstrated. Table 8.2 shows how Carla completed the reading component for Ricardo to assess his reading performance throughout the unit.

Carla begins by identifying the type of reading task that Ricardo will perform, for example: *focus on providing text evidence of key ideas* or *make inferences*. Next, Carla identifies the types of general linguistic or language-specific performance she observes. In this case, Carla observes when Ricardo performs only in English, performs only in Spanish, or draws on the full features of his linguistic repertoire, including Mixteco. Next to each task, and according to each type of language use, Carla records the type of assistance Ricardo requires: IP, PMA, or NP. At the bottom of the form, Carla makes notes of the evidence that she collects

Table 8.2. Carla's Assessment of Ricardo's Work

Unit title: Cuentos de la tierra y del barrio			
	General Linguistic Performance	Language-Specific Performance (English)	Language-Specific Performance (Spanish)
Reading Can the student:			
Focus on providing text-based evidence of key ideas	PMA*	NP	NP
Make inferences	IP	NP	IP
Identify main ideas and relationships in complex texts	PMA	PMA	PMA
Recognize the text's craft and structure (e.g., chronology, comparison, cause/effect)	PMA	NP	NP
Associate knowledge and ideas from multiple sources and texts	PMA	PMA	PMA
Conduct research to build knowledge	IP	NP	IP
Evidence	With assistance (technology, texts, peers, teacher) Ricardo can • Provide many details, evidence, and examples in a text (expanding) • Identify main ideas and relationships (expanding) • Recognize text structure (expanding) • Associate from multiple sources/texts (expanding) Independently, Ricardo can • Make inferences (expanding) • Conduct research (expanding)	With assistance (technology, texts, peers, teacher) Ricardo can • Identify some relationships (developing) • Associate from multiple sources/texts (developing) Without assistance, Ricardo can only • Refer to a few details, evidence, and examples from a text (emerging) • Locate some language associated with inferences (entering) • Start outlining his ideas in English (emerging) • Recognize the text's craft (emerging)	Independently, Ricardo can • Make inferences (expanding) • Conduct research (expanding) Without assistance, Ricardo can only • Provide few details, evidence, and examples from a text (emerging) • Compare and contrast language associated with inferences (emerging) • Write an essay in Mixteco and translate into Spanish (emerging)

*IP, independent performance; NP, novice performance, even with assistance; PMA, performance with moderate assistance.

to support her assessment. In this case, Carla identifies the patterns she observes along three dimensions: (1) type of task, (2) type of language performance (*entering, emerging, developing, expanding, bridging* and *reaching*), and (3) type of assistance (*with assistance, independently,* or *without assistance).*

Ricardo's performance in English on many of the reading tasks, even with assistance, is still considered novice (NP). However, when using Spanish, Ricardo can make inferences and do research independently (IP)—the two tasks that are not directly related to text analysis. In the evidence section, Carla evaluates Ricardo's Spanish language performances on these types of tasks (making inferences and doing research independently) as *expanding.* Recall that Ricardo's school in Mexico had provided him with little experience in finding text-based evidence and analyzing the text's craft. As a result, Ricardo's performance on text-based tasks in Spanish, even with assistance, is still novice (NP). However, when Ricardo is permitted to use his entire language repertoire, his performance is greatly enhanced on the text-based tasks. Looking at Ricardo's general linguistic performance, we see that he reaches the *expanding* stage on all types of reading tasks evaluated in this unit, although sometimes he requires assistance from other people or material. The Teacher's Assessment Tool allows Carla to understand clearly that developing Ricardo's reading performances in English is going to require much more than simply learning a new language. It is going to require that Carla provide opportunities for him to practice using his home languages—Spanish and Mixteco—to find text-based evidence and analyze the text's craft.

The evidence that Carla collects using the Teacher's Assessment Tool paints a much more complex portrait of Ricardo's reading performance than that drawn from standardized assessments. Carla uses this document as the jumping-off point to build Ricardo's language arts portfolio, and she includes samples of student work to demonstrate what Ricardo can do using the full features of his linguistic repertoire alongside what he can do in Spanish and English. Carla makes instructional and assessment decisions for Ricardo based on his performance on different types of tasks over time. This documentation is important because the DLBE spaces for English and the language other than English (LOTE) are now "strategically accompanied by spaces in which translanguaging is used intentionally to have a more holistic understanding of the child as learner" (Sánchez et al., 2017, p. 7).

Turning now to the students in our other focal teachers' classrooms, we see how Justin and Stephanie also utilize the Teacher's Assessment Tool to understand what their students know and can do, beginning with Justin's assessment of the reading performance of his student Pablo. Recall that Pablo has recently arrived in Los Angeles from Argentina and that he is a student in the math class that Justin supports as an ESL teacher. Before coming to the United States, Pablo had taken private after-school English lessons and was enrolled in a private school in Buenos Aires. Pablo has been in the United States approximately the same period of time as Ricardo in Carla's class. He can do all the tasks of the reading assessment inventory in Spanish only, using the full features of his language repertoire independently. Pablo's general language performance, as well as his performance in Spanish, is *commanding*. Because of his strong general language performance, Pablo is able to complete the English reading tasks with moderate assistance.

Here are a few more examples from Justin's and Stephanie's translanguaging classrooms to highlight how teachers can use the Teacher Assessment Tool to make informed decisions about their students in their very different classroom contexts:

- ***Yi-Sheng*** is a newcomer from Taiwan in Justin's class, and she needs assistance all the time when she has to perform reading tasks in English. However, Yi-Sheng performs the same types of reading tasks beautifully and independently when she uses Mandarin.
- ***Luis*** is a recent arrival from El Salvador in Stephanie's class, and he speaks only Spanish. As a result of his limited schooling in El Salvador, Luis' reading and writing performances in Spanish are *transitioning*. Luis therefore needs assistance when performing literacy-based tasks in Spanish.
- ***Fatoumata*** is a student in Justin's class who needs assistance whether using all her language resources or using one language or another. Despite her oral fluency in Pular, Fatoumata does not have any experience using this language for academic purposes. Although she speaks fluent French, in the schools she attended in Guinea she had never been asked to find text-based evidence or to write an argumentative essay.

The Teacher's Assessment Tool directs teachers' attention to what students can do with language on different types of academic tasks, with assistance and independently, which in turn helps them identify specific supports their students need. Teachers need to provide students with external resources to support them in performing tasks so that they can carry them out independently. Teachers also need to be able to differentiate how those scaffolds and supports relate to students' performances with their entire language repertoires or to performances in one language or another.

ASSESSING FROM MANY ANGLES

Teachers in translanguaging classrooms emphasize the importance of dynamic, authentic, and holistic assessment from many angles. The constituents of the translanguaging design for assessment, the student, peer group, family, and teacher, are shown in Figure 8.5. This section illustrates these angles in action and concludes with the teacher's inclusive class

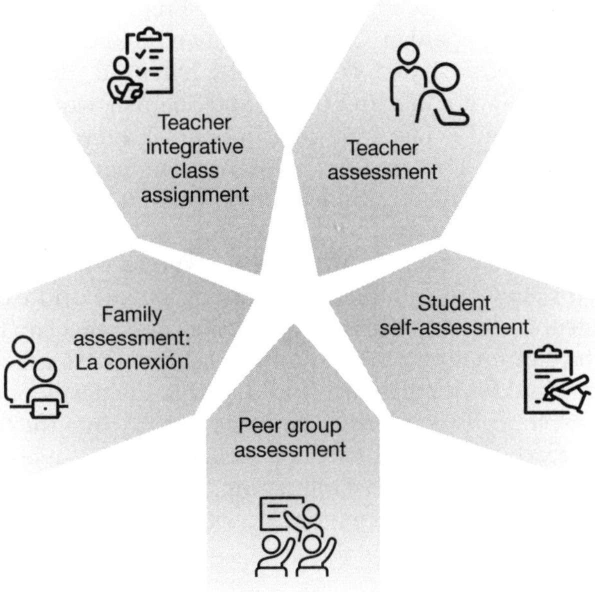

Figure 8.5. Demonstrates assessment from many angles. (Courtesy of Jamie Schissel)

assessment. As you read, consider how you can use a translanguaging lens[3] to assess your bilingual students' performances throughout a translanguaging unit of instruction.

Student Self-Assessment

Student learning is at the center of the translanguaging pedagogy, and students must be involved in documenting and assessing their own learning. An initial step to doing this is to engage students in designing their own autobiographical translanguaging portraits. In addition, the *Student Self-Assessment Tool* asks students what essential questions they can answer, what new vocabulary or language structures they can use, whether and how they've used translanguaging to learn, what standards they've addressed, how they've collaborated with peers, their teacher's and families' roles in their learning, and what outside resources they've used. Students are also asked to evaluate their content and language performances, whether they think the culminating project was an appropriate way of assessing their learning, and what new questions they have. Because all of Carla's students use Spanish and English, the questions on the Student Self-Assessment in Appendix 8.2 are in both languages. Teachers whose students speak other languages can translate the questions as necessary.

Students can complete the questions on this self-assessment in writing, or, if necessary, the teacher can ask students the questions orally and write down their answers. Or students can do so for each other or use a recorder. For example, Ricardo completes the self-assessment task orally, largely in Spanish, with some Mixteco and a few words and phrases in English. When Carla hears Mixteco on the self-assessment recorder, she invites Ricardo to discuss what he means in Spanish.

[3]It is unrealistic for every teacher to assess every student from each of these different perspectives during each unit and then to integrate all this information. Furthermore, some perspectives may be more important than others at different times throughout the instructional unit. Teachers, especially novice teachers, should try out one assessment at a time with different students. An important advantage of having different constituents involved in assessment is that the teacher does not have to do all the work in isolation, but can share responsibility for assessment with the students themselves, peers, and families.

The situation is different in Stephanie's class because she does not speak or read her students' home languages. For her Spanish-speaking students, for example, she asks her Spanish-speaking colleagues to translate to English any parts of the responses that are written or spoken in Spanish. Other students who know their classmates' home languages can also help with translation. For example, *Teresita*, a student in Stephanie's class who is a strong reader and writer in both English and Spanish, works with *Luis*, who recently arrived from El Salvador and is just emerging in Spanish literacy, to complete his self-assessment orally while she writes his answers in English. Stephanie uses the information derived from the self-assessment to determine what new content and language each individual student now understands and can use.

Bilingual students can use this tool to express what translanguaging means for their learning, with attention to how they draw on people and external resources for support, communicate their needs for future instruction, and reflect on the design of the assessments, including the culminating project. Bilingual students are asked to articulate new questions that have emerged for them, which could lead to the development of a new unit or topic for students to explorar. This information feeds directly into the teacher's instructional design, enabling the teacher to set a different instructional course and to understand how individual bilingual students use translanguaging, as well as how they use people resources (e.g., peers, family, and teacher) and external resources (e.g., printed, media texts and technology) to support their learning.

Peer Group Assessment

A collaborative instructional design must correspond to a collaborative assessment design. This means that peers are also asked to evaluate the group's work. A blank Peer Group Assessment Tool is in Appendix 8.3, and the questions are written in Spanish and English. It is important to emphasize that this assessment is *not* of individuals by peers; instead, it is an assessment of the group's collaborative learning and the group's ways of working. This form could be filled out by one group member in consultation with the others after extensive discussion, or individual group members can take turns filling out different questions. As with individual students' self-assessments, the group is asked to assess its learning of essential ideas and questions; of content, language, and translanguaging objectives; of its use of other resources; and of the culminating project.

For one of the activities in Carla's class, a group consisting of Erica, Moisés, Jennifer, and Ricardo searched the Internet for information on local farming in Albuquerque. Jennifer and Erica searched the web in English, while Ricardo and Moisés did so in Spanish. When they came together, they read from each other's notes, and the ensuing dialogue used both English and Spanish as they quoted text-based evidence. When they filled out their peer group assessment, Jennifer wrote the group's answer to question 2 as: "We know now many things, but especially that it will be difficult to eat chiles verdes because there are not enough farmers." For question 3, she wrote: "We were awesome! Ricardo read in Spanish, and Moisés, Erica, and Jennifer in English. There is more stuff in English." Carla was especially interested in the group's response to question 7, to which Ricardo recorded: "Excellent! We discussed excellent! Y ahora sabemos más. Y abajo con una, y arriba con dos." By having students take responsibility for assessing their learning and their ability to work together, Carla is motivating them to take the initiative to learn and to reflect on how language works. The students not only take pride in being bilingual, but also realize that "una" certainly doesn't mean "más," and so they actually lift their bilingualism as they are propelled to greater learning.

This assessment fosters group collaboration and consciousness of each other's learning while giving the teacher opportunities to assess whether the grouping is successful. A review of this group assessment by the teacher will inform grouping decisions the teacher makes for subsequent instructional units, activities, and assessments.

Family Assessment: La Conexión

The assessment of students' bilingualism and learning by families is often very different from that of school, as was demonstrated in Chapter 4 when Noemí's parents rated her as a more experienced bilingual than did her teacher, Stephanie. When family members assess their children's learning, they shine light on the translanguaging corriente that connects students' homes and communities with the school, and they contribute to a more holistic view of the bilingual child. A *Family Assessment Tool* is provided in Appendix 8.4 that families can use to share their perspectives on students' content and language learning. The questions are in Spanish and English.

The Family Assessment Tool, however, is not only a way to ask family members what their children have learned and what they have learned from their children. It also taps the families' funds of knowledge and provides a vehicle for sharing their own understanding and resources with children in school. Thus, the translanguaging design for assessment recognizes families as learners *and* teachers, emphasizing the families' potential to extend their own children's understanding of content and language, as well as that of other children in the class. The family assessment is an important conexión.

As with the Peer Group Assessment Tool, the Family Assessment Tool is collaborative. It is designed so that family members work with children to complete the form. Parents can either write their own responses or share their answers with their children, who then record them. In this way, parents and children are engaged in the assessment process as learners and teachers. Furthermore, when family members identify a fund of knowledge from their home or community that they would like to share, they can indicate this on the form, and teachers can invite family members to the classrooms to help students make important home-family-community-school connections.

For example, Ricardo shared the form with his mother. Ricardo read the questions in Spanish, while his mother spoke to him mostly in Mixteco with some Spanish. She also asked him to read the questions in English. Ricardo's mother was proud of her son's ability to read in English, and she proudly repeated some words: "son," "child," "song," "story," some of which Ricardo gently repeated back. Ricardo filled out the form as best he could with his mother's words in Spanish and Mixteco. When Ricardo's father came home from work, his mother showed him the conexión and all of Ricardo's writing. She also showed him the corn plant that she had drawn on the back of the form. She spoke with excitement about the English words she learned from her son and about her pride in her son's progress in English. Then they discussed the last question. Both of them had grown corn in their tierra back in Oaxaca. They decided that they would tell Ricardo that they could visit the class to tell his classmates about their cosecha de maíz.

Teacher's Integrative Class Assessment Tool

The information provided by the different constituents of the translanguaging design for assessment—the students themselves and their families, peers, and teacher—has to be integrated into instruction. The *Teacher's Integrative Class Assessment Tool* is provided in Appendix 8.5. Teachers can use this template to organize the assessment data they have collected from different constituents on different tasks. Teachers may include assessments of the students' understanding of content, their language use, use of resources, and intellectual curiosity and creativity. This information then supports the teacher's translanguaging instructional design.

Teachers are the ultimate assessors of student learning. If they pay close attention to what students say and do, teachers can surely say a lot more about their students than a score on a standardized test. However, translanguaging for assessment requires that the teachers' assessment of students is not based solely on their own evaluation of student learning, but that this assessment is done in collaboration with others, especially those who know the students best—the students themselves and their peers and families. It is then important to integrate the teacher's evaluation with the student's self-evaluation and those of the peer group and families. The equitable and fair assessment of bilingual students also requires that teachers evaluate students' performances according to their general linguistic and language-specific performances.

In Table 8.3, Carla has filled out the Teacher's Integrative Class Assessment Tool for Ricardo. A few obvious patterns emerge. Ricardo is a lot more critical of his academic performances than the rest of the constituents. His parents are his biggest fans and evaluate his performance as *commanding*. His peers are also quite proud of the group's performance. His

Table 8.3. Completed Integrative Assessment for Ricardo

Indicate for each of these five measures whether the student's performance has been evaluated as:
3 = Advanced
2 = Satisfactory
1 = Needs work
Leave blank if you do not have the data to make this determination.

1. Add up each column for a *total sum per constituent*.
2. Divide by the number of categories you can assess in the column. This gives you the total *average per constituent*.
3. Add the averages per student and divide by 4.
4. Give the *integrative score* on the next line.

Student's Name: Ricardo

Categories	Constituents			
	Self	Group	Family	Teacher
Content use				
Essential ideas	2		3	2
Language use				
General linguistic performance	3	3	3	3
Language-specific performance (Spanish)	3	2	3	2
Use of resources	2	3	3	3
Creativity/Curiosity	2	3	2	3
Total sum per constituent	12	11	14	13
Total average per constituent	2.4	2.75	2.8	2.6
Integrative scores and comments	2.63: Ricardo's self-evaluation is harsher than that of the other constituents. He is well-liked by members of his group, who evaluate him as having *expanding* performances. But he is especially well positioned based on his parents' evaluation. The teacher's evaluation falls between the poorer self-evaluation and the positive ones given to him by family and peers. A 2.63 score means that Ricardo is well poised because of support from his family and peers to advance to meet standards. All he needs is self-confidence to continue to perform.			

teacher's evaluation falls between the *transitioning* one of Ricardo and the *commanding* one of his parents. Overall, however, his total integrative score of 2.63 indicates that Ricardo's performances in school are approaching *commanding* and, therefore, that he is on the road to academic success.

Managing Assessments

Realistically, teachers do not have to use all of these assessment tools at all times for every child in the classroom. They are offered here as opportunities to help teachers get to know students and improve instruction. It is possible to try out the Peer Group Assessment Tool in one unit and the Student's Self-Assessment Tool in a different unit, or to send the Family Assessment Tool home to families once a month or once a week. It might also be possible for the teacher to do a full assessment of three to five students for every instructional unit. What is important is that teachers gather evidence of student performance on different tasks, from different perspectives, at different times and then use that evidence to improve instruction and assessment of bilingual students.

TRANSLANGUAGING SHIFTS IN ASSESSMENT

Teachers in translanguaging classrooms understand that assessment is not simply a standardized test score that each child has for the year. Rather, assessment has to be flexible and responsive to students' learning needs. In addition to formally assessing students' understanding from different perspectives, teachers in translanguaging classrooms shift their focus as they assess different moments from students' work.

Teachers in translanguaging classrooms vary in the ways they use assessment tools. Sometimes, for example, the self-assessment is given to students after the teacher has evaluated their learning and shared the assessment with them. Sometimes teachers use different tools to assess children; they choose and adapt them for the specific learning opportunity and the characteristics of the student being assessed.

Teachers in translanguaging classrooms think about the design of their assessment, but they also assess students informally as the opportunities arise. For example, when Carla taught the jardín lesson discussed earlier, Ricardo preferred to perform in Spanish. Carla showed Ricardo her own evaluation of his work, in which English was often left blank. Ricardo objected and said that he was able to use English—he had just not done so for that particular task. Carla then gave Ricardo the opportunity to work in English and then assessed his performance, which showed he was able to use English, with moderate assistance, for most tasks.

Assessment in translanguaging classrooms is never just handed down. It is discussed with the learners, and advice is sought for the future. Students are given a voice in their assessment through self-reflection and self-evaluation. Furthermore, students' performances are assessed on different tasks, from different perspectives, over time. Teachers' shifts in assessment are purposeful; they allow students to perform what they know and can do through different modes—drawing, speaking, writing, pointing, the use of technology, and so forth—and they encourage students to use different language practices. In these cases, collaboration means adaptation and adjustment, as teachers make moment-by-moment decisions about what counts as knowledge and how to assess it.

After carefully designing and planning the use of assessments, all teachers must go with the flow of the translanguaging corriente to ensure that students are being assessed fairly and accurately. Assessment works for the child and not the other way around. When in doubt about assessment, go with the flow of your students' needs, inquiries, and abilities.

CONCLUSION

Teachers in translanguaging classrooms design assessments carefully. They do not see themselves as the sole expert/evaluator but as one of many caring observers, ensuring that students, peers, and families also have a role in assessment. Knowledge is collaboratively constructed, and students are given opportunities to perform certain tasks independently or with the assistance of others or other resources. For bilingual students, language is an interrelated repertoire, not simply the autonomous use of English or Spanish, as illustrated in the autobiographical translanguaging portraits. Thus, assessments of bilingual students must not only assess the use of two languages independently, as schools most often require, but also include the perspective of bilingual children using their entire language repertoire. It is important for teachers to know whether a child's emergent performance on a task reflects an incomplete understanding of content, an emergent performance level in the school language, or an emergent general linguistic performance. When teachers can clearly assess the specific challenges that their students face (content, named language A or B, general linguistic performance), they are in a stronger position to support and scaffold students' learning and to transform their capacities.

An important lesson to draw from this chapter is that even though assessments are often thought of as fixed and rigid, they too are shaped by the translanguaging corriente. In fact, it is the flexibility afforded by translanguaging that allows teachers to assess what students know and can do using different language practices.

Translanguaging in assessment requires a strong juntos stance, careful design, and well-orchestrated shifts. There cannot be a simple linear arrangement where teaching comes first and assessment last. Instruction and assessment need to work juntos as interlocking gears to strengthen students' performances. The translanguaging corriente mobilizes students' bilingual resources, and the teacher uses flexible assessment instruments to accelerate student learning.

REFLECTION QUESTIONS AND ACTIVITIES

1. Think about the two general principles of a translanguaging assessment design, as well as the four elements of identifying and evaluating bilingual students' language performances. Which feel realistic for you to include in your own assessment design? Why? Which seem more difficult? Why?
2. Engage your students in producing their own autobiographical translanguaging portraits and invite their reflections on their language practices.
3. Describe the difference between general linguistic and language-specific performances in assessment. Is this a useful distinction? Is it a difficult distinction to make?
4. Can you think of a time when it is not a good idea to allow students to use their entire linguistic repertoire to respond to assessment? Explain your answer.

TAKING ACTION

1. Now that you have read about assessment, see if you can add to the boxes on assessment and general and language-specific performances in the translanguaging unit plan that you produced using Appendix 6.1.
2. Select three students. After a lesson, have each of them fill out the Student Self-Assessment (see Appendix 8.2), have the group fill out the Peer Group Assessment (see Appendix 8.3), send home the Family Assessment: La Conexión (see Appendix 8.4), and fill out your own assessment (see Appendix 8.1). What did you learn from these various assessments? How would you adapt or change your instruction based on this new information?

APPENDIX 8.1

Teacher's Assessment Tool for Translanguaging Classrooms

Student Name: ______________________________

Instructions
Indicate the type of linguistic performance (general linguistic or language-specific) that the student demonstrates in performing each task by indicating whether the student can do each task *with assistance* or *independently*.
Indicate in the appropriate area:
PMA, performance with moderate assistance: Can do with assistance from other people (peers or teachers) or resources (technology, books, posters, etc.)
IP, independent performance: Can do task without assistance from other people or resources*
NP, novice performance: Only beginning to emerge, even with assistance
Leave blank if it doesn't apply.

	***General* Linguistic Performance**	**Language-*Specific* Performance (English)**	**Language-*Specific* Performance (LOTE)****	**Observations/ Comments**
Translanguaging Design for Assessment	Using all language resources	Using features from English only	Using features from the LOTE only	
Essential Ideas				
How is the student demonstrating know-how of the essential ideas of the content/topic?				
Creativity/Curiosity				
Has the student demonstrated further curiosity about or transformation of the content/topic?				
Reading				
Can the student: • Focus on providing text-based evidence of key ideas? • Make inferences? • Identify main ideas and relationships in complex texts?				

Reading (continued)				
• Recognize the text's craft and structure (e.g., chronology, comparison, cause/effect)? • Associate knowledge and ideas from multiple sources and texts? • Conduct research to build knowledge?				
Writing				
Can the student: • Produce texts of opinion? • Produce texts of information? • Produce texts of explanation? • Produce narrative texts?				
Speaking and Listening				
Can the student: • Comprehend knowledge and ideas? • Orally present knowledge and ideas collaboratively?				

* For more on IP and PMA, see Bodrova and Leong (2019).

** To be filled out only by bilingual teachers or other teachers who share a LOTE with the student (e.g., world/heritage language teachers).

APPENDIX 8.2

Student Self-Assessment Tool

WHAT AND HOW I LEARNED AND WHAT I CAN DO
LO QUE APRENDÍ Y COMO Y LO QUE PUEDO HACER

Student Name: ____

	I CAN/YO PUEDO
¿Qué ideas esenciales comprendes ahora? ¿Qué preguntas esenciales puedes ahora contestar? [What essential ideas do you now understand? What essential questions can you now answer?]	
¿Qué vocabulario o estructura lingüística aprendiste? ¿Lo aprendiste en una o dos lenguas? Si estudias en dos lenguas, ¿Qué notas de cómo funciona el inglés en comparación con el español? [What vocabulary or language structures did you learn? Did you learn those in one or two languages? If you learned bilingually, what do you notice about how English works that is different from or the same as how the Spanish language works?]	
Reflexiona sobre tu uso lingüístico. Si usaste translanguaging cuándo, por qué, y cómo te hizo sentir? Si no lo usaste, por qué no? [Reflect on your use of language. Did you use translanguaging at any time? If so, when, why, and how did it make you feel? If not, why not?]	
¿Podrías identificar algún estándar de lectura, escritura, comprensión o expresión oral que se enlace con tu aprendizaje? [Can you identify any reading, writing, listening and speaking, and content standards to which your learning was linked?]	
¿Cómo te ayudaron tus compañeros para aprender? ¿Cómo colaboraron? ¿Qué podían haber hecho diferente? [How did your classmates help you learn? How did you all collaborate? What could you have done differently?]	

	I CAN/YO PUEDO
¿Qué rol tuvo tu familia en tu aprendizaje? ¿Qué podrían haber hecho diferente? [What role did your family play in your learning? What could they have done differently?]	
¿Qué rol tuvo tu maestra(o) en tu aprendizaje? ¿Qué podría haber hecho diferente? [What role did your teacher have in your learning? What could they have done differently?]	
¿Qué recursos externos usaste para aprender (textos, el web, videos, periódicos, diccionarios, realia, etc.)? [What external resources did you use to learn (texts, the web, videos, newspapers, dictionaries, realia, and so forth)?]	
¿Cuáles de tus actuaciones durante este tiempo demuestra mejor lo que has aprendido? [Which of your performances during this time best demonstrates what you have learned?]	
¿Fue apropriada el proyecto culminante para saber qué aprendiste? [Was the culminating project appropriate to evaluate your learning?]	
¿Cómo evaluarías tu actuación en el área de contenido? ¿Pudiste expresarte oralmente o a través de la escritura con éxito? ¿Pudiste expresarte usando solamente las formas de una lengua específica? [How would you evaluate your performance in the content area? Were you able to carry it out orally and/or in writing successfully? Were you able to carry it out successfully using only the features of a specific language?]	
¿Qué nuevas preguntas tienes ahora de este tema? [What new question do you now have about this topic?]	

APPENDIX 8.3

Peer Group Assessment Tool

WHAT AND HOW DID WE LEARN? / ¿LO QUE APRENDIMOS Y CÓMO?

Names of individuals in group: ______________________________

1. ¿Qué se discutió en tu grupo (en términos de contenido y/o lengua)? ¿Qué aspectos fueron más fáciles o difíciles para el grupo?
   [What did you discuss among yourselves in the group (in terms of content and/or language)? What aspects were easier or more difficult for the group?]

2. ¿Qué preguntas esenciales (sobre contenido y/o lengua) puedes ahora contestar después de hablarlo en el grupo que no hubieras podido contestar antes?
   [What essential questions can you now answer (about content and/or language) after having discussed it in the group that you couldn't have answered before?]

3. Reflexiona sobre el uso lingüístico de tu grupo. Si usaron translanguaging ¿cuándo, con quién, por qué, y cómo te hizo sentir? Si no lo usaste, por qué no?
   [Reflect on your use of language in the group. Did you use translanguaging at any time? If so, when, with whom, why, and how did it make you feel? If not, why not?]

4. ¿Cómo te ayudaron tus compañeros para aprender? ¿Cómo colaboraron? ¿Qué podían haber hecho diferente?
   [How did your classmates help you learn? How did you all collaborate? What could you have done differently?]

5. ¿Qué recursos externos usó tu grupo para aprender? Textos, el web, videos, periódicos, diccionarios, realia, etc? ¿Qué fue más útil para tu grupo y por qué? ¿Qué no fue útil?
   [What external resources did your group use to learn? Did you use texts, the web, videos, newspapers, dictionaries, realia, and so forth? What was most helpful to the group and why? What was unhelpful?]

6. ¿Cómo fue el proyecto final para tu grupo? ¿Fue apropriada el proyecto final para saber qué aprendió tu grupo?
   [How did your group do with the culminating project? Was it appropriate for evaluating your learning?]

7. ¿Cómo evaluarías la actuación de tu grupo en el área de contenido? ¿Cómo se expresaron oralmente y en escritura? ¿Cómo se expresaron cuando tuvieron que utilizar una sola lengua?
   [How would you evaluate your group's performance in the content area? How did the group do using oral and written language? How did the group do using only one language or the other?]

8. ¿Qué nuevas preguntas tiene tu grupo ahora sobre este tema?
   [What new question does your group have about this topic?]

Family Assessment Tool: La Conexión

<table>
<tr><td colspan="2">Hoy su hijo(a) le mostró algo que aprendió en la escuela. Muéstreme con un dibujo, escriba o dígale a su hijo(a) lo que aprendió de él/ella.

[Today your child showed you something they learned in school. Show me in a drawing, tell me, or write what you learned from what your child shared.]</td></tr>
<tr><td>¿Cree Ud. que su hijo(a) comprendió la lección si o no? ¿Cómo lo sabe?

[Do you think your child understood the lesson well or not? How do you know?]</td><td>Sí
No
Por favor, explique cómo lo sabe.
How do you know?</td></tr>
<tr><td>¿En qué lengua le habló su hijo(a)? ¿En español? ¿En inglés? ¿En los dos? ¿Qué opina Ud. del lenguaje que usa su hijo(a)?

[In which language did your child speak to you? In English? Spanish? Both? What do you think of the language used by your child?]</td><td>Español/Spanish
Inglés/English
En los dos/Both</td></tr>
</table>

¿Qué otra cosa le gustaría saber de este tema a su hijo(a)? ¿A Ud.? [What else would your child like to know about this topic? How about you?]	Escríbelo aquí/Write it here.
Tal vez Ud. sepa algo que se relacione a lo que su hijo(a) aprende en la escuela. Por ejemplo, tal vez Ud. sabe cómo hacer algo, conoce una canción, un dicho, un cuento, que nos ayude a entender major la lección. ¿Podría compartirlo con la clase? Díganos. [Maybe you know something that is related to what your child is learning in school. For example, maybe you know how to do something, or maybe you know a song, a saying, or a story that would help us understand the lesson better. Would you be able to share it with the class? Tell us.]	Díganos aqui/Tell us.

APPENDIX 8.5

Teacher's Integrative Class Assessment Tool

Indicate for each of these five measures whether the student's performance has been evaluated as:
3 = Advanced

2 = Satisfactory

1 = Needs work

Leave blank if you do not have the data to make this determination.

1. Add up each column for a *total sum per constituent*.
2. Divide by the number of categories you can assess in the column. This gives you the total *average per constituent*.
3. Add the averages per student and divide by 4.
4. Give the integrative score on the next line.

Student's Name:____

	Constituents			
Categories	**Self**	**Group**	**Family**	**Teacher**
Content use				
Essential ideas				
Language use				
General linguistic performance				
Language-specific performance (Spanish)				
Use of resources				
Creativity/Curiosity				
Total sum per constituent				
Total average per constituent				
Integrative scores and comments				

9

Translanguaging Pedagogy in Action

LEARNING OBJECTIVES

After reading this chapter, you will be able to:

- Identify the key components of a translanguaging pedagogy.
- Explain how the three translanguaging strands—stance, design, and shifts—work together and have a transformative effect on the daily life of a classroom.
- Describe the teacher's juntos stance toward students, languages, and content.
- Explain how teachers leverage the translanguaging corriente during instruction and assessment.
- Give examples of moment-to-moment shifts that teachers make in response to the translanguaging corriente.
- Use a reflective tool for adopting a translanguaging pedagogy in your classroom.

The daily life of the translanguaging classroom mirrors the daily lives of bilinguals outside of the classroom. When the world of the classroom reflects the everyday lives of bilingual people, educational opportunities for bilingual students open up. Rather than simply using students' home languages as scaffolds to English, teachers in translanguaging classrooms recognize and create opportunities for students to language, learn, express themselves, and forge relationships in unique ways. If translanguaging, as García and Leiva (2014) write, can "dissolve solid differences while create[ing] new realities" (p. 203), a translanguaging pedagogy reshapes the classroom space, enabling teachers to transcend traditional rules about language, learning, and teaching to foster new social realities in their classrooms. In other words, a *critical* translanguaging pedagogy has transformative potential; it can reconfigure power, disrupt established knowledge, and develop Latinx students' **critical consciousness** (Hamman-Ortiz, 2023; Sánchez & García, 2022). This chapter illustrates the integrated whole of the translanguaging classroom with attention to the stance, design, and shifts in instruction and assessment. This holistic portrait of the translanguaging pedagogy in action prepares us to reimagine and *transform* what it means to teach, learn, and assess.

A CLOSER LOOK AT CLASSROOM PRACTICE

We visit ***Stephanie***'s 11th-grade English-medium social studies classroom to illustrate the integrated nature of the stance, design, and shifts of the translanguaging pedagogy for instruction and assessment. Stephanie introduces students to a new genre, public service announcements (PSAs), as part of her social studies unit "Environmentalism: Then and Now." One assignment within this unit is for students to create their own PSAs, which they can then use to raise awareness about social issues faced by people living in their local communities.

Students First

Although Stephanie is not bilingual, and the official language of instruction in her class is English, Stephanie grouped together five of her bilingual students—Eddy, Luis, Mariana, Noemí, and Teresita—so that they could leverage their Spanish and English language resources to engage with complex content and texts and develop linguistic practices for academic contexts. Let's look more closely at the profiles of these students, which Stephanie has continued to flesh out based on their autobiographical translanguaging portraits (see Chapter 8) and her ongoing, holistic assessment of their performances in her class this year:

Eddy's family is from the Dominican Republic, and he was born and raised in a predominantly Dominican neighborhood in New York City. His parents moved to the United States when they were very young; they speak to Eddy and his siblings mostly in English. Though he understands Spanish, listens to reggaeton and bachata, and can "mess around" with his friends in Spanish, he feels more comfortable using English at school. Eddy's English literacy, especially in writing, is below grade level. Stephanie was curious about his Spanish literacy level, so she asked the Spanish language teacher about it. Stephanie found out that although Eddy was studying Spanish in the Spanish for heritage speakers class, he had never received instruction in Spanish before this time. Stephanie tries to partner or group Eddy with newly arrived Spanish-speaking students for two reasons: he can lend his excellent oral English skills to support students who are beginning to learn English, and he can learn from their Spanish-speaking strengths.

Luis arrived from El Salvador in the 10th grade, and he is officially designated as an English language learner (ELL). His family was from a rural area, and Luis's experiences with formal schooling are limited. Luis is now classified as a **student with incomplete or interrupted formal education (SIFE)**. When speaking with his peers and his teachers in Spanish, it is clear that he is funny, smart, creative, and tech savvy. However, Luis produces written text at a level well below his peers in both Spanish and English. Luis enjoys comic books and sports magazines, but he struggles to read academic texts in English or Spanish. Stephanie works hard to include different content entry points for Luis, such as music and video clips in Spanish, visuals, and realia. Stephanie also pushes Luis to share his ideas in Spanish while he learns more English.

Mariana's family is from Puebla, Mexico. Though she was born in Mexico, Mariana has been raised in the United States all her life. She is a strong translator and constantly helps her family and friends navigate tasks that require English, like going with her mother to the doctor, talking to her father's boss on the phone, and helping her younger siblings with homework. Although Mariana can perform these tasks outside of school in English, her literacy in English is not at grade level. Mariana was labeled an ELL when she first entered school and has yet to test out of this status. Now in high school, Mariana struggles on literacy assessments, even though she has a strong grasp of content. In school she is now classified as a long-term English language learner (LTELL), although she prefers English to Spanish for schoolwork. Mariana is in the same Spanish for heritage speakers class as Eddy; she is quite fluent orally in Spanish, but her teacher describes her literacy skills in Spanish as weak.

Noemí and her family came to the United States from Ecuador when she was in eighth grade. When Noemí first arrived, she was one of only a few students in her class classified as an ELL. Though she got help from her teachers to learn English, she was often bored by the rote, grammar-based instruction. In her pull-out English as a second language class, her teacher, who did not speak Spanish, did not seem to understand that Noemí was a strong reader. Now in 11th grade, Noemí uses English orally with *commanding* performances, but she still struggles with literacy, especially in writing, and she is still classified as an ELL. Noemí finds it helpful to prewrite in Spanish before writing an essay in English and to annotate an English text with questions or ideas in Spanish.

Teresita was born in Guatemala but moved to the United States when she was very young. Though she always spoke Spanish at home, she learned English from her older siblings and television programs before she entered kindergarten. Teresita is a strong reader and writer in both English and Spanish. She consistently scores well on high-stakes exams and is a voracious reader in both languages, though she prefers reading books in English. Teresita also likes to write poetry in both languages, but she says that Spanish poetry comes more easily to her. Because she is highly proficient in English, some of her teachers don't even know that she can read and write in Spanish.

These five bilingual students have a wide range of expertise in oral and written Spanish and English. Despite the raciolinguistic ideologies that particularly pervade perceptions of students labeled SIFE and long-term English language learners (Flores & Rosa, 2015), all five students language in highly sophisticated ways. Stephanie carefully documents her students' language performances, using her understanding of what her students can do with Spanish and English, individually and in collaboration, to structure activities in her classes.

Structuring Activities A longer vignette from Stephanie's "Environmentalism: Then and Now" unit demonstrates how she makes space for translanguaging and uses it strategically to (1) introduce the PSA genre to her bilingual students in this English-medium class, (2) encourage students' critical engagement with this new genre, and (3) provide opportunities for students to produce this new genre. Focus on how Stephanie structures whole class and small group activities that leverage students' bilingualism, with particular attention to Eddy, Luis, Mariana, Noemí, and Teresita. At a more general level, this activity series illustrates how Stephanie's classroom practices address the four purposes of translanguaging—supporting students as they engage with complex content and texts; providing opportunities for students to develop language practices for a variety of purposes, including academic ones; supporting students' bilingual identities, socioemotional development, and critical consciousness; and making space for all students' language practices and ways of knowing to build an inclusive classroom.

Stephanie started her lesson by showing a video of a model PSA in English about human trafficking in the United States (see the Brookes Download Hub for access to the video; Figure 9.1 shows screenshots). Stephanie then played the Spanish language version of the PSA to ensure that all her Spanish-speaking emergent bilingual students could draw on their entire linguistic repertoires to comprehend the minute-long PSA. This second viewing also served as a reinforcement for her English-speaking students, especially those who were bilingual.

After watching both the English and the Spanish versions, Stephanie encouraged the class to discuss the end of the PSA, where a man trips over a woman and says in English (in both the Spanish and English versions): "Sorry, I didn't even see you." Stephanie asked the students, "How did the shift to English in the Spanish PSA affect your understanding? Why do you think the creators of the video made this choice?" To encourage deep thinking about the use of language, Stephanie asked students to discuss these questions in their groups using Spanish or English. This way, the groups that were stronger in Spanish could benefit from its use and explore this question deeply and participate in the discussion.

Stephanie then asked her students to come up with a definition of the PSA genre and to discuss whether the PSA they watched was effective and why. She provided the groups with printed texts about PSAs—in English only for some groups and in English and Spanish for others (e.g., for our focal group that includes Eddy, Luis, Mariana, Noemí, and Teresita). Stephanie then told the groups to look up other PSAs on the web and encouraged those who spoke Spanish to find some in Spanish. During the research,

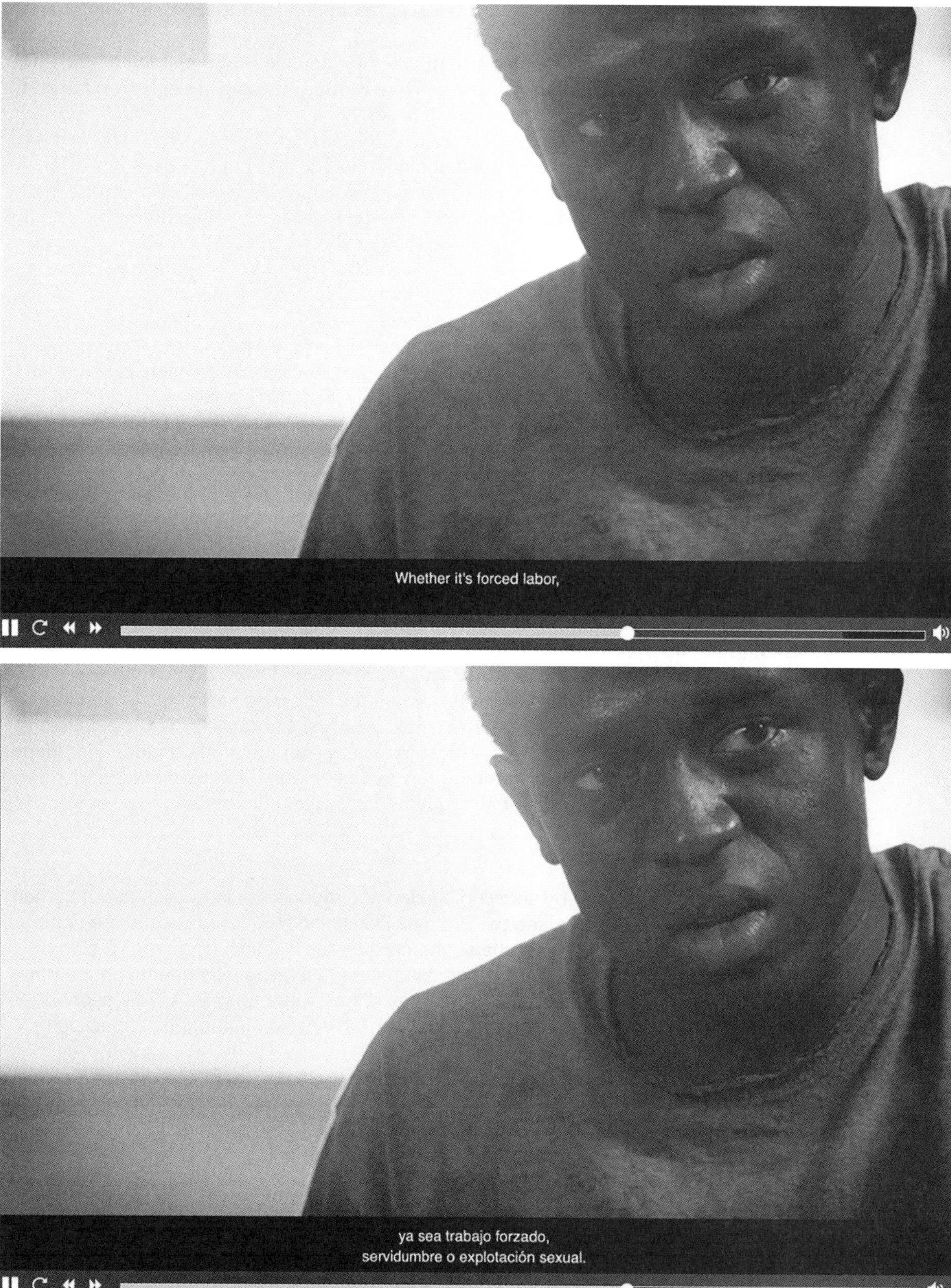

Figure 9.1 Shows screenshots of the PSA "Human Trafficking Victims Are Closer Than You Think" / "Las Víctimas de la Trata de Personas Están Más Cerca de lo que Piensa Ud."

students in the focal group conducted their discussion and reading of other texts in Spanish and English.

After the groups shared their thoughts in English with the entire class, Stephanie formally introduced the PSA genre by synthesizing students' definitions and ideas. She then facilitated the discussion while students brainstormed characteristics of the genre. Mariana shared that to be effective a PSA had to "be a little shocking." Stephanie agreed and rephrased, saying, "That's true—PSAs often focus on controversial topics." Luis raised his hand and asked, "Pero todos los PSAs son videos así?" A student translated his question [Are all PSAs videos like this one?] and Stephanie responded that PSAs could be on the radio, in print, or in video form. Stephanie then transitioned the discussion to the use of persuasive language and tactics in PSAs. She emphasized that different kinds of persuasive language and tactics are used for different audiences, similar to the way English and Spanish are used for different audiences.

Next, Stephanie gave each group a different PSA to analyze, some in English and some in Spanish. Some of the PSAs focused on environmentalism, and some focused on other high-interest, controversial social issues. Students were told to discuss the model PSAs and to think about purpose, message, audience, and persuasive language and tactics, as well as the PSA's effectiveness. To support their work, Stephanie gave each group a handout that included the same five questions, which were intended to support each group's academic conversations:

1. What is the purpose of this PSA? What message is it trying to convey?
2. Who is the audience for the PSA? How do you know?
3. What persuasive language and/or tactics are used in this PSA?
4. What is the emotional effect of this PSA on this audience?
5. Is this PSA effective? Why or why not?

Each handout also included three different languaging options:

1. Discuss your PSA in English; write down your answers in English.
2. Discuss your PSA in Spanish and English; write down your answers in English.
3. Discuss your PSA in Spanish and English; write your answers in English and Spanish (e.g., write down a word/phrase in English and expand on it in Spanish).

Students could choose the languaging option that allowed them to individually and collectively leverage all of their language resources to complete this task.

Eddy, Luis, Mariana, Noemí, and Teresita were given a PSA from a campaign to raise awareness about teen pregnancy in Chicago (Figure 9.2).

The group shared their first reactions to the image. Eddy thought the PSA was "weird" and "unexpected." Luis did not understand the word "unexpected," and Teresita offered "inesperado, que no se espera." When he understood the meaning, Luis said, "OK, ahora entiendo. Es muy unexpected que el muchacho esté embarazado!" [OK, now I get it. It's very unexpected that the guy is pregnant!] All students worked collaboratively to answer the questions, and those in the focal group moved between Spanish and English to discuss their thoughts and, eventually, write down their answers.

After the groups had shared their thinking on their PSAs, Stephanie opened up the discussion to the whole class to see if anyone had anything else to add. A student from another group asked angrily, "Why'd they have to make him Spanish, though?" Luis volunteered an answer immediately, saying "Porque siempre los Latinos cargan con la culpa." [Because Latinos are always blamed.] Teresita added that the PSA played on stereotypes about Latinx and teen pregnancy. Stephanie jumped in, sharing that this playing on stereotypes, as well as its controversial image and short, blunt text, made it a very effective PSA—even if it made them mad.

After all the groups shared their assigned PSAs, Stephanie told them that they would be creating their *own* PSAs for their group's chosen social issue. She told students that

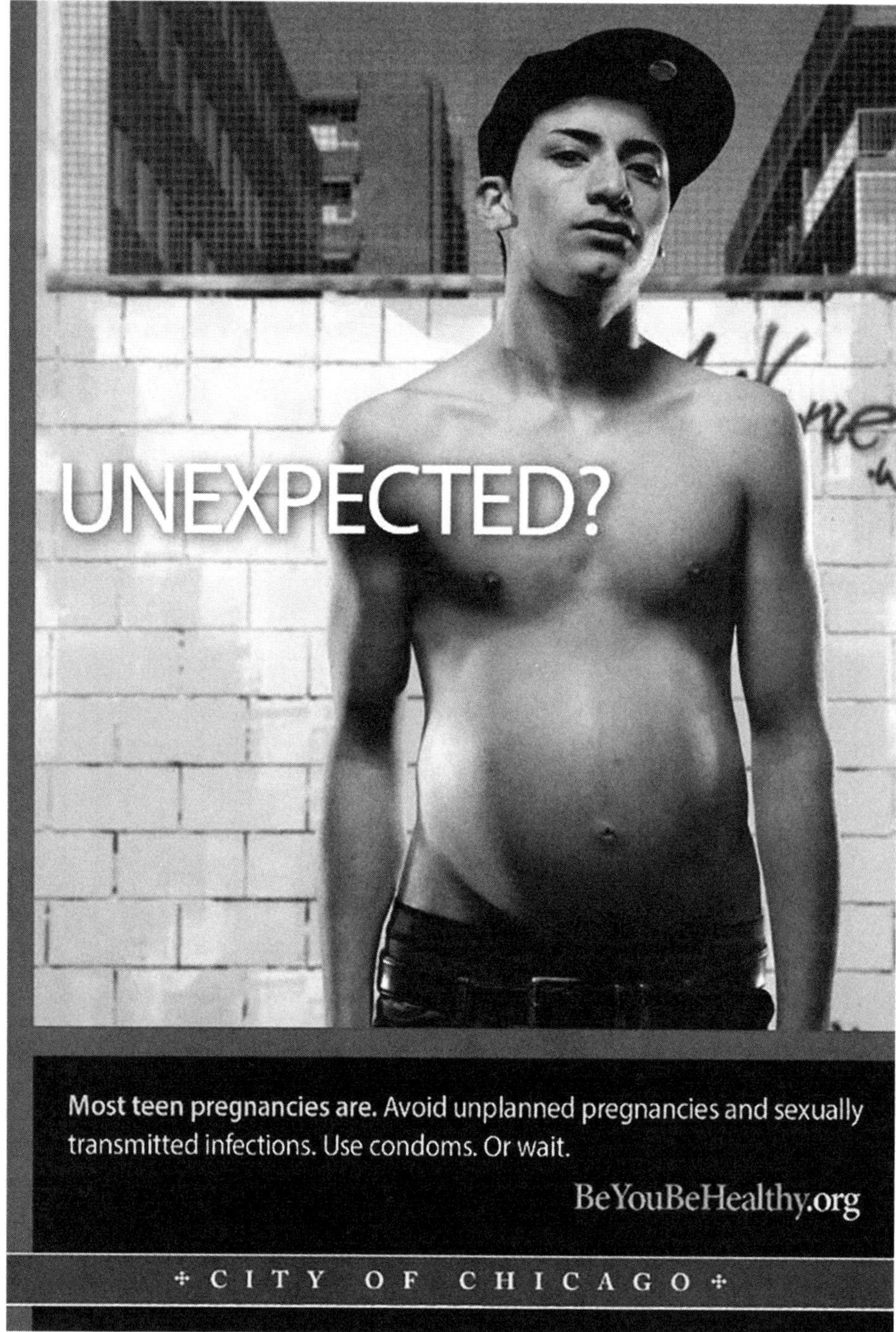

Figure 9.2 Shows a PSA released by the city of Chicago to raise awareness about teen pregnancy.

they should focus their work not only on the PSA's content, but also on its *language* and *style*. Because the focal group chose an environmental issue that specifically affected Latinx, Stephanie asked students to create their PSA using English and Spanish. This meant that students had to keep two different audiences in mind and make appropriate linguistic and stylistic choices.

When students finished drafts of their bilingual PSAs, they made short, informal presentations to the class. Stephanie required every student in the group to participate in the presentation. Noemí, for example, introduced her group's PSA. Stephanie explained to Noemí that she should do her best to explain the work in English, but that she could use Spanish to expand on or clarify ideas. When Noemí spoke in Spanish, Stephanie relied on students like Mariana and Teresita to translate so that she could fully understand Noemí's contributions.

Each group then filled out the Peer Group Assessment Tool for the work they did. Each student in the group also completed a Student Self-Assessment Tool. Stephanie then asked the students to show their families the bilingual PSA that their group had produced. The families assessed what they learned, as well as what they thought the students had learned, by filling out the Family Assessment Tool: La conexión (for more on these assessments, see Chapter 8). These evaluations contributed to Stephanie's holistic assessment of students' performances and helped engage students and their families in the assessment process.

After students presented to the class, Stephanie asked her principal if they could post their PSAs around the school. The principal agreed and asked Stephanie if students would explain the project to the community during the morning announcements. Stephanie asked Mariana and Luis to work together to come up with an explanation of the PSA assignment in both Spanish and English that they would read during the announcements the following week.

This rich vignette provides an opportunity to look closely at how the translanguaging strands—stance, design, and shifts—are manifested in Stephanie's classroom. Important principles in each of the strands are highlighted to keep in mind as you develop your own translanguaging classroom.

STANCE: STUDENTS, LANGUAGE, AND CONTENT JUNTOS

The translanguaging stance informs all our classroom work. Though each of our translanguaging stances will be a little different, there are three fundamental elements that are integral to the stance of any teacher working with bilingual students. As discussed in Chapter 5, these three core beliefs are as follows:

1. Students' language practices and cultural understanding encompass those they bring from home and communities, as well as those from school. These practices and understanding co-exist, work juntos, and enrich each other.
2. Students' families and communities are valuable sources of knowledge and must be involved in the education process juntos.
3. The classroom is a democratic space where teachers and students juntos create knowledge, challenge traditional hierarchies, and work toward a more just society.

Stephanie's translanguaging stance is reflected in many aspects of the classroom vignette. For example, Stephanie's choice to strategically group students heterogeneously in terms of their English language performances illustrates her belief that all students have something important and meaningful to contribute to the classroom work, regardless of what they can do with oral and written English. Returning to the focal group, Noemí's more experienced literacy performances in Spanish help Eddy with his writing in Spanish, and Eddy's strong oral language performances in English provide Luis with an opportunity to grow more confident using English. Luis's comfort with technology and his ability to find things on the Internet make him the resident expert on research, even though, as you recall, he has been classified as a SIFE. Mariana and Teresita, both of whom have strong Spanish and English, love explaining ideas to the group in both languages.

Putting these five students into one group juntos builds on their different linguistic strengths. This kind of strategic grouping also fosters strong relationships and enables each student to leverage their entire language repertoire. These relationships can also help address tensions that often exist between Latinx newcomer students and Latinx students who have been in the United States longer and speak more English, as well as among Latinx students from different national origins. Rather than segregate newcomers from experienced English speakers, Stephanie chooses to integrate them, which enriches the group's learning and contributes to their intellectual and socioemotional growth. It is also an important way of supporting students' bilingualism and biliteracy in this English-medium classroom.

A second aspect of the lesson that illustrates Stephanie's translanguaging juntos stance is how she views the use of one language or the other. To the administration, Stephanie teaches in English. However, Stephanie believes that all her students learn more when they can use the full features of their language repertoires. Thus, she presents the PSA in two languages juntos in order to enable her bilingual students to learn more about topics and to become familiar with different discourses and genres. Allowing students to make different language choices to express what they know demonstrates her belief in the interrelationship of language practices. This kind of focus on genre, audience, and language also raises students' metalinguistic awareness, one of the major benefits of translanguaging.

A third aspect of the lesson that illustrates Stephanie's translanguaging juntos stance is her choice of content. A focus on PSAs allows students to put their research to work in an authentic, real-world genre and pushes them to think critically about both audience and discourse. By "hooking" students with model PSAs that are high-interest, controversial, and relatable, like the one that focused on teen pregnancy, Stephanie sets them up to create their own PSAs on topics related to the unit. Asking students questions about a text's expected audience, purpose, impact, and effectiveness moves them past simple comprehension. These kinds of questions challenge students to "read the word and the world" (Freire & Macedo, 1987) more critically, to assess *everything* they encounter with a critical lens. These kinds of tasks ask students to use their unique ways of knowing and languaging to foster a critical consciousness that helps them recognize, challenge, and transform the structures that uphold the status quo and stand in the way of social, racial, and cognitive justice.

Stephanie's juntos stance is also manifested in her use of assessment, which, like her instruction, is collaborative. She not only evaluates students' learning herself, but also gives the students themselves, their peer groups, and their families opportunities for assessment, which makes everyone co-learners and co-teachers. Stephanie's assessment practices evaluate whether students can perform tasks with moderate assistance or independently, and they also differentiate between students' understanding of language and content. By allowing students to perform tasks using English and Spanish at times and English only at other times, Stephanie also differentiates between the students' general linguistic and language-specific performances. These translanguaging practices also greatly benefit her English-speaking African American students, who are learning some Spanish from their peers. Also, they are no longer judged solely on whether they can use English language features considered "standard," but rather on the *kind* of language users they are, regardless of specific language features.

DESIGN: PURPOSEFUL AND STRATEGIC

Incorporating translanguaging into instruction and assessment design is a powerful means of enhancing bilingual students' learning opportunities, because translanguaging enables students to engage with complex content and texts and develop linguistic practices for academic contexts. Simply put, if students are limited to the use of only part of their language repertoires—especially the part that is considered their *weaker* language—their ability to learn is also limited. Teachers can use a translanguaging design to tap into and leverage the translanguaging corriente in ways that enhance bilingual students' content and language learning at school.

It has taken some time, but I have explained to my co-teachers that practicing biliteracy and active engagement of students' entire linguistic repertoire actually helps them learn language faster and more efficiently. In classrooms where we incorporate students' translanguaging, there is a huge difference in their motivation and success. They are interested in the work because it's more accessible to them and the higher grades prove it.

—Nicole Salisbury, ENL teacher, Math, Science, and Technology Preparatory School #197, Buffalo, New York

This section looks more closely at the vignette from Stephanie's classroom to examine her translanguaging design. First, Stephanie's translanguaging instructional unit design, "Environmentalism: Then and Now," is introduced. Then the focus shifts to the stages of the translanguaging instructional design cycle that structure and sequence student learning in her unit plan. Finally, Stephanie's classroom is used to illustrate the myriad opportunities for translanguaging assessments present in everyday instruction. These assessments, some small and informal, others more formal, give Stephanie authentic information about what her students know and can do with content and language and enable her to learn from their languaging and build on their strengths so that all students can meet or exceed the unit goals and objectives.

Translanguaging Unit Design

Start by looking at the vignette through the lens of Stephanie's translanguaging instructional unit design, which is shown in Table 9.1. This unit design is the flexible structure that Stephanie uses to enact her translanguaging stance and pedagogy in the classroom. Stephanie's stance is reflected in the four essential questions that connect social studies content to students' everyday lives, relate contemporary issues to the historical context, and work to address social justice issues.

Table 9.1. Stephanie's Translanguaging Unit Design—Environmentalism: Then and Now

Essential Questions	• What does it mean to live sustainably? • How does our environment influence our lives and actions? • How have people fought for what they believe in throughout history? • In what ways can we make change on the local level?	
Content Standards	New York State Next Generation Standards and New York State Social Studies Framework Next Generation Reading (RH) and Writing (WH) Standards for History/Social Studies RH 1. Cite specific textual evidence to support analysis of primary and secondary sources, connecting insights gained from specific details to an understanding of the source as a whole. RH 7. Integrate and evaluate multiple sources of information presented in diverse formats and media (e.g., visually, quantitatively, as well as in words) in order to address a question or solve a problem. WHST.5. Conduct short as well as more sustained research projects to answer a question (including a self-generated question), analyze a topic, or solve a problem; narrow or broaden the inquiry when appropriate; synthesize multiple sources on the subject, demonstrating understanding of the subject under investigation. Social Studies Framework Social Studies Practice F. Civic Participation F.2. Participate in activities that focus on a classroom, school, community, state, or national issue or problem. F.5. Participate in persuading, debating, negotiating, and compromising in the resolution of conflicts and differences. F.6. Identify situations in which social actions are required and determine an appropriate course of action. Social Studies Curriculum, 11.10 b. Individuals, diverse groups, and organizations have sought to bring about change in American society through a variety of methods.	
Content and Language Objectives	*Content Objectives* • Students will trace the development of the U.S. environmental movement from the early 20th century to today. • Students will make connections between the environmental movement and larger societal events and developments in recent U.S. history. • Students will relate ideas, such as sustainability, to their own lives as young people in an urban environment. • Students will create an action campaign that attempts to solve a local school- or community-based issue related to environmentalism and sustainability.	*Language Objectives* *General linguistic* • Students will read and synthesize a variety of text sources in order to make connections and draw conclusions. • Students will use appropriate and relevant text evidence to support their ideas. • Students will create action plans that they will present both orally and in writing in ways that persuade an audience to support their position. *Language-specific (English for English-medium class)** • Students will use content-specific vocabulary, both orally and in writing, to explain their ideas and connections to the content. • Students will use a structured essay-writing format for persuasive writing that includes an introduction, two supporting body paragraphs, a counter-claim paragraph, and a conclusion. • Students will present their action plans orally in English.
Translanguaging Objectives	• Students will use oral and written Spanish and English to analyze and critique both the content and discourse of bilingual PSAs. • Students will create bilingual PSA texts across a variety of genres (announcements, posters, persuasive essays, oral presentations, and short dramatic plays) and rationalize their linguistic choices.	

(continued)

Table 9.1. *(continued)*

Culminating Project and Assessments	*Culminating project* Students will create bilingual action plans and presentations for improving the environmental sustainability of the school or local community in a way that would reach and be understood by diverse, bilingual audiences.	*Other assessments* Teacher's Assessment Tool: Teachers assess the student's content understanding and linguistic performances, with attention to what the student can do with or without assistance, using all the features of their repertoire (general linguistic performance) or language-specific features. Student Self-Assessment Tool: Throughout the unit, students provide feedback and self-assessment via questions about their own learning, language development, and content understanding in English and their home languages, orally and in writing. Peer Group Assessment Tool: Members reflect on their work as a group via questions about their content learning, languaging performances, and further questions the group has about the unit theme. Family Assessment Tool: La conexión: Students and their families assess what the students learned about the unit topic at school and what families learned from students about the topic. Families also identify relevant funds of knowledge that they might share with the class.
Texts	*In English* • 11th-grade U.S. history textbook • Various content area readings from newspapers, magazines, blogs, and websites • Documentary film • Readings on César Chávez and the Farm Workers Association • Podcasts and music • Content-related fiction/creative nonfiction	*In the home language(s)* • 11th-grade U.S. history textbook (Spanish version) • Documentary film with Spanish subtitles • Readings in Spanish on César Chávez and the Farm Workers Association • Supplementary readings on the same content-area topics in Spanish (found via teacher's research and students' online research)

Stephanie's unit design is clearly aligned with state standards, and she includes content and language objectives, as required by district and school administration. Stephanie's plans for translanguaging in this unit of instruction are reflected in the **translanguaging objectives**, culminating design, and assessment from many angles. This flexible design provides the structure and space that Stephanie needs to leverage students' bilingualism for learning.

Translanguaging Instructional Design Cycle

Now look at the vignette of Stephanie's classroom practices through the lens of the translanguaging instructional design cycle, which, as explored in Chapter 5, includes five stages: explorar, evaluar, imaginar, presentar, and implementar. These stages provide a way of envisioning an active, engaging, and responsive instructional unit. Here, the translanguaging instructional design cycle, shown in Figure 9.3, is used as a framework for examining a cycle of instruction within Stephanie's "Environmentalism: Then and Now" translanguaging unit. If students are to be active learners throughout a unit, instruction must be designed so that they are *constantly* engaged in exploring and evaluating what exists, imagining something new, and presenting and implementing new ideas outside the four walls of the classroom.

In the following sections, each stage of the translanguaging instructional design cycle is broken down and ways Stephanie and her students used translanguaging within each stage during this cycle of instruction are discussed. We illustrate how to use this design cycle as a tool to plan the "big picture" of the unit, as well as the smaller instructional designs that occur from week to week *within* a unit. At each stage of the cycle, we identify concrete translanguaging pedagogical practices that Stephanie uses to open up space for translanguaging and help her students learn.

Explorar The first stage of the translanguaging instructional design cycle is explorar, which encourages students to explore a new topic or theme, follow their natural interests and questions, and build their background knowledge. Multifaceted exploration occurred

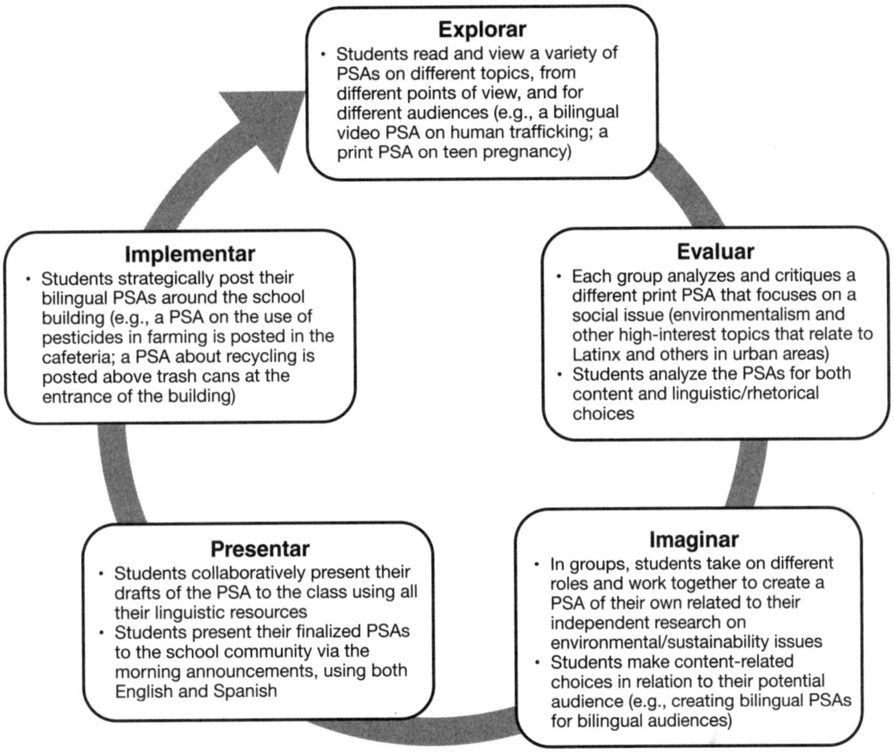

Explorar
- Students read and view a variety of PSAs on different topics, from different points of view, and for different audiences (e.g., a bilingual video PSA on human trafficking; a print PSA on teen pregnancy)

Evaluar
- Each group analyzes and critiques a different print PSA that focuses on a social issue (environmentalism and other high-interest topics that relate to Latinx and others in urban areas)
- Students analyze the PSAs for both content and linguistic/rhetorical choices

Imaginar
- In groups, students take on different roles and work together to create a PSA of their own related to their independent research on environmental/sustainability issues
- Students make content-related choices in relation to their potential audience (e.g., creating bilingual PSAs for bilingual audiences)

Presentar
- Students collaboratively present their drafts of the PSA to the class using all their linguistic resources
- Students present their finalized PSAs to the school community via the morning announcements, using both English and Spanish

Implementar
- Students strategically post their bilingual PSAs around the school building (e.g., a PSA on the use of pesticides in farming is posted in the cafeteria; a PSA about recycling is posted above trash cans at the entrance of the building)

Figure 9.3 Illustrates Stephanie's translanguaging design cycle for a 3-week unit.

throughout the "Environmentalism: Then and Now" unit as a whole. Stephanie worked hard to provide her students with multiple content entry points through a variety of texts (in both Spanish and English and representing different perspectives) and a variety of modalities (e.g., film, print, Internet sources). These design choices reflect her belief that one must view a topic from multiple perspectives to understand it. They also reflect her understanding that all students, but especially emergent bilinguals, benefit from rich, thematic, interdisciplinary instruction. Stephanie organized each unit around a central theme, bringing in social studies events and ideas from a variety of time periods. This helped her students to see the connections across historical periods through today, as well as to better understand the breadth of a topic.

In the unit of instruction depicted in the vignette, students explored a new genre, the PSA, in a variety of ways. They were given models or "mentor texts" of PSAs in both video and print form. They collaboratively defined the genre, working from the models to formulate ideas about audience and purpose as well as linguistic and stylistic characteristics. As they explored, Stephanie opened up space for and leveraged students' translanguaging in a number of ways, including the following:

- Stephanie showed the PSA in English and in Spanish. Both short videos had subtitles so that students were able to read the text as they watched.
- Students shared questions and comments in English and Spanish; Stephanie took notes for the class in English.
- In groups, students analyzed print PSAs in Spanish and English.
- To answer the five questions about the model PSAs, students discussed, debated, and analyzed in Spanish and English, and they were given three options, including translanguaging options, to arrive at their answers in English.

Evaluar As students explore, they also evaluate what they are learning. This second stage in the instructional design cycle is important because it helps students strengthen their ability to read texts critically. In Stephanie's classroom, students focused on comprehending the content of the PSAs and on the tactics and discourse used within them to play off a potential audience's fears and deep-seated prejudices. This evaluation of the content deepened learning and helped students think critically and develop a social and racial justice lens. Though students were evaluating PSAs in this lesson, they could just as easily have evaluated a content-specific reading. This kind of critical evaluation of texts both expands and localizes the traditional curriculum, making it more complex and more specific to bilingual students' lives. The translanguaging pedagogical practices that Stephanie used facilitated the process of evaluar in the following ways:

- In groups, students used Spanish and English to express their thoughts and analyze the PSAs. The emergent bilinguals performed better in English on the handout because they were able to first use Spanish to engage with complex content and texts.
- Stephanie drew students' attention to specific linguistic and stylistic choices made within the PSAs. This raised students' metalinguistic awareness and helped them identify these choices in other texts.
- Stephanie chose model PSAs that portrayed situations or social issues that Latinx bilingual students might relate to (i.e., directly related to Latinx or directly related to young people in urban contexts). This allowed students to bring their local knowledge to the analysis of the texts and think critically, developing a critical consciousness and a justice-oriented lens.

Imaginar The third stage of the translanguaging instructional design cycle is imaginar, which supports and informs new ideas and new ways of using language to learn. Students are encouraged to use what they have learned in the explorar and evaluar stages to imaginar something new. During the "Environmentalism: Then and Now" unit, students in Stephanie's class were asked to imagine a PSA related to the groups' independent research on environmental or sustainability issues. Our focal group members worked together to build on what they had learned from the PSA on teen pregnancy and in other activities in this unit. In the group, students were able to draw on their strengths to carry out different tasks and translanguage in different ways. Here are some of the ways that Noemí, Eddy, Teresita, Luis, and Mariana contributed their translanguaging and participated meaningfully within the imaginar stage:

- Noemí contributed ideas orally in Spanish to the group's bilingual PSA. She also took the lead in writing the Spanish text, choosing the evidence from the group's research that was most persuasive.
- Eddy contributed ideas orally, mostly in English but also in Spanish. He lent his creativity to the task of writing a short but powerful "hook" that would catch a reader's attention. He drafted versions of this hook in English and worked with the group to edit it for the final draft.
- Teresita used her experienced bilingualism to synthesize group members' comments in English and Spanish. She worked closely with Luis to translate his ideas from Spanish into English. She also translated a quote from a newspaper article from English to Spanish.
- Luis contributed many content-related ideas orally in Spanish. Though he did not have strong writing skills in English or Spanish, he had creative ideas for the visual format of the PSA. He sketched out plans, explained his vision, and worked with the whole group to brainstorm the look of the PSA.
- Mariana worked on both the English and Spanish texts for the PSA. She helped Teresita translate pieces of their research from English to Spanish. Together, they imagined how to construct a PSA that would be understood by both Spanish-speaking and English-speaking audiences.

Presentar The fourth stage of the translanguaging instructional design cycle is presentar, which involves students in peer editing, conferencing, rewriting, and presenting their work, with attention to the choices they make about using language. Stephanie's translanguaging design helped students pool their linguistic resources and present their work orally in English in several ways. First, she had groups present *collaboratively*, rather than individually. This was beneficial for two reasons. First, it lessened the anxiety that some students felt about presenting. For those students newer to English, like Noemí and Luis, sharing responsibility with three other people enabled them to participate in the presentation with much less worry. Second, it gave *all* students an opportunity to practice their oral language for an authentic purpose. The following list includes some of the steps that Stephanie and her students took to make these presentations successful.

- Stephanie provided specific sentence frames for students that supported their presentations. Students whose performances in English were emerging, like Luis, first expressed themselves in Spanish and then used the English sentence frames and added short English responses with the help of other group members.
- During presentations, Noemí and Luis read their prepared English responses but clarified and expanded on their thinking in Spanish.
- Teresita, Mariana, and Eddy presented in English and built on Noemí's and Luis's Spanish comments by summarizing them in English.

The importance of making any presentation an opportunity for *all* students to practice English and the other language orally for a variety of audiences (monolingual audiences, bilingual audiences made up of monolingual speakers of one language or another, and bilingual-speaking audiences) cannot be overstated. This participation improves students' confidence as public speakers and gives them practice in adapting language to the needs of listeners.

Stephanie carefully guided her students' performances throughout the unit so that each task would provide a foundation for the public presentation. First, students made an informal, in-class presentation for their bilingual peers using the full features of their linguistic repertoires. Second, they made a more public presentation, using English and Spanish, during the school's morning announcements. Third, they prepared a formal presentation in English for the larger school community. Finally, they made a presentation to the local community outside of school, leveraging translanguaging practices to engage the diverse community. These different types of task-based performances provide bilingual students with opportunities to make the "same" presentation to diverse audiences, drawing on their language resources to reach a larger and more diverse audience than a monolingual English or Spanish presentation would allow. These presentations, or performances, provide opportunities for authentic assessment and documentation throughout the unit.

Implementar The implementar stage moves students' work from the classroom to the larger community. This action-based step does not have to be monumental—it merely means that students' work should be applied in authentic ways. In this instructional unit, Stephanie used a number of translanguaging pedagogical practices to encourage her students to implementar, for example, displaying their bilingual PSAs around the school building. Because students' PSAs were both bilingual *and* geared toward the local audience of the school (fellow students, teachers, administrators), their placement around the building contributed to the multilingual ecology of the school and raised awareness about important issues that affected community members. In addition, when Mariana and Luis used the school's morning announcements to explain the genre of the PSA and the purpose of their work in both Spanish and English, they used their bilingualism to communicate with their school community about important issues of sustainability and environmentalism as well as the broader goals of social and racial justice inherent to their work. Rather than mere social studies students, Mariana, Luis, and their classmates became *activists*, informing their community at the local level. The following translanguaging pedagogical practices were present in Stephanie's instructional design at the implementar stage:

- Students posted their bilingual PSAs around the school building, strategically placing certain PSAs in particular locations (e.g., a PSA on the use of pesticides in farming and the dangers to the environment and to health was posted in the cafeteria; a PSA about recycling was posted above trash cans at the entrance to the building).

- Mariana and Luis prepared a bilingual statement explaining the PSA genre and the class's work with the genre. They gave examples of PSAs that were posted around the school and previewed the larger culminating design that their class would present.

Like Stephanie, teachers in translanguaging classrooms can use the translanguaging instructional design cycle to plan and deliver their week-to-week instruction within a specific unit of instruction *and* to plan and deliver their entire unit.

ASSESSING FROM MANY ANGLES

Like Carla's assessment practices, discussed in Chapter 8, Stephanie's unit assesses through different tasks, at different times, and from different angles. Stephanie's authentic assessment of student learning is never done in isolation, nor does it rely only on English, despite English being her language and medium of instruction. Her assessment practices include *all* of students' linguistic resources as well as the students themselves, the group, and students' families so that she gains a more holistic, inclusive understanding of what the students are learning. And because her instruction leverages authentic collaborative performances in groups, she can also use her own assessment tools to gauge whether students are performing independently, with moderate assistance from other people or resources, or at an emergent stage.

As was demonstrated in the opening vignette, Stephanie's informal assessment practices differentiate between language and content understanding by ensuring that specific language features do not become a barrier to assessing what students know about content. Moreover, when assessing language performances, Stephanie makes sure to differentiate between students' ways of using language to express complex thoughts, make inferences, associate ideas, explain, persuade, and so forth—their general linguistic performance—and the use of specific English language features. Although Spanish is not an official language of instruction in Stephanie's class, her design for formal and informal assessment reflects the power of translanguaging for learning in this English-medium classroom.

When teaching or assessing within a translanguaging unit, a teacher taps into their stance, enacts the design, and uses the third strand—shifts—to weave the strong rope that pulls students' learning forward along their translanguaging performances.

SHIFTS: GOING WITH THE FLOW OF THE TRANSLANGUAGING CORRIENTE

Throughout the translanguaging instructional design cycle, Stephanie served as facilitator for the class's inquiries and learning. Rather than present a scripted, teacher-centered lesson, Stephanie provided students with information (the model PSAs and questions that made students think about those PSAs) and let them run with it. For example, when a student in the class voiced his anger about the Latinx youth portrayed in the teen pregnancy PSA, Stephanie built on that anger to help the class understand the purpose of the genre. Rather than deflect the question or avoid a difficult conversation, Stephanie opened the question up to the presenting group and facilitated an important discussion of how ideology is transmitted through discourse. This unplanned shift, and others like it, contributed to the sense that Stephanie and her students were a part of a small, tight-knit community of thinkers who were, as Stephanie puts it, "moving and shaking our society." This kind of shift is also clearly connected to Stephanie's stance, in that she believes that the *classroom is a democratic space where teachers and students juntos create knowledge, challenge traditional hierarchies, and work toward a more just society.*

A second shift is Stephanie's linguistic flexibility, which is also tied, of course, to her stance. Because Stephanie is not a Spanish speaker, she could not always understand her students' contributions to classroom discussions around content. However, Stephanie knew how important it was for students to draw on their full repertoire at *all* times to make meaning and share their ideas. For this reason, Stephanie often encouraged students to use Spanish to express their content knowledge and relied on other students in the class for help understanding their comments. For example, when Noemí presented her group's PSA, she sometimes elaborated on her ideas in Spanish. Rather than impose a rigid language policy that forced Noemí to speak English only, Stephanie sat back and let her express herself on her own terms, bilingually. This shift, the embracing of flexibility in response to students' linguistic needs, contributed to the sense that all voices were welcome and valuable in the shared classroom space.

Like Stephanie, teachers in translanguaging classrooms must adapt their instruction to the flow of the translanguaging corriente. To do so requires that teachers think of their classrooms as a tight community of thinkers who are exploring content on their own terms. As co-learners, teachers in translanguaging classrooms also rely on students and other multimodal resources, such as technology, to ensure that all students learn.

ENACTING A TRANSLANGUAGING PEDAGOGY IN YOUR CLASSROOM

This integrated view of Stephanie's translanguaging pedagogy in action has been provided as a model to help you develop your own translanguaging pedagogy. To support your work, a blank protocol that aids teacher reflection and planning for translanguaging is included in Appendix 9.1. Teachers can use this protocol to document how they use (or do not use) translanguaging and to generate concrete ideas for new ways to use it. This tool encourages you to consider the various aspects of your pedagogy—your own stance, design, and shifts—and think critically about whether those aspects make space for the translanguaging corriente to flow. Specifically, when examining your own stance, to what degree do you:

- Think of students' languages and cultural practices as equally valuable and interrelated?
- Value and include students' families and communities in their education?
- Challenge traditional hierarchies, such as teacher/student, English/additional language, native/non-native speaker, and academic/non-academic language, and work toward a more just classroom (and society)?

When examining your own design, to what degree do you:

- Design the physical space of the classroom for collaboration and create a multilingual and multimodal ecology?
- Design instruction (e.g., in unit planning, activities, pedagogical practices) so that it makes space for and leverages translanguaging?
- Design assessments that differentiate between general linguistic and language-specific performances?
- Design assessments that holistically evaluate students through different tasks, at different times, and from different angles?

Finally, when examining the moment-to-moment interaction in your classroom, to what degree do you use shifts to allow for flexibility and changes to your design that are responsive to students' needs, interests, and language practices?

These are not easy questions, and you are encouraged to explore them within a professional learning community of teachers who are also thinking deeply about their own practice. Asking questions of and reflecting on our own pedagogy helps us grow as educators, which can only benefit the bilingual students in our classrooms.

CONCLUSION

In this chapter, you explored a unit of instruction in Stephanie's translanguaging classroom, and you learned how her translanguaging pedagogy—her stance, design, and shifts—is integral to the success of her classroom. You also investigated how she uses specific translanguaging pedagogical practices across the five stages of the translanguaging instructional design cycle. This translanguaging instructional design was closely linked with her translanguaging design for assessment. Stephanie's integrated translanguaging pedagogy helped students draw on their linguistic strengths, connect new learning to their own local knowledge, and use their unique positions as Latinx bilinguals to analyze a new genre with a critical eye.

Stephanie's instruction was also drawn from in order to identify the general principles that teachers in translanguaging classrooms should hold within each of three strands:

1. *Stance*: Bringing juntos students, languages, and content
2. *Design*: Purposefully and strategically including translanguaging in unit planning, stages of instruction, classroom activities, and student performance assessments
3. *Shifts*: Responding to students' needs and interests and the corriente

Lastly, this chapter provided you with a protocol for reflection and planning that you can use to think deeply about your own instruction. You can then use these reflections and observations to make positive changes that strengthen how you work with the translanguaging corriente in your specific context.

REFLECTION QUESTIONS AND ACTIVITIES

1. How do you envision translanguaging practices occurring in your classroom? What opportunities exist? What challenges? How might you build on these opportunities and work to address these challenges?
2. What kinds of texts, genres, or resources do you think lend themselves to translanguaging practices? How might you incorporate these into a unit or lesson?

TAKING ACTION

1. Design an instructional opportunity from a translanguaging lens. Work off of the instructional planning structures you already use and make space for translanguaging in each aspect of that instruction.
2. On your own or with a group of colleagues, fill out Appendix 9.1, Reflecting and Planning for a Translanguaging Pedagogy. Work through each strand of the translanguaging pedagogy (stance, design, and shifts) and discuss where you are now and how to make room for the translanguaging corriente in your classroom.

APPENDIX 9.1

Reflecting and Planning for a Translanguaging Pedagogy

Strand of Translanguaging Pedagogy	Reflected in My Teaching?*	How Can I Adapt My Current Pedagogy to Make Space for Translanguaging?
Stance		
To what degree do I. . .		
Think of students' languages and cultural practices as equally valuable and interrelated?		
Value and include students' families and communities in their education?		
Challenge traditional hierarchies (e.g., teacher/student, English/additional language, native/non-native speaker, academic/non-academic language) and work toward a more just classroom (and society)?		
Design		
To what degree do I. . .		
Design the physical space of the classroom for collaboration; design a multilingual and multimodal ecology?		

Strand of Translanguaging Pedagogy	Reflected in My Teaching?*	How Can I Adapt My Current Pedagogy to Make Space for Translanguaging?
Design instruction so that all learning promotes translanguaging (e.g., in unit planning, classroom activities, pedagogical practices)?		
Design assessments that differentiate between general linguistic and language-specific performances?		
Design assessments that holistically evaluate students through different tasks, at different times, and from different angles?		
Shifts		
To what degree do I. . .		
Allow for flexibility and changes to my design that are responsive to students' needs, interests, and language practices?		
Comments		

* 1, none; 2, some; 3, a lot.

III

Reimagining Teaching and Learning Through Translanguaging

10

Standards in the Translanguaging Classroom

LEARNING OBJECTIVES

After reading this chapter, you will be able to:

- Explain how teachers in translanguaging classrooms use mandated standards.
- Describe how a translanguaging perspective on standards helps teachers address the first purpose of translanguaging—to support students as they engage with complex content and texts.
- Explain how teachers can use their translanguaging stance, design, and shifts to help students meet and exceed the expectations of state and other content and language standards.
- Design instruction that expands and localizes the standards by drawing on and extending students' existing language and cultural practices.

Good teachers use standards to help them focus and organize their instruction. A set of standards can help you think big and highlight those practices that will help your students develop literacies and engage with content in deep, authentic ways. These days, however, it is easy to feel like standards are using *us* more than we are using *them*. It is important for all teachers, especially those teaching emergent bilingual students, to "take back" standards and to reclaim them as part of the toolkit of good instruction. This chapter explores how standards can be used in a translanguaging classroom and how they can be seen as a way to meet students where they are, leverage their linguistic gifts, and build paths toward new understanding.

In this chapter, we return to ***Stephanie***'s "Environmentalism: Then and Now" unit design and focus on how she uses content standards to set goals and create a strong, engaging, culturally and linguistically sustaining translanguaging instructional unit.

Looking more closely at Stephanie's classroom practices reveals how she uses these standards and her translanguaging stance, design, and shifts to address the first purpose of translanguaging—to support students as they engage with and comprehend complex content and texts. As you read about Stephanie's planning process using standards, you are encouraged to think further about how *you* would use standards in the development of your own translanguaging unit.

STANCE: JUNTOS TO "TALK THE TALK" AND "WALK THE WALK"

When standards affect everything from testing to graduation to teacher evaluations, teachers naturally come to view them as the benchmarks of academic success. Though helping students meet standards is important, it is essential to remember that these standards—especially the standardized tests used to evaluate student performance relative to these standards—are not infallible, particularly with regard to emergent bilinguals. If scores on standardized tests are thought of as the *only* measure of success, students may be viewed through a deficit lens—lacking something, missing something, behind, or below (Ascenzi-Moreno & Seltzer, 2021; Menken, 2008; Schissel, 2019). In other words, the standardized test lens emphasizes what students *do not have* rather than what they know and can do. This is especially the case for emergent bilinguals, whose developing English—often described in terms of a lack of English language proficiency—can become the defining characteristic of their academic identities in a standards-driven educational environment.

Developing a translanguaging stance means rejecting this deficit lens and embracing one that highlights students' strengths and ways of knowing. It means viewing students' dynamic bilingualism as an advantage, rather than as a problem to be solved. It also means leveraging that dynamic bilingualism to ensure that students learn. And it means starting by designing challenging and relevant instructional units while being mindful of standards, rather than starting with the standards themselves in isolation of content and purpose. In sum, developing a translanguaging stance means making the standards work for students, rather than the other way around. This stance toward standards is key to an additional purpose of translanguaging classrooms: disrupting ideologies that render bilingual students as deficient.

In the following vignette, notice how Stephanie's use of standards arose from her understanding of what her students knew, what they were passionate about, and what she thought would be important to their growth as thinkers and active, informed people with critical consciousness. Stephanie's stance toward the standards also reflects her passion and personal goal of living a life of which she can be proud.

In every unit she taught, Stephanie noticed that her 11th-grade students found ways to make connections between the content they were learning and current events, stories they had been told by their families, historical events from the United States and their home countries, and pop culture like music, movies, and TV. Seeing how excited they were when they brought up these connections, Stephanie knew she had to build on her students' knowledge, no matter what content she introduced in English. Recently, Stephanie was moved by a documentary she saw about a controversial aspect of the environmental movement and knew that her students would jump at the chance to discuss a part of history that is not usually afforded much time in social studies classrooms. Stephanie also knew that the New York State Social Studies Framework addresses the study of civics, so a unit on sustainability and environmentalism would help her students meet content-area standards. When looking through her textbook, however, Stephanie found the section on environmentalism to be lacking. There was a short discussion of the history of the environmental movement, but Stephanie could not find a trace of the kind of passion and urgency she had seen in the documentary. Thus, Stephanie went about designing a unit, "Environmentalism: Then and Now," that addressed both the New York State Next Generation Learning Standards[1] for literacy in history/social studies and the state content-area framework through the study of the past and present of the environmental movement. The unit included an action-based culminating project and, of course, a translanguaging pedagogical framework.

---

[1]In the time since the first edition of this book was published, New York State transitioned from using the Common Core State Standards to using the Next Generation Learning Standards. Stephanie's unit has been updated to reflect this change. Importantly, this state-level change, and the revision of this element of the book, reinforces our assertion that the process of using the standards should start with designing challenging, culturally and linguistically sustaining instructional units while being mindful of—not wholly reliant on—the standards themselves.

When asked about the inception of this unit, Stephanie recounted:

> I knew that the history of the environmental movement was often left out of social studies curricula, so I thought I'd design a unit that taught us about the history and pushed us to put ourselves into the movement *today*—"walking the walk" through culminating projects that could actually do something for the community.

This idea of "walking the walk" meant that Stephanie wanted her students to do *more* than just "talk the talk," that is, more than just meet the standards by learning about and discussing the environmental movement. Stephanie believed that deep student learning would occur from *taking action*. By encouraging her students to look at new content with a critical eye, designing a project that required local action, and using local ways of languaging, she hoped her students would be emboldened and inspired to think about real change. In this way, Stephanie used translanguaging to support her students' bilingual identities and work toward inclusivity and social justice.

Though Stephanie did not start with the standards themselves, they were an integral part of her planning. She knew that having state literacy and social studies standards in her unit were necessary for her and her students. Stephanie enacted her belief that designing a critical and creative unit on a timely and important issue would engage her students and allow them to meet the standards' requirements but prevent the standards from taking over the unit. She also believed that her emphasis on students' use of Spanish and English in interrelationship and the inclusion of community and families would play a similar role. Without access to both Spanish and English, many of Stephanie's students would be unable to engage with complex content and texts to meet the rigorous standards set forth by the state. Thus, Stephanie taps into the translanguaging corriente to ensure that students gain deep understanding of content. In addition to accessing the content, students' use of all their language practices allows them to go *beyond* the standards, opening up opportunities to hear different voices and stories, compare different perspectives, and take action that benefits the local, bilingual community. Furthermore, when bilingual and *all* language-minoritized students (including, for example, the Black students in Stephanie's classroom) can use the full features of their linguistic repertoires (i.e., their general linguistic performance), they are able to offer more experienced academic performances in English (and Spanish for her bilingual students) than if they are allowed only to use features from so-called "standard English." When teachers create this kind of flexible learning space, they communicate to students that they reject the notion that students' existing ways of languaging are at all unacademic or deficient.

When teachers adopt a translanguaging stance, their instruction can become *more* rigorous than when they rely exclusively on mandated standards. Furthermore, teachers can apply a translanguaging lens to their standards-aligned classrooms to open up a democratic co-learning space. Learning in translanguaging classrooms can become deeper and more authentic, enabling bilingual students to (1) meet and exceed state- and otherwise-sanctioned standards and complete school-defined tasks ("talk the talk") and (2) take action as informed, critical, and empowered members of their communities and families ("walk the walk").

DESIGN: EXPAND AND LOCALIZE THE STANDARDS

When thinking about the role of standards in translanguaging designs, it is important to reiterate that teachers use standards; standards do not use teachers. When designing instruction and assessment, it is important to take this point a step further and embrace what may seem like a paradox: to use standards well, teachers must both expand *and* localize them. They must enlarge the scope of the standards, moving past monolingual, monocultural, and decontextualized understandings to *make local* those understandings. This means carefully selecting standards and aligning them to an instructional unit that draws on students' language practices, funds of knowledge, communities, families, and concerns to help them understand and meet those standards *on their own terms and with their own language practices.* In this way, students' local questions, noticings, and community language practices are also (re)cast as intellectual and "academic," already meeting and *exceeding* the standards.

Designing a Translanguaging Unit Starting from the Local

Stephanie designs every unit by first drawing on her knowledge of her students. As she began gathering resources for her "Environmentalism: Then and Now" unit, Stephanie realized that a general study of the environmental movement would not be enough to engage and stimulate her students. In her words, she needed to find a lens that would "bring the issues home" for her students. It is important to reiterate here that though the focus here is on Stephanie's unit, which adheres to New York State's standards, the *process* of using standards that is described can be used by educators across contexts and frameworks.

After talking with her fellow teachers, running ideas by some of her students, and doing additional research, Stephanie decided that, in addition to learning the history of the movement, the unit would focus on current environmental issues that disproportionately affect Latinx and Black communities, such as air and water pollution and pesticide poisoning, as well as those that affect the students' local community in New York City. Because she knew that her students would already have connections to these topics, Stephanie saw this focus as a connection between what students already knew and what they would learn. She also saw this unit as an opportunity to help her students expand their passion for social justice and learn about how change could be made on the community level.

With this new emphasis on the "local," Stephanie turned her attention to the content understanding she wanted her students to grasp and the language and literacy she knew they would need to best express their understanding of these important topics.

In teaching the state standards for English Language Development, I guide teacher candidates to consider what they want to teach first, given their students' interests and language practices. Subsequently, they can pinpoint standards that correlate with their chosen teaching focus. This book has been critical in guiding this work since it helps educators plan instruction that addresses the purposes of translanguaging, which puts students—not standards—at the center of our planning for teaching and learning.

—Luz Yadira Herrera, Ph.D., teacher educator, co-author, En Comunidad, California

Using the Standards to Meet Students' Needs

Stephanie's planning around standards arose organically from the understanding she wanted students to gain from the unit. Once Stephanie had decided on her focus and found a few anchor texts in English, she looked for supplementary texts in Spanish and then asked her bilingual colleagues, as well as some of her experienced bilingual students, to check them out for her. She also looked for relevant passages on the topic in the social studies textbook and reviewed the New York State Next Generation Learning Standards for literacy in history/social studies.

As Stephanie read through the list of standards, she saw that many of them already applied to what she wanted her students to do in the unit. For example, one of the unit goals was for students to synthesize information from multiple sources—the documentary, textbook, public service announcements (PSAs), supplemental readings, music, and so forth—to get a holistic view of the topic. Stephanie could see this goal clearly in the Anchor Standards for Reading History/Social Studies (Standard 7), which reads, "Integrate and evaluate content presented in diverse media and formats, including across multiple texts." Next, she moved on to the state's Social Studies Framework and curricular goals for 11th-grade U.S. History and Government. Stephanie thought about the resources she already had—and the understanding she wanted the class to grasp—and, again, found standards that met her students' needs. For example, Stephanie found that her desire for students to use their understanding of environmentalism and sustainability to locate a problem in the school or community and come up with possible solutions aligned with the state standards (Social Studies Practice F: Civic Engagement). She also explicitly aligned her unit goals to the state's curricular focus on "Social and Economic Change/Domestic Issues (1945–present)," which explicitly covers the environmental movement. She determined that her unit would enable students to develop understanding of Standard 11.10b, which reads, "Individuals, diverse groups, and organizations have sought to bring about change in American society through a variety of methods."

Figure 10.1 shows how Stephanie expands and localizes content-area standards by choosing activities that connect this content standard to students' lives, in this case with a focus on one of the state's Next Generation Learning Standards for reading.

Stephanie also expanded and localized the standards through her choice of texts, an important element in her unit design. Stephanie used the required English language social studies textbook in the "Environmentalism: Then and Now" unit. However, she knew that to localize the content (as well as help build students' literacies), she would need to supplement with multimodal texts—videos, film, music, tables, graphs, maps, blogs, websites, and so forth—in English and Spanish. To this end, Stephanie chose high-interest texts from different genres and with different levels of complexity, as shown in Figure 10.2.

Seeing Content Standards Through a Language Lens

All teachers must identify the language practices necessary for all students to meet every standard successfully. This isn't always easy. As Gibbons (2009) writes, "the fish doesn't recognize the water in which it swims" (p. 46), meaning that many of us cannot point out the specific language practices that we use to communicate and make meaning on a daily basis. However, teachers of bilingual students—especially emergent bilinguals—can look closely at the content and literacy standards to highlight the kinds of language practices that different students will need to engage with and comprehend the complex content and texts included in an instructional unit.

New York State Social Studies Practices, Grades 9-12: A.2:
Identify, describe, and evaluate evidence about events from diverse sources (including written documents, works of art, photographs, charts and graphs, artifacts, oral traditions, and other primary and secondary sources).

Expand and Localize

- Analyze U.S. maps for areas of air pollution and compare to demographic factors, such as language, race, ethnicity, and socioeconomic levels.
- Survey school and local communities and make graphs and charts that represent percentages of people who suffer from pollution-related conditions like asthma and compare those to percentages in surrounding areas/across the United States.
- Survey Latinx and non-Latinx in the school and local communities, using both English and Spanish, and represent the percentages of asthma sufferers in each group.
- Integrate data collected by students and found through research to support plans of action for increased sustainability in school/local communities.

Figure 10.1 Connecting content-area practices to students' lives and local realities.

Standards-Based English Language Social Studies Textbook

Expand and Localize

- Newspaper articles from Spanish and English publications
- Public service announcements in Spanish and English
- Bilingual readings on César Chávez and the Farm Workers Association
- Excerpts from TIME's *Generation Now* and other documentaries that focus on youth participation in environmental/sustainability movements
- Bilingual music and poetry with messages about the environment, community action, and social change
- Thematically relevant podcasts in both English and Spanish
- Blogs, websites, social media, and other resources about local environmental/sustainability projects and campaigns

Figure 10.2 Supplementing a standards-aligned textbook with multimodal, multilingual texts.

The next vignette demonstrates how Stephanie views the content standards included in the "Environmentalism: Then and Now" unit through a language lens:

Prepared with ideas for content understanding, Stephanie began to think deeply about the language practices her students would need to meet the standards. She also thought about her students, who used English and Spanish differently. For example, even though Eddy was confident using English in class, he struggled with writing. Noemí was one of the strongest writers in class in Spanish, but her English literacy performances were still developing. Other students had different strengths and needed practice with different kinds of language. With her specific students in mind, Stephanie looked again at the Social Studies Framework and Next Generation Learning Standards she had chosen, the texts and resources she planned to use, and the project students would complete at the end of the unit and brainstormed what kinds of language practices all students would need to be successful.

Looking more closely at the standards Stephanie included in her translanguaging unit plan, it becomes apparent that the language demands of New York State's Social Studies Practices are particularly complex. As mentioned earlier, Stephanie has aligned her unit to several of these practices, namely F.6 Civic Participation: "Identify situations in which social actions are required and determine an appropriate course of action." To meet this content standard, students will need to use language for a variety of purposes, including those deemed "academic." For example, they might have to:

- Discuss with peers and come to a shared understanding of what it means for a situation to require social action.
- Define, and support with evidence, what social action is and what it can achieve.
- Propose a course of action and persuade different audiences that it will address the issue and/or resolve the problem.
- Develop an argument that supports a course of action with precedent (i.e., where has such social action been successful in the past?).

Stephanie knows that the complex language performances this standard demands require language practices that may be particularly challenging for her emergent bilinguals. Stephanie also knows that it is unrealistic for her to expect that some of her students, for example,

Eddy, Noemí, Mariana, Luis, and ***Teresita,*** will be able to perform these language functions with the same levels of expertise.

Stephanie determined how she would need to differentiate instruction and assessment for students in the different activities in the unit, considering their general linguistic performances and their language-specific performances in English and Spanish. Realistically, Stephanie couldn't create individual language objectives for each student. Therefore, she loosely grouped her students into the five different placements that align with designations set out by New York State: *entering*, *emerging*, *developing*,[2] *expanding*, and *commanding*. She used these groupings to think about the expectations, scaffolds, and assessments she would use throughout the unit to help her meet students where they were and enable them to access content, share their ideas, and strengthen their oracy and literacy performances in English.

Teachers can use any system/framework to get a preliminary idea of what students at different stages of development should be able to do with English (and other languages) relative to the content-area standards used in their state. For example, teachers can use Can Do Descriptors or model performance indicators articulated by their state-mandated English language development (ELD) systems (e.g., WIDA, ELPA 21).

Creating Translanguaging Objectives

Though various systems and frameworks—those focused on English language development and those aimed at bilingual development—can help teachers think about what students can do in each of their specific languages relative to content standards, these systems may still be interpreted as focusing on languages as separate and separable entities. However, teachers in translanguaging classrooms understand that bilingual students have one holistic language repertoire that includes general linguistic and language-specific performances, and they understand that they can leverage students' general linguistic performances for learning. Therefore, in addition to creating language objectives that target specific languages like Spanish and English, teachers must also create **translanguaging objectives**:

Stephanie looked for opportunities for her students to use all their language practices, not only to help them communicate and express their thinking, but also to look at the topic from multiple points of view, write for different audiences, and compare environmentalism and sustainability across different cultures. Thus, she chose texts, planned lessons and activities, and planned the details of the culminating design so that students could use all of their languages to dig deeper into the content and access it on a variety of levels. To keep students' language practices front and center in the unit, Stephanie challenged herself to create translanguaging objectives for the unit. This meant thinking of ways that students' existing language practices could be extended to meet content standards and learn school-sanctioned language practices in English. For example, Stephanie decided that students would be required to create bilingual culminating projects, action plans, and presentations for improving the environmental sustainability of the school or local community that would reach and be understood by a diverse, multilingual audience.

In addition to identifying the kind of language practices necessary for students to comprehend content in English, Stephanie knows how important it is for them to use all their language practices to engage deeply with that content. Stephanie believes that, more so than

[2]Stephanie uses the term *developing* rather than *transitioning*, the term used by New York State. As she developed her translanguaging stance, she found it difficult to adhere to the use of the term because she does not believe that students ever "transition" from one language to another; they always develop both languages side by side. Therefore, Stephanie chooses to use "developing" in her own planning practice.

monolingual students, bilingual students can understand a concept from more than one linguistic and cultural perspective. In effect, bilingual students have the ability to see multiple sides of an issue because of the multiple worlds they inhabit. Stephanie knew that this deeper understanding of the content would not only help students better meet the standards, but also engage them with the learning in a more meaningful way.

Stephanie's use of translanguaging objectives *expands* on the use of language objectives, which focus mainly on English and only occasionally on another language like Spanish. Translanguaging objectives leverage students' general linguistic performance, asking them to use all their language practices to do *more* with the standard than they could through the use of only one language. Translanguaging objectives also provide opportunities for all students to engage meaningfully with the content, no matter their experience with English.

Translanguaging objectives not only bring language in general to the core of lesson planning; they help candidates be more concrete about the specific language-inclusive approaches they will take. Especially for future teachers of English language arts and French as a second language, who often struggle to understand the difference between content and language objectives, asking them to consider translanguaging objectives in their lesson planning has proven effective in clarifying their questions about multilingualism and how to include all student languages in the classroom.

—Jeff Bale, Ph.D., language education policy researcher and teacher educator, University of Toronto, Ontario Institute for Studies in Education

There is an integral relationship between content standards and translanguaging objectives in the translanguaging classroom. Content standards are the "what" of instruction and translanguaging objectives are the "how," that is, how to leverage students' general linguistic performance for learning within this unit of instruction. As discussed earlier, one of the content standards targeted in the "Environmentalism: Then and Now" unit of instruction is Standard 7 of the Next Generation Learning Standards' Anchor Standards for Reading History/Social Studies, which asks students to "integrate and evaluate context presented in diverse media and formats, including across multiple texts." With this Anchor Standard in mind, Stephanie generated the following translanguaging objectives, which focus on how bilingual students would draw on their general linguistic performances to meet this standard:

- Students will use their oral and written Spanish and English to analyze and critique both the content and the discourse of bilingual PSAs.
- Students will select different drawings and images to integrate with the PSAs, reflecting on what the images add to the overall message.
- Students will create bilingual texts across a variety of diverse media/formats (PSAs, posters, persuasive essays, oral presentations, and short dramatic plays) and rationalize their linguistic choices (see Table 10.1; see also Chapter 9 for a full discussion of students' engagement with and creation of bilingual PSAs).

Because students would eventually create their own bilingual PSAs, Stephanie asked students to integrate different kinds of information into a relatively small space (a one-page print PSA) and use language persuasively to move an audience to think about an issue in a new light. Because students' audiences (the school and local community) were bilingual, Stephanie required students to look at PSAs in both languages to analyze persuasive tactics for these different audiences. Using textual evidence (i.e., the PSAs in both languages), Stephanie asked her students to demonstrate whether and how the PSAs directed at Spanish-speaking Latinx differ from those directed at English speakers. She also asked them to reflect on whether all images and drawings work with texts in English or Spanish. Then, using the concrete differences they identified in the texts, Stephanie asked her students to explain why one audience might be moved by one tactic rather than another. Through the use of both languages and with a critical focus on discourse, Stephanie was able to expand on this standard, deepening what it meant to *evaluate* sources of information and see information in *diverse formats*. Students were prepared to create bilingual PSAs using the most persuasive features for different audiences.

Table 10.1 Relationship Between Content Standards and Translanguaging Objectives

Content Standards: *The What*	Translanguaging Objectives: *The How*
Next Generation Learning Standards, Anchor Standard 7	
• Integrate and evaluate content presented in diverse media and formats, including across multiple texts.	• Students will use their oral and written Spanish and English to analyze and critique both the content and the discourse of bilingual PSAs. • Students will select different drawings and images to integrate with the PSAs, reflecting on what the images add to the overall message. • Students will create bilingual texts across a variety of diverse media/formats (PSAs, posters, persuasive essays, oral presentations, and short dramatic plays) and rationalize their linguistic choices.

SHIFTS: SEIZING THE MOMENT

To this point, we have seen how the translanguaging design for instruction and assessment allows teachers to purposefully and strategically leverage students' bilingualism to meet or exceed standards. This section turns to the moment-by-moment translanguaging shifts that teachers in translanguaging classrooms make to respond to the dynamic flow of bilingual students' language practices throughout the course of unit implementation. For example, teachers may shift course when they:

- Get informal feedback on unit planning and implementation through conversations with colleagues *and* students.
- Make spontaneous choices about language use in classroom activities, such as when to ask for translations of ideas and how to facilitate whole-class brainstorming and participation.
- Relinquish the role of "expert" and enlist the help of bilingual students.
- Seize the moment to make a specific language or content turn.
- Reference students' questions and connections throughout planning and instruction.

The shift focused on here is Stephanie's way of using language in the classroom. Remember that Stephanie is one of the few people in her classroom who is not bilingual—a fact she thinks about often. When Stephanie plans activities to help students meet standards and engage with complex content and texts, she knows that she needs to step back and allow students to use language in ways that benefit them the most. Other teachers and administrators constantly question Stephanie about her stance on language in the classroom. When asked about this, Stephanie said:

> When I first started teaching, I was really nervous that I couldn't understand everything my students said. I kept thinking, "How can I teach them if I can't understand them?" Now though, I just let them go if they're on a roll—if I can tell they're really into a discussion or a debate, I just sit back and listen. Later, if I feel like it's something I can build on, I'll ask a student like Teresita or Eddy to fill me in on what I missed.

Stephanie sees her flexibility as integral to her strong relationships with students, to students' rapport with one another, to the high levels of engagement and participation she sees, and, of course, to students' ability to tackle rigorous, complex content and demonstrate their understanding in ways that align with standards. By stepping back and allowing students to use language in their own ways, Stephanie is *seizing a translanguaging moment*, not only honoring the authentic language practices of her students, but also making space for them to grapple with ideas and make sense of new information in a deeper way than they could if they were forced to use only one language. She is also disrupting raciolinguistic ideologies that so often cast White, English-speaking teachers as linguistic experts/models who must actively "police" their racialized students' language practices (Flores et al., 2018).

Ceding control and leaning into the role of co-learner in the classroom is key not only to developing a translanguaging pedagogy but also to being an advocate for bilingual students. For more on how a translanguaging pedagogy can be seen through the lens of advocacy by monolingual English-speaking teachers, see Episode 2 of the web series "Teaching Bilinguals (Even If You're Not One)," which you can find via the Brookes Download Hub.

Aligning instruction to standards is important. However, teachers in translanguaging classrooms also know that they must make shifts in their instruction so that they can work with, and not against, the translanguaging corriente. Teachers can use translanguaging shifts spontaneously to make sure that bilingual students meet and *exceed* standards.

STANDARDS AND CURRICULA: A CAUTIONARY NOTE

One unfortunate result of the implementation of standards has been that many states have adopted commercial curricula that are prescriptive and preplanned. Most standards-aligned curricula have been developed for elementary schools, so fortunately Stephanie, a high school teacher, is still free to think creatively about how to align her curriculum and instruction to the standards. However, her friend ***Sarah*** teaches third grade in an elementary school in the same school district, and there the school administration has adopted a ready-made curriculum that all teachers must use in the same way. Although Sarah teaches in an English-medium classroom, there is tremendous linguistic diversity among her students. Some of Sarah's students come from homes where only English is spoken and others from homes where languages other than English are spoken. Some speak and write English very well; others speak English fluently, but their reading and writing performances in English are more emergent. Some of Sarah's students have been classified as English language learners (ELLs) and get support in English as a second language programs. Despite this diversity, Sarah is expected to follow the scripted curriculum in the same way for all her students, regardless of their individual language performances and cultural practices.

Sarah's colleague ***Lina*** teaches a Spanish-English bilingual third-grade classroom in the same school. Lina is also expected to use the district curriculum, but she has not found texts in Spanish that readily align to the topics of the English curriculum. Neither has she found a way to teach this curriculum in two languages that makes pedagogical sense. To teach bilingually, Lina is expected to translate the English anchor texts to Spanish, but, of course, something is lost in translation, and the texts in two languages are not in any way equivalent. Lina struggles to find a balance between English and Spanish in her dual-language bilingual classroom. The space for Spanish is shrinking every day, while attention is focused on getting students to achieve standards in English only. Not only are these scripted curricula taxing the bilingual children more than the monolingual children, but bilingual teachers are also being burdened. When these planned curricula are adopted without taking into account either the variation in bilingual students' language performances (in terms of general linguistic and language-specific performances) or the ways that teachers can leverage students' dynamic bilingualism for learning, these curricula burn out teachers and they fail children.

This, of course, creates inequalities among students and teachers. It is imperative that bilingual learners, including emergent bilinguals, meet college and career-readiness standards, but this cannot be done without stretching and transforming the standards-aligned curricula that publishers are producing and selling. Bilingual teachers cannot be expected to carry this burden alone. It is the responsibility of publishers to also produce bilingual curricula that acknowledge the complexity of the dynamic translanguaging of the students and that are aligned to what bilingual children know and can do, not simply to external standards. It is also the responsibility of districts to provide professional development for all teachers who work with bilingual students to learn how to leverage translanguaging for learning.

Developing standards-based translanguaging instruction as in Stephanie's classroom is not easy. It is perhaps faster and cheaper to buy scripted curricula than to prepare teachers who are creative and knowledgeable about translanguaging instruction. But the costs to children and to society are very high. Rather than using bilingual students' language practices to meet and exceed content and language standards, following scripted curricula without regard for the students' diversity will ensure that bilingual children are left behind, and bilingual teachers with them.

CONCLUSION

Standards shape much of what happens in classrooms. In Stephanie's translanguaging classroom, however, standards are shaped *by* the translanguaging corriente and are not blindly adopted. They are used, but always with a translanguaging *stance* informing their use. Stephanie not only "talks the talk," she also "walks the walk" by *designing* instruction and assessment that take up the standards, expand and localize them, and connect them with action-oriented, culturally and linguistically sustaining work, thus adapting them to the translanguaging corriente. Part of the adaptation involves the *shifts* Stephanie makes to seize moments of learning. These moments are unplanned, but they expand students' learning and language development opportunities, enabling them to meet standards. Stephanie is always on the lookout for ways to leverage the translanguaging corriente for learning.

For many, standards mean an emphasis on English-only instruction, with teachers forced to follow scripted curricula that is said to be aligned to those standards. But, as Stephanie demonstrates, this doesn't have to be the case. A translanguaging pedagogy, including a translanguaging stance, design, and shifts, can actually *expand* the power of the standards because teachers use instruction and assessment to leverage students' use of their entire language repertoires, not part of them, to meet their important goals.

REFLECTION QUESTIONS AND ACTIVITIES

1. How can teachers in translanguaging classrooms work with mandated, standards-aligned curricula? What design choices and shifts can they make?
2. How do you typically integrate mandated standards into your planning? What new thinking and considerations do you have now that you read about Stephanie's planning process?
3. How do you relate a translanguaging approach to mandated standards to the larger purposes of translanguaging classrooms, namely, the pursuit of racial, cognitive, and social justice?

TAKING ACTION

1. On your own or with a colleague, design a lesson or activity in which you *expand* and *localize* a particular standard through the use of translanguaging. If possible, use the translanguaging unit of instruction that you have been developing while reading this book. What differentiation strategies might you need for the bilingual students in your class to meet that standard?
2. Implement the lesson or activity. Reflect on how you used translanguaging to address the standards. In what ways did translanguaging help advance bilingual students' content and language learning, leverage their bilingualism, promote stronger socioemotional identity, and work toward racial, cognitive, and social justice?

11

Developing Literacies in the Translanguaging Classroom

LEARNING OBJECTIVES

After reading this chapter, you will be able to:

- Explore a translanguaging lens on literacy, particularly how it deepens student engagement and students' understanding and generation of texts.
- Explain how teachers can use translanguaging to develop students' literacies, specifically through their stance, design, and shifts.
- Design activities that support the development of bilingual students' literacy practices for academic purposes by leveraging their dynamic bilingualism.

Literacy is a very important part of schooling. It is in school that students learn how to interact with written texts in the ways that many academic contexts demand. School is also the place where bilingual students are too often exposed to rigid, monolingual conceptualizations of their literacies. Rather than the fluid, multimodal, translingual nature of their interactions with texts outside the classroom, students are frequently taught that reading and writing happen in one language or another and that certain ways of reading and writing (and certain ways of being readers and writers) are the expectation (Ascenzi-Moreno & Seltzer, 2021). Developing literacies through a translanguaging lens, on the other hand, means making space for bilingual students to "engage in literacy in ways that deepen their understanding of texts, generate more diverse texts, develop students' confianza in performing literacies, and foster their critical metalinguistic awareness" (García & Kleifgen, 2020, p. 561). This chapter delves into this translanguaging lens on literacy and discusses how teachers can take up such a lens in their practice, particularly when designing opportunities for students to develop literacy for academic purposes.

While all students must reach equally high standards in content, language, and literacy, bilingual students develop literacy differently than their monolingual peers. Emergent bilinguals who are developing literacies in an additional language will need explicit attention to differences in literacy practices across their languages. They, like all students, will also need to develop their literacies for the various school-based tasks that are set out for them—reading for information, writing for a variety of audiences and purposes, analyzing the deeper meaning of texts, and supporting their ideas with text-based evidence, to name only a few. A translanguaging lens on literacy is rooted in the belief that bilingual students are *already* sophisticated readers, writers, and creators of both the word and the world (Freire, 1970). In school, teachers must help them expand their repertoires so that they can read, write, and create in new ways, including those that will find them success in academic contexts.

A translanguaging lens also promotes an understanding of literacies *beyond* school-sanctioned tasks and performances. Such a lens can provide teachers with what author Kate and her colleague Cati de los Ríos (2021) describe as "counternarratives about bi-/ multilingual students' language and literacy practices" (p. 4). Rather than uphold ideologies that locate deficiency and lack in bilingual students' literacies, which can, as García and Kleifen (2020) write, "restrict rather than liberate students' meaning-making potential and often result in failure in school," a translanguaging approach "decolonizes these understandings about language, literacy, and bilingualism and incorporates thinking from, and being/listening with, racialized/ minoritized multilingual bodies" (p. 557).

Educating bilingual students equitably requires identifying and building on the specific content, language, literacy, and cultural strengths these students bring with them to school and leveraging their dynamic bilingualism and bilingual ways of knowing for a variety of purposes, including those deemed academic. There has been a proliferation of scholarship that has taken up this call since the first edition of this book was published. This research emphasizes that students' translanguaging must be "viewed as a strength that drives literacy" (Espinosa & Ascenzi-Moreno, 2021, p. 18) across all modalities and literacy tasks (see España & Herrera, 2020; García & Cervantes-Soon, 2023; Seltzer & de los Ríos, 2021, among many others). Yet despite this research and the longstanding work of teachers of bilingual students, the drumbeat of simplistic, monoglossic approaches to literacy—particularly, of late, in science of reading debates—continues. For more on this topic, see Durán and Hikida (2022) for a historical analysis of the "reading wars" and the recent joint statement (2023) from the Reading League and the National Committee for Effective Literacy for Emergent Bilingual Students, which clarifies the science of reading for emergent bilingual students.

This chapter focuses on ***Stephanie***'s English-medium 11th-grade social studies classroom in New York City. We see how Stephanie—who sees herself as a content-area and literacy teacher—structures activities that engage her students with complex, grade-level texts and literacy practices, affirm and extend students' dynamic translanguaging and translingual literacies, and develop their critical consciousness. To begin, we return to the bilingual profiles of our five focal students in Stephanie's class, which illustrate some of the variation teachers can expect to find in their classrooms:

- ***Eddy*** was born and raised by Dominican parents in a Dominican neighborhood in New York City. He has excellent English oracy and can speak Spanish. Eddy is below grade level in English literacy and is beginning to develop literacy in Spanish.
- ***Luis*** arrived from El Salvador last year and speaks Spanish. Luis is officially designated as an English language learner (ELL), has been identified as a student with incomplete/ interrupted formal education (SIFE), and struggles to read and write academic texts in English and Spanish.
- ***Mariana*** is of Mexican descent, was raised in the United States, and is more comfortable speaking English than Spanish. Mariana has been officially designated as an ELL since she entered elementary school and is considered a long-term ELL who struggles on literacy assessments in English and Spanish.
- ***Noemí*** moved to the United States from Ecuador in the eighth grade, is a strong reader in Spanish, and is still classified as an ELL. Noemí's English oracy performances are expanding, although she still struggles with English literacy, especially in writing.
- ***Teresita*** moved to the United States from Guatemala when she was very young, and her oracy and literacy performances in English and Spanish are commanding. She is a voracious reader in both languages, scores well on standardized tests, and loves to write poetry.

This chapter demonstrates how Stephanie's translanguaging stance, design, and shifts throughout the "Environmentalism: Then and Now" unit enable all of her students, particularly emergent bilinguals, to engage with and create complex texts. As you read, you are encouraged to think about how you can leverage your students' bilingualism to promote literacy in your classes.

STANCE: CONTENT AND LITERACY JUNTOS

A defining feature of all translanguaging classrooms is the teacher's juntos stance, which informs everything from how the teacher views students and their language and cultural practices to the way they plan instruction. Here, Stephanie's juntos stance is reflected in how she brings content and literacy together in her curriculum and instruction.

Throughout her unit on the history of the environmental movement, Stephanie constantly made connections between the social studies content and students' lives, interests, and concerns. One of the most important connections she made was putting Latinx people at the center of the curriculum. In addition to focusing on environmental issues that disproportionately affect Latinx communities, Stephanie incorporated readings about Latinx historical figures who were given little treatment in the standards-aligned textbook. For example, though her social studies textbook provided a short autobiography of César Chávez and briefly outlined his role in fighting for workers' rights, Stephanie felt it was too cursory for such an important voice in the struggle, or as her students referred to it, la lucha. Stephanie decided to devote a unit of instruction to learning about Chávez's life and contributions to both the environmental movement and the struggle for human rights.

Stephanie's stance, which included pride in her students' bilingual Latinx identities, strongly informed her instructional design and the ways she had students engage with texts. Her choice to *expand* the learning outside the bounds of the textbook was in response to her own and her students' belief that an important figure in la lucha had not been given adequate coverage. As discussed in Chapter 10, in *expanding* the learning beyond the standards-aligned textbook to focus on an important Latinx historical figure—whom some students had never heard of—Stephanie also *localized* the learning. This helped students connect and engage with content, learn about a person whose role in the movement was both important and controversial, and affirm the identities of her Latinx students. Though Chávez was Mexican American and most of Stephanie's Latinx students are Dominican or African American, all students expressed deep pride as they learned about his legacy. This change to the curriculum through the simultaneous expansion and localization of the content resonated with all students and made them more active learners. In this way, Stephanie used translanguaging to make space for students' ways of knowing, which supported their socioemotional development and bilingual identities. Her stance also reflects a social justice approach to teaching content. Stephanie supplemented the traditional curriculum with voices and stories that are often underrepresented, and she pushed her students to see themselves and people like them as powerful agents of change in society.

Stephanie's stance also influenced the way she approached texts. As she expanded the instruction past the textbook, she made important choices about texts that would supplement students' study of Chávez. Though her students' language and literacy performances differed, Stephanie knew that each one of them could engage with complex, grade-appropriate content. Here we see how Stephanie chooses texts:

Stephanie did some research and found several websites that had readings about Chávez in both English and Spanish. For example, the entire United Farm Workers website was in both languages and had a great deal of information on Chávez's work. Because she wanted her students to get a full picture of Chávez rather than the flat rendering she found in the textbook, Stephanie also found articles that examined Chávez's legacy from different angles. Some were glowing retellings of his role in the movement. Others highlighted criticism about Chávez and looked at some of the controversies around his life and work. While some of the readings she found were in Spanish, many were only in English. As such, Stephanie knew she would have to use different kinds of strategies to help her students—especially emergent bilinguals like Noemí and Luis—access the texts. She knew that her students could handle the content of such nuanced, complex readings; they just needed the language support to do so.

Stephanie does not "water down" or simplify the content and texts that she chooses; instead, she amplifies them (Gibbons, 2009), strategically scaffolding her instruction to support student learning. As demonstrated in the sections that follow, Stephanie sets her students up to participate successfully in rigorous literacy experiences that include and go beyond academic purposes, no matter what their experiences are with English.

Stephanie's view of bilingualism as a resource for creativity and criticality shines through all aspects of her thinking about content and literacy instruction. Rather than view students' languaging as a problem to solve, Stephanie plans her approach to literacy instruction so that students have authentic opportunities to use their bilingualism to understand texts in deeper ways than they would have if they only had access to English. These opportunities for students to use their bilingualism and ways of knowing make space for them to show off their linguistic strengths and cultural understanding and engage with texts in more meaningful ways.

DESIGN: ENGAGING WITH CONTENT-AREA TEXTS

To leverage the translanguaging corriente, Stephanie had to find ways to help *all* students—bilingual or not—engage with complex texts in English and create their own texts in English. Though her students had different experiences using English for academic purposes, Stephanie knew that the right designs would meet each student where they were and enable them all to meet the language and content demands of the "Environmentalism: Then and Now" unit of instruction. As described in the vignettes that follow, Stephanie makes sure that her instructional designs:

- Provide a variety of affordances,
- Model and encourage the production of multilingual and multimodal texts,
- Invite collaboration, and
- Make space for students to foster their critical metalinguistic awareness (García & Kleifgen, 2020).

Using Two Languages Side by Side to Increase Comprehension

Stephanie's translanguaging unit design provides opportunities for students to engage with multilingual texts and reflects her content and literacy juntos stance.

On the first day devoted to the Chávez study, Stephanie had students read a biography of Chávez that she found on the United Farm Workers website. The website had the short biography in both English and Spanish, so Stephanie created a handout that put the two versions side by side. After watching the trailer for a new movie about Chávez and having a short discussion about what, if anything, students knew about him, Stephanie distributed the reading handout (Figure 11.1), which contained an annotation system for reading and the side-by-side English and Spanish versions of the biography. Rather than giving some students English and others Spanish, Stephanie gave each student both versions, telling them that they could choose to read one or the other or both. Before they read, Stephanie went over the reading handout, especially the annotation and note-taking system the class had been working with, which was a way for students to track their thinking in *any* language and improve their comprehension. Stephanie reviewed the different annotations—circling unknown vocabulary, looking up and writing the meaning of unknown words in English or Spanish, underlining main ideas, putting a star next to important/interesting moments, putting a question mark next to moments of confusion or wondering. Stephanie also emphasized that students' notes could be taken in English, Spanish, or both, regardless of the written language of the text.

These design choices clearly illustrate how *any* teacher can leverage students' dynamic bilingualism to promote reading for academic purposes in English. Remember that

Student name ______________________________

Date ______________________________

Directions
Read the biography of César Chávez independently. Make sure you annotate and take notes on what you read. Your annotations can include the following:

- (Circling) unknown vocabulary words or Spanish/English cognates
- Writing the *meaning* of the word in English or Spanish
- Underlining main ideas
- Putting a star (★) next to things you think are interesting or important
- Putting a question mark (?) next to your questions, wondering, or moments of confusion

Your note-taking can include the following:

- Noting and explaining things you agree or disagree with
- Writing down your questions or wondering
- Making connections
- Making predictions
- Summarizing or writing out the main ideas

You can make notes in English, Spanish, or both, regardless of the written language of the text!

The Story of César Chávez
The Beginning

The story of César Estrada Chávez begins near Yuma, Arizona. César was born on March 31, 1927. He was named after his grandfather, Cesario. Regrettably, the story of César Estrada Chávez also ends near Yuma, Arizona. He passed away on April 23, 1993, in San Luis, a small village near Yuma, Arizona.

He learned about justice, or rather injustice, early in his life. César grew up in Arizona; the small adobe home where César was born was swindled from them by dishonest Anglos. César's father agreed to clear eighty acres of land, and in exchange he would receive the deed to forty acres of land that adjoined the home. The agreement was broken and the land sold to a man named Justus Jackson. César's dad went to a lawyer who advised him to borrow money and buy the land. Later, when César's father could not pay the interest on the loan, the lawyer bought back the land and sold it to the original owner. César learned a lesson about injustice that he would never forget. Later, he would say, "The love for justice that is in us is not only the best part of our being but it is also the most true to our nature."

La historia de César Chávez
El principio

La historia de César Estrada Chávez empieza cerca de Yuma, Arizona. César nació el 31 de marzo de 1927. Lo llamaron como su abuelo, Cesario. Lamentablemente, la historia de César Estrada Chávez también termina cerca de Yuma, Arizona. Falleció el 23 de abril de 1993, en San Luis, un pueblo pequeño cerca de Yuma, Arizona.

Aprendió sobre la justicia o más bien la injusticia temprano en su vida. César creció en Arizona; unos Anglos deshonestos les quitaron la casa pequeña de adobe en dónde nació. El padre de César aceptó limpiar ochenta acres de terreno a cambio del título de propiedad de cuarenta acres de terreno que colindaban con su casa. El acuerdo no se cumplió y los Anglos vendieron la tierra a un hombre llamado Justus Jackson. El papá de César fue a un abogado que le aconsejó pedir un préstamo y comprar el terreno. Después, cuando el padre de César no pudo pagar el interés del préstamo, el abogado volvió a comprar el terreno y se la vendió al dueño original. César aprendió una lección sobre la injusticia de la cual nunca se olvidaría. Después diría, "El amor por la justicia que está dentro de nosotros no sólo es la parte mejor de nuestro ser pero también es la parte más verdadera de nuestra naturaleza."

Notes/Notas

Figure 11.1 Reading handout.

Stephanie does not speak Spanish and that English is the official language of instruction in this social studies classroom. Stephanie brought in many affordances, including readings in English and Spanish on the same topic, and set up opportunities for students to draw from their full linguistic repertoires, regardless of the text's written language. The use of side-by-side English and Spanish texts also provided *all* students with an important opportunity to develop and display **critical metalinguistic awareness**. For the students who were bilingual, putting their two languages next to one another allowed them to compare syntax, vocabulary (including Spanish/English cognates), word choice, and discourse structure. For those who were monolingual, seeing one text in two languages raised their linguistic awareness and enabled them to see how many similarities exist between languages that they may have thought of as totally separate and different. Drawing explicit attention to language helps *all* students—bilingual or not—think more deeply about language in relation to literacy practices.

Through the use of an explicit strategy for annotating their ideas, Stephanie also encouraged students to be in dialogue with their intrapersonal translanguaging voices while they read independently. As students read the English and/or Spanish texts, some annotated and took notes in English, some did so in Spanish, and some used both languages.

Using a Reading Jigsaw to Differentiate Content-Area Literacy Instruction

Stephanie has the same high standards, goals, and objectives for all of her students. However, not all students perform equally in oracy and literacy in English and in Spanish. Teachers therefore need to differentiate their content, language, and literacy instruction to meet students where they are individually and engage all students in learning. The next vignette demonstrates how Stephanie encouraged collaboration, strategically grouping her students and providing affordances so that all students can engage with complex content and texts, develop language practices for academic contexts, and strengthen their metalinguistic awareness.

Later that week, Stephanie organized a "jigsaw" of different readings in English. First, she thought about her students' translanguaging and assigned students to five different groupings according to their English language development. Though the groups' assigned readings were at different levels, each dealt with the legacy that Chávez left behind, and the three questions they had to answer were the same. This ensured that when students went back to more heterogeneous groups, their discussions and comparisons would be aligned.

Once students had settled into these more-or-less homogeneous groups, Stephanie explained the activity and distributed the reading activity handout (Figure 11.2).

Stephanie told students that they would:

- Read their assigned text independently, using the annotation and note-taking procedures they had been practicing.
- Discuss their annotations and notes with the group.
- Answer the three questions on the handout.

Stephanie also told her students that after they completed the questions on the handout, they would join a new group to report on what they had read. Stephanie reminded the students that they would be the only expert on their reading when they joined the new group, because members of the new group had read a different article.

After students read their assigned English language texts about Chávez independently, they discussed what they had read with group members who had read the same text and prepared to report as experts on their reading. Some groups used both English and Spanish, but they used the languages in different ways that reflected the translanguaging corriente flowing through each group. For example, some students annotated texts and took notes in Spanish about the English texts they had read, while others annotated texts and took notes in English. Other students annotated texts and made notes

READING ACTIVITY HANDOUT FOR GROUP WORK

Student name ____

Date ____

Directions

After you have read your assigned text independently and used our annotations and note-taking strategies:

1. Share your thoughts and questions with your group.
2. In your group, answer the following questions about your assigned text (write in English, Spanish, or both):
    1. What do you think is the most important idea from this reading?
    2. What is the message about César Chávez given by the author?
    3. Do you agree or disagree with this message? Why?

Remember: Once you join your new groups, you will be the only expert on your reading, so make sure you know what you're talking about!

Figure 11.2 Reading activity handout for group work.

in the same language as the text, but then discussed what they had written in the other language. Group members worked together to jot down some notes for each of the three questions, in both English and Spanish, preparing to report back in English to their new groups. The bell rang just as students were finishing up their work, so Stephanie told them to review their readings and notes for homework in preparation for the second part of the jigsaw the next day.

When students arrived to class the following day, they went back into their groups to review and ensure that everyone was prepared to present their ideas. Stephanie instructed students to discuss each of the three questions they had answered. Students took notes, sometimes in English and other times in Spanish, as they listened to others sharing. Once the groups had finished discussing the three questions, they collaborated to write a summary of their reading in English (which they negotiated in both languages in many cases), and they were prepared to report as experts on their reading.

Afterward, Stephanie sent all students to groups composed of students at different progression levels who had read different texts. Thus, in each group, there were five different points of view on the issue of Chávez's legacy, reflecting the five different texts they had read.

Stephanie purposefully used the structure of a jigsaw activity to leverage the translanguaging corriente in her class and engage all of her students with complex content and texts in English, particularly those who are emergent bilinguals at earlier stages of English development.

First, Stephanie made strategic choices as she grouped her students and assigned texts and tasks throughout the jigsaw activity. The objective for the first part of this activity was to have all students read a text written in English about César Chávez and respond to the same three questions about the text they had read. Though Stephanie generally preferred to organize her students heterogeneously, she understood that students with *expanding* English literacy performances on this type of task needed to be challenged with higher level texts, while those with *entering* or *emerging* English literacy performances on this type of task needed practice with less linguistically complex texts. Stephanie therefore organized students into more homogeneous groups for this first activity, and she gave each group a text with a different level of linguistic complexity. The texts were also differentiated across modalities—for example, one group of students gathered around a laptop cued up to a short, accessible video on Chávez in English with Spanish subtitles, while another read a piece of written text in English. In this way, Stephanie supported those students who needed a less complex English text as well as those who could take on something more linguistically challenging, so that every student would be able to engage with the same complex content in English.

There is strong evidence of the translanguaging corriente in this activity. Though all the texts for this jigsaw were in English, Stephanie encouraged students to collaborate and use all their language resources to take notes, discuss and analyze the texts, and answer the discussion questions. When students utilized all of their languages to engage with those texts, they were able to comprehend and analyze them on a much higher level. Students like Noemí and Luis, who were bright and curious but did not yet have the ability to comprehend complex texts written in English, were not left out. Instead, Stephanie's purposeful design, which leveraged students' translanguaging and provided them with meaningful affordances, gave them access to both the texts and the conversations occurring around those texts.

After this first stage of the jigsaw activity, Stephanie sent students to different groups, where students were organized more heterogeneously. She distributed her jigsaw activity handout (Figure 11.3). In those groups, every student was able to learn about all of the texts. Though some groups had engaged with more complex English texts that others would not have been able to understand, they were able to access the content by listening to their group members' reports. They answered the questions using all their language resources. Each group wrote summaries of what they had learned from all five texts in English, which they then presented to the whole class.

Re-Presenting English Texts with Translanguaging

Though it was very important that students comprehended the content-area texts in English, Stephanie knew it was equally important for them to generate texts that interacted with the content and showcased students' translanguaging and uniquely bilingual ways of knowing. Through the combination of engaging with texts and creating new texts, students were able to learn about and "talk back" to the content, which made them active and engaged learners. Rather than assign only a traditional writing assignment like an essay, Stephanie designed an opportunity for students to *re-present* a text they had read with different language practices and in a different genre. She wanted students to re-present complex, linguistically challenging texts such as primary source documents, textbook chapters, and scholarly journal articles as dramatic dialogue, poems, stories, interviews, advertisements, newspaper articles, emails, or postcards (to name only a few). Walqui (2006) writes of text re-presentation:

> It has been argued . . . that there is a progression in the ability of language users to use different genres within academic discourses. In terms of language use, this continuum starts with asking students to say what is happening (as in drama or dialogue), then what has happened (narratives, reports), then what happens (generalisations in exposition) and, finally, what may happen (tautologic transformations, theorising). In this fashion, students can access content presented in more difficult genres by . . . transforming it into different genres, especially those that are more easily produced. (p. 213)

Stephanie's design for re-presenting academic texts in new genres and with new linguistic practices helped students extend their learning and draw on their bilingualism and bilingual understandings of texts.

HANDOUT FOR JIGSAW ACTIVITY	
Student name____________________ Date____________________	
Jigsaw Group Work	
Reading	My Notes Write down what you learned about the other texts your group members read; notes can be written in English, Spanish, or both.
Reading 1:	
Reading 2:	
Reading 3:	
Reading 4:	
Reading 5:	
Summary paragraph (written in English) ____________________ ____________________ ____________________ ____________________ ____________________ ____________________	

Figure 11.3 Handout for jigsaw activity.

Stephanie paired students to create imagined dialogues between César Chávez and another character from the readings they had done throughout the week. To get them started, Stephanie modeled a short dialogue she had written between César Chávez and the writer of a particularly critical article one group of students had read for the jigsaw. Stephanie showed students how she was taking what she had read and presenting it in a new way—through a dramatic dialogue. She pointed out a part of her dialogue that used a specific piece of textual evidence from the article, which she had re-presented as a line of dialogue in her scene. She told students that they could choose any character—for example, Chávez's wife, a farmworker who joined the movement, or the owner of a large farm—and that their dialogues should represent an aspect of Chávez's legacy. Stephanie explained that they should include in the dialogue at least two direct quotes from the texts they had read that were relevant and appropriate to the character and scene. She also told students that depending on whom Chávez was talking to, he might use English, Spanish, or both. Thus, students' dialogues could be written in either or both languages. Students worked in pairs, co-creating their dialogues, which they later performed for the class.

By re-presenting what they learned about César Chávez in the form of a dramatic dialogue, students were able to create multimodal, *translingual* texts that enabled them to demonstrate their knowledge and understanding in an engaging way that was accessible to all.

Performing these dialogues helped students teach one another more about Chávez and his legacy and provided Stephanie with an important assessment opportunity. Listening to her students perform their co-created dialogues helped Stephanie understand the extent to which they had comprehended the texts they read without the burden of writing a linguistically complex, decontextualized genre like an essay. Though Stephanie appreciates the importance of teaching students how to write in all genres, she believes that students' understanding of texts could be better assessed without relying solely on decontextualized written tasks in English.

In addition, Stephanie took Walqui's ideas a step further by making space for students' re-presentations to include translanguaging. Because Chávez was Mexican-American and interacted with his family and many of the farmworkers he organized in Spanish, their imagined dialogues were authentic opportunities for students to create translingual texts. Encouraging students to use all of their languages while interacting with an English text served a number of purposes. First, it gave emergent bilinguals like Noemí and Luis the opportunity to express their knowledge in the language they knew best. It also opened up space for *all* students, including those who spoke English only, to draw from their entire language repertoires, making the dialogues more interesting, nuanced, and authentic. Lastly, it provided an opportunity for students to develop and demonstrate their critical metalinguistic awareness, as Stephanie asked students to reflect on why they made the linguistic choices they made. As students explained their rationale for including certain words or phrases in one or the other language, Stephanie could assess what they knew about how to use Spanish and English for different audiences and purposes.

See how one English as a new language teacher promotes the use of graphic novels to develop her bilingual students' literacies in this video from the CUNY-NYSIEB web series "Teaching Bilinguals (Even If You're Not One)." You can also get many more ideas for teaching writing in the CUNY-NYSIEB guide, *A Translanguaging Pedagogy for Writing.* You can access both these resources via the Brookes Download Hub.

There are many pedagogical practices that teachers can use—in any content area, program, or classroom type—to set the course of the translanguaging corriente with texts, including the following:

- Purposefully create groups or partnerships so that students can read various texts, use different language practices, and engage in activities that differ but that are on similar topics.
- Supplement the curriculum with texts that are linguistically and culturally relevant to students.
- Look for or create versions of English texts in students' home languages (and vice versa).
- Use the Internet as a resource for finding bilingual texts on the same topic, perhaps reflecting different perspectives.

- Supplement the reading of texts with multilingual film clips, music and other audio, art and other visuals, and realia.
- Explicitly teach students how to annotate and take notes on a text in the language in which they are most comfortable, regardless of the text's written language (e.g., students can annotate an English text with a LOTE or vice versa).
- Encourage students to be in dialogue with their intrapersonal voice as they read and write, no matter the language of the text.
- Encourage students to work in groups and use all their language resources in collaborative dialogue to make meaning of complex texts.
- Assess students' understanding of texts by having them re-present those texts with different language practices and in different genres (e.g., a textbook chapter in English as a dramatic bilingual dialogue or a scholarly journal article in English as a poem in English or a LOTE).

When teachers enact a juntos stance through their translanguaging designs that brings content and literacy together and that leverages the translanguaging corriente for learning, bilingual students can engage more meaningfully with complex texts and build their literacy practices for and *beyond* academic purposes.

SHIFTS: ENHANCING CONVERSATIONS AROUND TEXT

Stephanie made several shifts that helped her follow the translanguaging corriente flowing through her classroom as she focused on her bilingual students' literacy performances. On the first day of the Chávez study, Stephanie made copies of excerpts from his biography in both Spanish and English. Stephanie had intended for students to work on the English text and only refer to the Spanish text if they needed additional help for comprehension. However, she soon realized that this approach might unintentionally stigmatize Spanish and support the idea that students use Spanish *only* if they are incapable of using English. Stephanie's stance toward Spanish and English is that they are of equal status, and she wanted her classroom practices to reflect that. She had first thought of creating a handout with the two texts on separate sheets, but she then decided to put the languages side by side. Right before the lesson, Stephanie decided not to tell students which text to read, contributing to the sense that Spanish was *always* available to *all* students, no matter their performances in English.

Stephanie also made important moves that demonstrated her ability to shift in response to her students' translanguaging. Stephanie's flexibility with language enabled *all* students to participate meaningfully in the literacy activity:

After students read the short biography of Chávez independently, Stephanie told them to discuss their annotations and notes with their groups. Students jumped into conversations about the reading while Stephanie circulated around the room, listening in, contributing ideas, answering questions, and jotting down things she heard that she wanted to bring up with the whole class. After the groups talked, Stephanie asked them to come up with one question and one comment about the reading to share with the class. She asked that they prepare to share in English, but she told them they should know how to explain their ideas in Spanish as well. When it came time to share, Stephanie asked Luis to share his group's answer in English; recall that Luis is an emergent bilingual with limited formal schooling, and he struggles with the grade-level literacy performances expected of him in school. Referring to his notes, Luis was able to explain the group's thinking in English, saying, "César Chávez's father was a victim of discrimination." After he finished, Stephanie asked Luis if there was anything he wanted to add in Spanish. Luis expanded, "que eso que le pasó al papá de César continúa pasando hoy también. Le pasó a un amigo mío." [What happened to Cesar's father continues to happen today. It happened to a friend of mine.] Though Stephanie did not understand most of what Luis said in his follow up, she saw that many students were nodding in agreement. She asked Mariana to translate Luis's comments, which she praised in English.

Although Luis had successfully completed the task in English, Stephanie sensed he had more to say than what he shared in English. By asking Luis if there was anything he wanted to add in Spanish, Stephanie made space for him to expand on what he said in English in the language with which he was more comfortable.

This shift illustrates how attuned Stephanie is to her students. Rather than limit emergent bilinguals like Luis to what they can express in English, Stephanie consistently pushes students to use Spanish to expand on their comments in English. Though she does not always understand what is said, she allows the translanguaging corriente to flow, leveraging students' bilingualism for learning and making space for increased comprehension and production of content-area texts. There are many different kinds of shifts that teachers can use to teach content while building literacy, including the following:

- Help students make meaning from texts by providing on-the-spot translations and explanations. If you are not bilingual in students' home languages, you can use translation apps, online or print dictionaries, and/or bilingual students and staff members.
- When students seem stuck, use strategies like "turn and talk" that permit pairs of students to use all their language resources privately to clear up confusion and spark conversation about texts.
- Encourage students to add to and expand their understanding of texts in English with discussion or writing in their home languages whenever they need to.
- Help students make connections to texts by providing culturally relevant examples or metaphors or asking students to supply them whenever necessary.

Overall, particularly when focusing on students' literacies, it is important that teachers make shifts that position them as co-learners and as open "to multiple ways of knowing, languaging, and experiencing" (García & Kleifgen, 2020, p. 566). In this way, "texts, both read and written by students, [also] remain open; their meanings are not constituted a priori, because meaning emerges in interactions with other people, texts, and other artifacts that may be available as activity enfolds" (p. 566). These important shifts—highly connected to stance—have the power to transform the development of literacies in classroom learning.

CONCLUSION

The main lesson of this chapter is that all teachers must see themselves as content and literacy teachers. Some teachers claim that students must be proficient in the language of the text before they can engage with complex grade-level content and skills. However, this is simply not the case. Almost every classroom is multilingual, and the bilingual students in these classrooms have very different experiences and expertise with language and literacy practices for academic purposes—in English and other languages. Thus, *all* teachers must recognize students' dynamic bilingualism and leverage it to help them engage with complex content and texts.

The chapter identifies the stance, design, and shifts of one teacher, Stephanie, in a translanguaging classroom. Stephanie teaches content and literacy juntos, and she draws heavily on local interests and understanding as she works to expand students' language and literacy practices in her English-medium 11th-grade classroom. Important characteristics of Stephanie's literacy teaching include the strategic grouping of students for collaborative tasks, the use of multimodal texts in English and students' home languages, an emphasis on different language practices and genres, and a commitment to developing students' critical metalinguistic awareness and affirming their bilingualism and bilingual identities. Stephanie's translanguaging classroom demonstrates how teachers can engage students with literacy more effectively when they do not restrict students to working exclusively with the language of the text. When teachers make space for students to draw on the full features of their linguistic repertoires, they have more opportunities to develop language and literacy for a variety of contexts and purposes, including those deemed academic, push the boundaries of school-based literacies, and disrupt ideologies of deficiency and lack.

REFLECTION QUESTIONS AND ACTIVITIES

1. Review the excerpts from Stephanie's classroom practices in this chapter. What else could Stephanie have done to expand her students' literacy performances?
2. Why did Stephanie include readings of a Chicano historical figure? Do you think this is useful for *all* students, Latinx/Chicanx or not? How could you localize the content you are teaching?
3. Discuss the kinds of moment-to-moment shifts that teachers can use to go with the flow of the translanguaging corriente and teach content while building literacy. Do you engage in any of these shifts in your own instruction? What additional shifts have you taken to respond to your students' language practices to engage them with complex content and texts?

TAKING ACTION

1. Design a jigsaw activity or a text re-presentation activity for your classroom that explicitly includes translanguaging, ideally as part of the translanguaging unit design that you have been working on while reading this book. What resources do you need? How will you structure activities throughout the jigsaw or text re-presentation to leverage the translanguaging corriente in your class?
2. Implement your chosen activity and then think about the following on your own or with a group of colleagues:
   a. How did the ways that you grouped students, differentiated texts, and provided affordances support students' efforts to engage with complex content and texts?
   b. How did students make use of their own translanguaging throughout the activity?
   c. What shifts did you make to go with the flow of the translanguaging corriente as you implemented this activity?

12

Biliteracy in the Translanguaging Classroom

LEARNING OBJECTIVES

After reading this chapter, you will be able to:

- Describe how translanguaging reshapes traditional conceptualizations of biliteracy.
- Analyze the differences between traditional models of biliteracy and the flexible multiple model of biliteracy used in translanguaging classrooms.
- Describe how teachers can implement a flexible model of biliteracy through their translanguaging stance, design, and shifts.
- Design and implement activities that use translanguaging to engage students with complex biliteracy texts in your classroom.

Biliteracy is an explicit goal and anticipated outcome in bilingual education programs; students are expected to read and write in two languages across content areas. Biliteracy, as described by Hornberger (1990), is a highly important element of all translanguaging classrooms—bilingual *and* English-medium. For Hornberger, biliteracy includes "any and all instances in which communication occurs in two or more languages *in or around writing*" (p. 213, italics added for emphasis). Many examples throughout this book illustrate how ***Stephanie*** and ***Justin*** leverage students' bilingualism in and around literacy in their English-medium classrooms. Here, we look more closely at how ***Carla*** uses a flexible, dynamic model of biliteracy in her dual-language bilingual education (DLBE) classroom.

This chapter begins with a broad look at different models of biliteracy found in bilingual schools today and reimagines what biliteracy—as an explicit instructional goal and as a language practice—might look like from a translanguaging perspective. Then, returning to Carla's DLBE classroom, you will see how she leverages the translanguaging corriente to promote biliteracy in her class through her stance, design, and shifts. As you read, you are encouraged to consider how you could use translanguaging to strengthen biliteracy in your bilingual classroom.

DYNAMIC BILITERACY

The concept of biliteracy has a long history (Goodman et al., 1979; Hornberger, 1990; Pérez & Torres-Guzmán, 1992; Reyes, 1992, among others). Perhaps the most consequential model for understanding biliteracy not simply as the acquisition, learning, and teaching of texts in two languages was Nancy Hornberger's *continua of biliteracy* (1990). Hornberger proposed that the process of acquiring biliteracy is *dynamic,* existing within a multidimensional changing space that is shaped by individual, interpersonal, and societal forces. The expansion of Hornberger's *continua,* co-authored by Ellen Skilton-Sylvester (2000) proposed that each continuum was embedded in a historical matrix of power relations that impacted how communication around two languages in or around writing took place.

The goal of biliteracy is slowly but surely being embraced in the United States. DLBE programs are more popular than ever, and the Seal of Biliteracy continues to be adopted in an increasing number of states (currently 48 states and the District of Columbia offer biliteracy seals, and approximately 91,000 seals were earned nationwide in 2018 [Arellano, 2022]). However, a clear definition of biliteracy is not found in most policy discussions, nor are clear articulations of different pathways to biliteracy.

Models of Biliteracy

García (2009) posited four models of language and literacy use in biliteracy practices found in different types of bilingual education programs. They are as follows:

1. **Convergent monoliterate model.** This model uses two languages (English and a language other than English [LOTE]) to discuss an English language text. The objective, however, is simply comprehension of the English written text. In this sense, it is not truly a biliterate model.

   English and LOTE ——————> English text/literacy

2. **Convergent biliterate model.** This model uses texts in two languages with a goal of literacy in English. Although texts written in two languages are used, minority literacy practices are simply calqued or copied from majority literacy practices. For example, in many English-Spanish bilingual programs, initial literacy in Spanish is often taught in ways that mimic the reading strategies used to decode English, based on phonemic awareness and phonics. But Spanish, unlike English, is considered a transparent language because of the consistency in pronunciation and the written form. Thus, in learning to read Spanish, it is the syllable that is key. Yet little attention is paid to the syllable in many English-Spanish bilingual programs because the goal is not really biliteracy, but simply literacy in English.

   English and LOTE calqued on English ——————> English text/literacy

3. **Separation biliterate model.** Here, one language or the other is used to interact with a text written in one language or the other, but there is strict separation based on the sociocultural and discourse literacy norms of the cultures that the texts represent. In practice, however, sociocultural and discourse norms of Spanish-speaking cultures are rarely reflected in bilingual programs. This is the biliteracy model found in many dual-language bilingual classrooms where there is strict separation of languages.

   English ——————> English text/literacy
   LOTE ——————> LOTE text/literacy

4. **Flexible multiple model.** In this case, the two languages are used to interact with texts written in both languages and in other media, according to a bilingual flexible norm capable of both integration and separation.

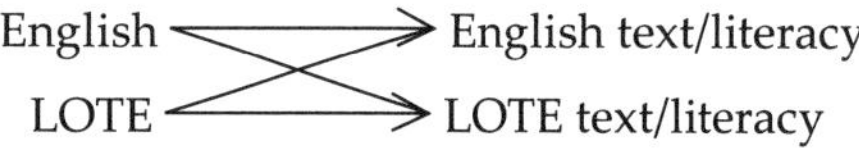

Traditional bilingual education classrooms most often follow either the convergent biliterate model or the separation biliterate model. The convergent biliterate model is generally found in **transitional bilingual education** classrooms, where reading and writing are performed in two languages but usually following the reading and writing norms of English, since the goal is literacy in English. As noted before, the separation biliterate model is generally found in DLBE classrooms, where the use of English and Spanish in literacy activities always occurs separately. Students read in one language and write in the same language.

In contrast to the convergent and separation biliterate models, the **flexible multiple model** reflects the type of biliteracy that is found in translanguaging classrooms, whether officially English-medium or bilingual (for more on how this model of translanguaging biliteracy is recognized in practice, see Johnson & García, 2023). Translanguaging pedagogical practices in instruction and assessment encourage bilingual students to draw on the full features of their linguistic repertoires to read texts in different languages as they think, discuss, interact with, and produce oral and written texts. The flexible multiple model reflects the type of biliteracy that Escamilla et al. describe in *Literacy Squared* (2014), where literacy contexts and topics across languages are interrelated and cross-language connections are made. It also aligns with recent biliteracy research from many scholars who attest that students' translanguaging must be "viewed as a strength that drives literacy" (Espinosa & Ascenzi-Moreno, 2021, p. 18; see also Bauer et al., 2020; España & Herrera, 2020; García & Kleifgen, 2020; Kabuto, 2022). This model is also enacted, as demonstrated later in this chapter, in Carla's DLBE classroom as she teaches for biliteracy.

Though they often follow the separation biliterate model, some DLBE classrooms do create *translanguaging spaces* within programmatic language policies. See how former teacher and current researcher Dr. Gladys Aponte did this in her fourth-grade DLBE classroom in the CUNY-NYSIEB web series "Teaching Bilinguals (Even If You're Not One)." You can access the video via the Brookes Download Hub.

Broad Notion of Texts and Literacies

The written texts used in a translanguaging classroom have a myriad of forms. Sometimes the texts are *monolingual* and are discussed using language practices that are different from those featured in the text. Sometimes the texts are *bilingual*, meaning they have translations with different layouts—often formatted side by side, sometimes top and bottom, and other times at the end. Sometimes the texts have been *constructed using translanguaging*, meaning that the two languages are used in relationship with each other throughout the text. For example, the dialogue between characters in a story is presented in different languages or with features that are considered two languages. (For a discussion and typology of how language and language ideologies are presented in bilingual children's books, see Przymus & Lindo, 2021.) The features of what are traditionally thought of as belonging to two different autonomous languages are used sin fronteras to enable bilingual voices to emerge.

Keep in mind that texts are not only in print format. Sometimes they are audio-based, in the form of oral interactions, or visual, in the form of videos or movies. Most of the time texts' multimodalities are experienced simultaneously. For example, shared reading practices enable students to see, listen to, and speak about the text at the same time. It is also possible to view a video clip, read its subtitles, and listen to the text in the language of the subtitles or the video itself. When we write, we read silently to ourselves, listen to what the text says and the way it sounds in our heads, and often use internal dialogue or make notes as we read the text. So how we interact with text requires all our meaning-making resources to make sense of texts and to create new ones. In the case of bilingual students, this means leveraging all their language and semiotic (meaning-making) resources to engage with and produce complex texts.

Translanguaging is important in developing biliteracy because a bilingual's inner voice (the **intrapersonal voice**) always contains features that are traditionally considered two languages but that, to the bilingual, are a single, complete language repertoire. That is, even with a monolingually written text, a bilingual student is always *constructing meaning bilingually* to make connections to themselves, their worlds, and to the texts of those worlds. When teachers require bilingual students to use only one language as they engage with texts inter- and intrapersonally, they limit these students' opportunities to learn.

Translanguaging offers a way for students to draw on the diverse aspects of Hornberger's **continua of biliteracy**. Hornberger (2005) adds, "Bi/multilinguals' learning is maximized when they are allowed and enabled to draw from across all their existing language skills (in two+ languages), rather than being constrained and inhibited from doing so by monolingual instructional assumptions and practices" (p. 607). A translanguaging classroom helps students use their entire language repertoires to develop a dynamic biliteracy, a way of interacting with texts that focuses on how and why texts are used. Teachers sustain and shape the many ways that translanguaging generates thinking, expression, and creativity as they encourage and enhance students' biliterate performances.

Multiple Pathways

In a traditional bilingual classroom that uses traditional biliteracy instruction for emergent and experienced bilinguals, the course from home language to new language is generally represented as linear and unidirectional, moving from home to school. Even in DLBE programs where Spanish literacy is a goal, the ways of using Spanish permitted in schools move away from local varieties of Spanish used in U.S. Spanish-speaking communities and toward a more "standard" Spanish. Acquiring a new language in any type of program is also generally represented as a linear, stage-like process, with students moving from, for example, *entering* to *emerging* to *developing* to *expanding* to *commanding*. From this perspective, students at particular stages of new language development are expected to be able to do certain things with language and not others; thus, teachers often deny students access to texts that are beyond their level. Because learning is represented as more-or-less straightforward and linear, the roles of teachers and students in reading instruction are often described in terms of three stages: teacher-directed (the teacher reads *to* the students), shared responsibility (the teacher reads *with* the students), and independent production (texts are read *by* the students). That is, the teacher first leads the actions and then turns over the actions to the students.

The movement in the translanguaging classroom is very different. Students do not have to wait to act by themselves until they reach a particular developmental stage. The translanguaging design for instruction and assessment allows teachers to move seamlessly among the three roles (reading *to* students, *with* students, and *by* students) because students are always actively performing tasks, even when they are new to English. Teachers use translanguaging strategies and shifts to adapt to the ecology of the classroom, the tasks at hand, and the individual student's positioning with regard to the content and language demands of the text. Teachers continually identify what students and their families know and can do with content, language, and literacy, and they help students make connections between home language and literacy practices and the language-specific practices required at school. Because students' language and literacy practices are so varied, and because the translanguaging corriente differs across contexts, teachers in translanguaging classrooms emphasize multiple pathways to biliteracy.

STANCE: RE-MEDIATING LITERACY JUNTOS

Since the enactment of No Child Left Behind (2001), and with current trends in English literacy around science of reading, the literacy education of emergent bilinguals has been increasingly remedial and prescriptive, devoid of important linguistic and cultural practices (Hruby, 2020), and focused solely on the teaching of basic skills. It has also followed ways of teaching reading in English, a language written in Latin script. However, many emergent bilinguals use languages that are not written in Latin script, and many of these languages, such as Chinese, have ideographic systems. Although Spanish, like English, is written in Latin script, it also behaves differently from English.

Rather than take up a remedial approach to teaching literacy, Carla's translanguaging stance leads her to focus on *re-mediating* literacy. Gutiérrez et al. (2009) refer to the concept of re-mediation as "a framework for the development of rich learning ecologies in which all students can expand their repertoires of practice" (p. 227). Carla understands that literacy is not an autonomous skill, that it is also *mediated* by social, cultural, political, and economic factors (Street, 1984) as well as the actors and elements involved in the literacy act. Carla's translanguaging stance demands that reading to learn has to be done juntos—using all students' language practices and with the help of other people and technology—while acknowledging the influence of culture on literacy practices.

Recall that Carla teaches in a DLBE program in New Mexico that stresses the separation of Spanish and English for instructional purposes, similar to many such programs in New Mexico and throughout the United States. However, Carla has carved out a space for translanguaging where she and her students bring Spanish and English together and draw on their bilingualism and ways of knowing. Carla calls this space Cuéntame Algo. During this instructional time, Carla and her students draw on the full features of their linguistic and cultural repertoires as they make connections between home, school, and community language and literacy practices.

Carla's translanguaging stance reflects her understanding that there is no such thing as academic language per se (although there are ways of using language differently for academic purposes), or even English or Spanish per se (although there are ways of using what is known as English or Spanish in certain settings). Instead, Carla recognizes that her bilingual students develop their language and cultural practices as they move between home, school, and other key contexts in their everyday lives. Thus, when bilingual students use language for academic purposes in either English or Spanish at school, we can expect to find language features generally associated with home and community settings. Likewise, when bilingual students use language for specific purposes at home and in the community, listeners are likely to find features that are associated with academic settings. Teachers can also strengthen these home, school, and community connections by encouraging the translanguaging corriente to flow.

Carla's teaching also reflects her stance that biliteracy practices are jointly constructed with others in communicative activities through two or more languages around writing. For example, she provides students with bilingual and multimodal texts (both fiction and nonfiction) from published sources and from the community. She integrates the language used in academic texts in one language or the other with those of bilingual community members, and she encourages her students to take a holistic view of their bilingual linguistic repertoires, using different linguistic features to strengthen their literacy performances and develop their voices.

Carla's ideological orientation is enacted by how she treats the language and literacy practices of the home and community as resources in her pedagogy, encouraging the translanguaging corriente to flow freely. In her classroom, knowledge is drawn not only from the school but also from home, as teacher and students work *jointly* to include cuentos from home, community, and school in the translanguaging unit of instruction, Cuentos de la tierra y del barrio. Works of fiction are experienced not just as cuentos de hadas [fairy tales]. Rather, they are placed alongside nonfiction texts—including the oral histories of family and community members—so that fiction can be seen as a mirror of life and nonfiction can be understood as another cuento. Thus, Carla constructs biliteracy in her classroom using home, school, and community practices juntos.

On a personal level, Carla is a bilingual, bicultural educator who understands the language practices of her students at home—neither solely English nor Spanish, neither solely oral nor written. Carla knows that her students' literacy practices are varied and include texting, posting on social media, using the Internet, using artificial intelligence, and reading from iPhones and other screens, all performed using their entire language repertoires. The space provided during Cuéntame Algo encourages students to value, support, and enact their biliteracy learning como la corriente. In so doing, students develop their bilingual identities as they leverage their bilingualism and ways of knowing.

DESIGN: BILITERACY ACOMPAÑAMIENTO

In traditional English as a second language (ESL) spaces, whether push-in, pull-out, or structured English immersion, classrooms students are given texts in English and asked to make sense of them (and produce them) in English only. In traditional bilingual classrooms, much biliteracy instruction is sequential, which means that students learn to read and write in one language first (usually their home language) before they are introduced to reading and writing activities in the additional language. Thus, when students are reading in a language that they are just learning (e.g., at the *entering* or *emerging* stages), they are only expected to perform low-level actions—"point," "draw," "sequence the pictures"—to demonstrate their comprehension of complex content and texts. In those cases, the teacher has to come up with a way of scaffolding literacy instruction that often seems artificial.

In a translanguaging biliteracy classroom, all students are expected to analyze, infer, synthesize, present evidence, and perform other higher order activities by drawing on the full features of their linguistic repertoires. At all times, even when students are reading or producing monolingual texts, they are using all their language resources, including the other language, to make meaning. Translanguaging classrooms enable bilingual students to display a wide range of general linguistic performances from the very beginning, including the following:

- Offering opinions on issues raised by texts, regardless of the language of the text
- Questioning the texts, regardless of the language of the text
- Discussing relationships among ideas in bilingual texts
- Evaluating different language features in the bilingual texts and explaining their meanings
- Comparing and contrasting language features and discourse structures in bilingual texts
- Extending their engagement with published texts by making connections to those produced by community members
- Using artificial intelligence to translate, interpret, and create texts

As students draw on their bilingualism and ways of knowing to demonstrate what they can do with their general and language-specific performances, they also have opportunities to develop their metalinguistic awareness and deepen their cultural understanding.

Students in Carla's classroom draw on the full features of their language repertoires as they participate in meaningful dialogue, conduct research, perform important literacy tasks as translators and linguists, create their own cuentos and scripts, make multimedia presentations, and even write sophisticated argumentative texts. Recall the varied profiles of our four focal students:

- ***Erica*** was born in New Mexico, although her parents were born in Puerto Rico. She speaks mostly English at home. Erica can speak, read, write, and comprehend Spanish and English. Her reading and writing in Spanish and English are just about grade level, but she is much more comfortable speaking English than Spanish.
- ***Jennifer*** is of Mexican descent, was born in the United States, and is learning Spanish at school. At home, Jennifer speaks English to her mother and siblings and Spanish to her grandmother. Jennifer reads at grade level in Spanish and above grade level in English.
- ***Moisés*** emigrated from Mexico 2 years ago, can read and write at grade level in Spanish, and is officially designated as an English language learner (ELL). At home, Moisés communicates with his parents mostly in Spanish because they do not speak much English; however, with his siblings he most often uses both languages to interact and play.
- ***Ricardo*** emigrated from Mexico (where he learned through Spanish and Mixteco at school in Oaxaca) last year, is officially designated as an ELL, and scores below grade level in reading in Spanish and English. Ricardo communicates in Mixteco and Spanish with his family but uses some English with his younger siblings.

It is important to remember that in a traditional DLBE program, Erica and Jennifer would both be considered English dominant, and Moisés and Ricardo would both be considered Spanish-dominant ELLs. The bilingual profile that Carla uses allows her to find bilingual resources in every case that are masked by traditional labeling conventions. For example, Jennifer was identified as a student with a disability, which Carla knew often came with deficit perceptions of what Jennifer knew and could do. Carla used the bilingual profile tool to provide her with data that demonstrated that Jennifer's bilingualism and biliteracy scores were far from deficient; they were on or above grade level.

As demonstrated in Carla's translanguaging unit plan, "Cuentos de la tierra y del barrio," in Chapter 8, Carla taught fiction and nonfiction texts in multiple modalities in her literacy instruction. The unit included a large number of books in both English and Spanish about farming and soil conservation. For example, Carla chose the following texts in Spanish:

- Rudolfo Anaya's *The Santero's Miracle*
- Literature about gardening written by a local community leader
- Readings about local/global farming practices from websites and magazines
- Videos about local and global farming practices

In English, she chose the following:

- Fourth-grade social studies textbook
- Fourth-grade science textbook
- Readings about local/global farming practices taken from websites and magazines
- Videos about local and global farming practices

We turn now to Carla's classroom to see how she skillfully conducts **biliteracy acompañamiento** in ways that engage students deeply with texts.

Read-Aloud: Linking Language and Cultural Practices

During the Cuéntame Algo translanguaging space, Carla read en voz alta *The Santero's Miracle*, a bilingual cuento written by a local New Mexican writer, Rudolfo Anaya. In the story, Don Jacobo and his grandson are finishing a wood carving of San Isidro Labrador, the santo patrón of farmers, as a heavy snowstorm hits New Mexico. San Isidro works a miracle for the grandfather by clearing the road, making it possible for an ambulance to reach his sick vecino and for his children to get home for Christmas.

In the book, Anaya's English text has been translated into Spanish, and the English-Spanish texts are laid side by side or top and bottom. Carla reads some paragraphs in English and others in Spanish, and students participate in the collaborative dialogue that ensues without regard to the language in which she reads. As they read el cuento en voz alta, they drew the action of the text on chart paper (Figure 12.1). Although the book was written in both languages, and Carla read some text in English and some in Spanish, the dialogue was mostly in Spanish, so she decided to write the action of the text on the chart paper in Spanish.

Notice in the following vignette how a student's questions about the use of Spanish lead to a metalinguistic discussion about differences between Spanish and English, and about challenges with translation:

"Is 'm'ijo' even a word?" Jennifer asked. Ricardo responded that this was a word in Oaxaca. They then looked it up in the dictionary and couldn't find it. Moisés then said that it meant "mi ijo," but he still couldn't find "ijo" in the dictionary. Then Jennifer pointed out that "hijito" had an "h" and they wondered if this was why they couldn't find the word. They looked up "hijo" and found it. Jennifer said, "The problem is Spanish. In English we hear the 'h,' so we wouldn't be confused." After much disagreement with Jennifer's statement, they discussed what "hijito" meant. Ricardo said that his family often called him "Ricardito," and then Jennifer chimed in, "I call my grandmother abuelita." They asked Carla why some Spanish words use "ito/ita," and together they decided it meant "little." Carla told them this was called a "diminutive."

Carla then gave them a sentence from the cuento: "Don Jacobo se bajó de la cama, se vistió y fue a la ventana para ver el pueblo entero." She asked the students to add the suffix "ito/ita" whenever possible and discuss what it did to the meaning of the sentence. She then asked them, "What is necessary to create the same sentence in English?" The class came up with an English translation with which they were totally

unsatisfied. For example, Jennifer said, "Little village is not the same as a pueblito. You love a pueblito, and that's why you add 'ito.' It has nothing to do with size!" Carla then talked about the complexities of translation. She pointed out that this particular book had a translator. The class discussed the well-respected (and well-paid) profession of translator. Erica said that she was always translating for her family and didn't get paid! Although they all laughed, they agreed that they did much translating in their families and that this was a valuable skill.

Carla then engaged students in a metalinguistic discussion of how bilingual authors make choices about language having to do with what they want to express. They also discussed the importance of biliteracy. Referring back to the cuento, Carla reminded them that Don Jacobo and his grandson worked all day on the wood carving of San Isidro and spent a lot of time selecting and mixing the colors to get the right shade. She then told them, "It says in the story: 'All day they worked at painting the carving.' Authors have to do the same thing with their words." And Erica exclaimed, "Yes, but as bilinguals we can paint with more colors. We have to use all our colors!"

As demonstrated in this vignette, reading, writing, listening, and speaking are experienced en acompañamiento, as are all the linguistic features of the children's two languages. Carla's use of translanguaging with her bilingual students in the discussion following the read-aloud provided many opportunities for metalinguistic analysis. The strict separation of the two languages that we see in traditional DLBE programs would have made this kind of opportunity unavailable.

In the following excerpt from the same class discussion, students' questioning of the text leads to an exploration of cultural practices and ways of knowing, again made possible by translanguaging:

During the reading of the story, Erica heard the word santero and jumped up. She told the class that in Puerto Rico, where her family came from, a santero was not someone who carved images of santos, but someone who practiced a religion that she was unfamiliar with and who dressed in white. Moisés got very excited and said, "Mentira. Mi mamá es católica, y ella siempre le reza a sus santos, y no se viste de blanco." [That's a lie. My mother is Catholic, and she always prays to her saints, and she doesn't dress in white.] Carla decided that she needed to respond to Moisés in Spanish and that this would be a good topic to pursue for research—the meanings of santeros and santos. In Spanish, she gave the class an assignment. They were to go home and interview their family members about their understanding of the words santos and santero, take notes on what the families said, and be ready to do an oral report to the class.

Carla is always looking for ways to build student engagement with texts, especially when students question the text or each other. Carla goes with the flow of the translanguaging corriente and adds a new activity to the unit—the family interview—to help students understand differences in the terms santos and santeros and gain a deeper understanding of associated cultural practices and ways of knowing.

This next excerpt is another example of how the read-aloud can engage students with each other and with the text when they discover shared background experiences and knowledge:

When Carla got to the part in the story where the grandfather repeated a well-known prayer to San Isidro, she made sure to read the rhyme in Spanish. Immediately Moisés said, "No es lo que digo" [It's not what I say], and he added, "San Isidro Labrador, quita el agua y pon el sol." [Saint Isidro the farmer, take away the rain and make it sunny.] And Erica exclaimed, "That's also what we say in my family when we want the rain to stop!" They then had a discussion about the role of the rain and the sun in farming.

In this case, Moisés questions the text because the prayer that he knows is not what is written in the text. His engagement with the text functions to bring Moisés and Erica closer together, because their families (one Mexican that uses largely Spanish at home and the other Puerto Rican that uses largely English at home) say the same prayer for sun.

After the discussion, which focused primarily on the meaning of the text, Carla invited her students to reflect on how the author chose to use translanguaging in his text. Anaya's text in English was peppered with words that some would call "Spanish" but that for many bilinguals are just part of their lexicon. Carla pointed this out to her students, and together they made a list of those words. In groups of four they then discussed why these words and not others were written in Spanish. The groups reported back to the class, and with Carla's help they came up with these categories:

- Informal greetings and interactions: "Buenos días," "Vamos," "Gracias," "Entre" "¿Qué pasa?"
- Terms of relationship and endearment: "abuelo/a," "hijito," "compadre," "m'ijo," "mujer," "amor"
- Food: "tortillas," "posole," "biscochitos"
- Other cultural practices: "santero," "santo"

Carla and her students discussed ways that authors use language to involve particular audiences in the texts they create, in this case using Spanish to invoke authentic cultural practices in U.S. Latinx homes.

Assessing Learning: Writing a Research Report Carla pays attention not only to instruction, but also to the close assessment of how her students engage with texts and use language (general linguistic and language-specific performances) to describe, explain, question, report, and so forth. Carla uses the *Teacher's Assessment Tool* (see Appendix 8.1), which she complements with other assessments, to yield a more holistic portrait of what students can do with content, literacy, and language on different tasks throughout the translanguaging unit of instruction. For example, one of Carla's culminating projects asks students to individually write a research report about local farming practices using text-based evidence, local sources, and human resources to support their positions. Students present their arguments to their peers and then to the school community during the annual open house.

First, Carla told her students to go home and share what they had learned about the story with their families, using the *Family Assessment Tool: La conexión* (see Chapter 8). Carla specifically had students ask their families for stories about farming and legends of San Isidro.

Carla then put students into groups of four and asked each group to write a research report putting together the findings from their families on cultural practices about farming and San Isidro. She also asked them to conduct Internet research using websites in English and Spanish. Carla instructed some groups to write in Spanish and others to write in English. She also told them to quote directly from the texts they had gathered from friends, family, and the Internet in whatever language they had read or heard them. Carla reminded them that Rudolfo Anaya had chosen some words to render in Spanish and that they could do the same. She explained to them that they would then use their research reports to make a public oral presentation to the school community.

The culminating research report for this part of the unit reflects Carla's juntos stance. For Carla and her students, reading *The Santero's Miracle* was a translanguaging literacy event where they strategically used Spanish and English juntos, orally and in writing. Carla's translanguaging design also enabled the bilingual students to make use of all their language and cultural resources juntos, while bringing home and school experiences juntos. These translanguaging practices encouraged students to engage with complex content and texts while deepening their experiences reading and writing monolingual and bilingual texts. Students demonstrated their performances through different tasks leading up to and including the research report that each group wrote.

I was educated to see language separation as an ideal practice. And just like Carla, I spoke my students' home languages and adhered to the macro-level language policy of my school. Following Carla's example, I regularly used translanguaged text readings along with translanguaged writing activities in practice. I noticed that translanguaged writing activities helped my students worry less about making mistakes, and thus they wrote for longer and provided many details using their whole linguistic repertoire during the writing process.

—Maira Klyshbekova, former English language teacher in a trilingual school in Kazakhstan and current Ph.D. candidate, University of Sheffield, Sheffield, United Kingdom

Close Reading: Using the Full Features of Students' Linguistic Repertoires

Later in the unit, Carla formed heterogenous groups of four students, taking into consideration the details of their language profiles, their autobiographical translanguaging portraits, and their different performances in Spanish and English. Each group read a different story about farming and soil conservation. Some groups read in English and others in Spanish, although each group had access to resources in both languages, including peers who could translate, iPads, and bilingual dictionaries. Carla grouped both Moisés and Ricardo, students whose English literacy performances were still developing, with two more experienced bilinguals so that they would have access to peers who would facilitate their reading of the English text. In this case, Carla wanted to make sure that Moisés and Ricardo grappled with a complex text in English, and she supported their work by providing additional Spanish texts on the same topic. Carla included both Jennifer and Erica in the group that was reading in Spanish because they were both more comfortable reading in English, and Carla knew that they needed the extra challenge of reading in Spanish. Jennifer and Erica were supported by peers with more literacy experience in Spanish and other resources. Students worked in their groups to do a close reading of their assigned texts:

Although groups of students were reading a text in either English or Spanish, they were using all their language resources to make meaning. That is, they were actively using translanguaging as they discussed and strategically raised questions about the text being read and provided answers. They also took notes with all their language resources for a later discussion.

Carla, working with individual groups, some in English, some in Spanish, through this close reading activity reminded them to use the general questions that were visible in a large classroom poster. These questions, in both English and Spanish, included the following:

- What picture or drawing could help me understand this text? [¿Qué fotografía o dibujo me puede ayudar a entender este texto?]
- Visualiza. ¿Qué sientes, hueles, o oyes? Explica. [Visualize. What do you feel, smell, and hear? Explain.]
- What does the text remind you of? In your life or experiences? In other texts that you've read? [¿De qué te recuerda el texto? ¿En tu vida? ¿En otro texto que hayas leído?]
- ¿De qué se trata el texto? [What is the text about?]

Carla also encouraged students to seek her support, as well as that of each other, as they read and took notes about the topic. As she walked around the room, she supported the students by paraphrasing ideas in Spanish or English, as appropriate, and reminded them to use their iPads and bilingual dictionaries.

Besides the close reading of bilingual published texts that told cuentos about farming and soil conservation, Carla and her students drew on cuentos from community and family members about the history of farming practices in New Mexico. Carla wanted her students to understand that la tierra y los barrios go through changes. For homework, the students were told to ask family or community members for cuentos de la tierra in New Mexico (or Mexico or other countries) and to take notes on the cuentos told by different people in various ways and with different language practices. Carla wanted to ensure that her students understood that reading meant engaging not only with published written fiction and nonfiction texts that they read at school but also with oral stories from their homes and the larger community.

Assessing Learning: Writing an Argumentative Essay Prepared with the deep knowledge that came from examining texts closely, both established ones written by published authors and those produced by community members, the students were ready for the culminating project of the unit's lessons—the writing of an argumentative essay. To do this, the students kept in mind the following essential question listed in Carla's translanguaging unit plan: how do communities interact with one another and their environments?

In their groups, students shared ideas and brainstormed about the position they would take in their collectively written argumentative essay on whether farming and the soil in el jardín del barrio was better or worse than in the time of their parents and grandparents and to consider and engage with other voices, possibilities, and perspectives. They were told to identify text-based evidence to support their positions as they debated the topic and came to agreement about which position they would support in their essays.

Carla referred the class to the bilingual bulletin board, where she had placed two mentor texts, one argumentative essay in English and one in Spanish, which had been written by students from her previous fourth-grade class. She read each example, giving students opportunities to ask clarifying questions and make recommendations as to how to extend the arguments made.

The students were then asked to choose one language in which to write, rendering the final argumentative text in only one language. To help them make this determination, Carla asked the groups, "Which audience are you writing for? To whom are you making the argument?" She continued, "The answer to these questions will help you determine the language and language practices that you would want to include in your essay." Once the groups had selected the language of publication of their argumentative essay,

Carla reminded them that it was possible to use the other language to make the writing more authentic, in the same way that Rudolfo Anaya had done.

Individual students then prewrote in the language of their choice. For example, as expected, Moisés and Ricardo prewrote in Spanish, but Erica and Jennifer did so in English. In their groups, they read each other's prewriting and made observations on how to extend arguments and use evidence. They then started to write their group's argumentative essay in the language they had selected for their chosen audience.

Writing in Carla's classroom is always accompanied by collective thinking, speaking, listening, and reading. That is why so much time is spent leveraging the students' collective language and literacy practices to discuss and find text-based evidence in readings. Carla's biliteracy acompañamiento approach allows her to continuously assess what students know, inviting their self-reflection and that of the peer group, and also inviting family members to contribute.

Strategies for Deep Engagement with Texts

The teacher's translanguaging unit plan and the translanguaging design cycle provide structures to support students' efforts to generate questions and think deeply about texts, interact meaningfully with texts, and design and perform texts for specific purposes. These types of literacy practices are key to academic success and beyond.

Carla provides students with opportunities to learn and use these kinds of strategies throughout the unit design cycle. For example, Carla uses bilingual read-alouds and multimodal texts and encourages her students to engage in discussion of the texts that they read, using their own voices and language practices, not just those of the chosen text. Carla also observes and documents the concrete strategies that her students use to engage with texts:

- Moisés made sense of the text by doing a close read and jotting notes and questions in the margins in English and Spanish. To better understand the main ideas and concepts, he asked his peers for help and used his iPad for translations.
- Erica read the Spanish text that was assigned to her group, but she wrote notes and questions in English.
- Jennifer collaborated closely with Moisés by reviewing the main ideas and concepts that he had written in Spanish. She asked clarifying questions in both English and Spanish to make sure she understood what he wrote.
- Ricardo translated key terms from English to Spanish in the text he was reading. He frequently asked questions of his peers, asked Carla for help, and looked for other resources on the iPad.

These are just a few of the ways that teachers can use the translanguaging design to enact biliteracy acompañamiento in the bilingual classroom. This approach to teaching for biliteracy accomplishes much that is impossible when the two languages are kept strictly separate. Carla's translanguaging design for biliteracy instruction and assessment meets students where they are, links home and school language and cultural practices, identifies and builds on students' general linguistic and language-specific performances, strengthens students' metalinguistic awareness and cultural understanding, and propels their content, language, and literacy learning forward.

SHIFTS: MOVING "UNMOVABLE" TEXTS

Carla makes moment-by-moment shifts in her instruction and assessment as she strategically adapts her language practices to those of her students. This does not mean that Carla uses one or the other language randomly. Rather, Carla plans the language of the texts that they read and write, but she frequently goes outside of the design that she had planned in order to follow the translanguaging corriente more freely. For example, when Moisés reacted in Spanish to Erica's meaning of santos, Carla immediately understood that she needed to discuss this matter, and follow it up, in Spanish, although this was not part of her design.

Teachers in translanguaging classrooms challenge the notion that written texts are often considered "unmovable"—written in one language or the other in static ways. Translanguaging enables teachers to strategically shift the course of instruction and assessment to put the readers (and not simply the authors of the texts) in charge of the text. Furthermore, translanguaging allows readers to "hear" the written text in their heads a través de/through their own language practices. Only by creating an intimate relationship with the text can readers generate deep meaning and create new texts. Teachers have to engage in these moment-by-moment shifts because they cannot possibly anticipate all of their students' responses to texts.

CONCLUSION

Translanguaging enables bilingual students to become better readers and writers in two languages, precisely because all their language resources are put in the service of (re)constructing text in their own voices, even when the text is monolingual. Unlike traditional bilingual classrooms, translanguaging classrooms take up a flexible multiple model of biliteracy. When students own the language of the text itself—even if only "in their heads"—they can become good readers and writers, especially in two languages.

At times, translanguaging classrooms also promote the use of language features that are considered two languages when constructing texts. By representing the language practices of bilinguals in the same text, the translanguaging classroom legitimizes students' dynamic bilingualism. Translanguaging is not just a scaffold for one language or the other. Reading and writing translanguaged texts show the potential of a bilingual repertoire for both academic and home functions. It also enables a student to write using their own voice, one that is bilingual and expresses multiple, dynamic ways of knowing el texto y el contexto.

REFLECTION QUESTIONS AND ACTIVITIES

1. Consider the four models of biliteracy posited by García (2009) and reviewed in this chapter. What models have you observed or worked with?
2. Identify the types of texts that use translanguaging and consider how you can use them in your classes.
3. Do you see translanguaging as simply a scaffold to literacy in an additional language or as a resource for becoming better readers and writers in an additional language or in two languages? Explain the reasons for your answer.

TAKING ACTION

1. Where do you see an opportunity to move toward a flexible, multiple model of biliteracy in your context? Work with a group of like-minded educators in your teaching context to carve some space for translanguaging within your programmatic language policies.
2. Design a lesson, ideally within the context of the unit plan you are developing while reading this book, and implement that lesson. If possible, videotape your lesson and look closely at the video, thinking about the following questions:
    - How does your lesson reflect a flexible, multiple model of biliteracy?
    - How do you use translanguaging strategies to promote dynamic biliteracy among your students?
    - How do your students take up these opportunities?

13

Socioemotional Well-Being and Social Justice

LEARNING OBJECTIVES

After reading this chapter, you will be able to:

- Describe how translanguaging supports bilingual students' socioemotional well-being through valorización.
- Explain how translanguaging classrooms can advance social, cognitive, and racial justice.
- Identify how you can use translanguaging to foster your students' socioemotional well-being and critical consciousness and grow their understanding of raciolinguistic ideologies.

The translanguaging corriente is the key to translanguaging classrooms. To feel the translanguaging corriente, all you have to do is take a step back from your daily routine and listen and look. Listen hard to what your students say to you and their peers inside the classroom, hallways, and cafeteria and on the playground. If you listen hard enough, you might be able to perceive their intrapersonal voices (what they're saying in their heads, in imaginary dialogues with themselves and their friends). Listen also to the conversations that take place when their families and peers are present; try to hear what is being said and how it is said, as well as what is not being said and why. Look at what they're doing with their bodies. Examine their gaze, their gestures, how they are relating to others. Listening, looking, and perceiving in this way allows you to understand your students' voices anew and puts you in touch with the flow of the translanguaging corriente, even if it is not obviously at the surface of your classroom.

Look at your students through a translanguaging lens. Focus so that you see, as Patricia Carini (2000) always says, the whole child. Observe closely so that you can describe fully what the student is doing with language. When, with whom, and where is the student languaging in certain ways? Let the students' language practices bloom by giving them control of the tasks at hand or putting them in situations where they're interacting freely with others. After listening deeply to the students in your class and seeing them in their entirety, you become aware of their languaging. And if your students are bilingual, you will come into contact with the translanguaging corriente. Let the translanguaging corriente flow through your classroom. What happens? What is the translanguaging corriente able to do for your teaching and your students' learning? How do we nurture the intellectual abilities of our students by tapping into their corriente?

Once you feel the translanguaging corriente, you are unable to ignore it, and you learn to use the translanguaging pedagogy purposefully and strategically to:

1. Support students as they engage with complex content and texts.
2. Provide opportunities for students to develop linguistic practices for a variety of purposes and contexts, including those deemed academic.
3. Support students' bilingual identities, socioemotional development, and critical consciousness and disrupt ideologies that render bilingual students as deficient.
4. Make space for all students' language practices and ways of knowing, thus building a classroom and society that is inclusive of linguistic, racial, gender, and ability differences.

Your teaching will then acquire a higher purpose, advancing social, racial, and cognitive justice, ensuring that bilingual students, especially those who come from language minority groups, are instructed and assessed in fair and equitable ways.

This concluding chapter highlights two fundamental reasons for education—upholding and supporting the socioemotional strength of students and advancing social justice for the improvement of society as a whole. Placing these two goals alongside each other emphasizes that it is impossible to uphold and support the socioemotional strength of each individual student without also considering the sociopolitical and economic context in which bilingual students are being educated.

STANCE: CON RESPETO, CON CARIÑO, COMO FAMILIA, Y CON ACOMPAÑAMIENTO

The development of students' socioemotional well-being is an important part of teaching, for one cannot learn without feeling secure in one's own identity and performances. A translanguaging classroom provides extended opportunities for bilingual students to be valued participants who draw on rich linguistic and cultural resources for learning. Thus, a translanguaging classroom enables students to create identities for themselves that are also academic.

Teachers in translanguaging classrooms believe that, as ***Carla*** put it, "la enseñanza y el aprendizaje comienzan valorizando a nuestros estudiantes." [Teaching and learning begin with valuing our students.] This valorización derives from teachers' understanding about what their students can do and from how translanguaging both uncovers and strengthens those assets. Here, four elements of the translanguaging classroom for socioemotional support are identified—con respeto, con cariño, como familia, y con acompañamiento:

1. *Con respeto* refers to the respect that needs to be shown for the struggles and ways of life of bilingual communities. This was the title of Valdés' (1996) study of 10 Mexican American families, mothers in a U.S.–Mexico border town. Translanguaging is a tool to teach con respeto because the students' language and cultural practices are valued, leveraged, and strengthened.
2. *Con cariño* means the authentic caring between teachers and students that is the core of the successful education of bilingual Latinx students.[1] However, con cariño goes beyond care; it builds on the love that brings juntos teachers, students, school, and community and English and other languages. Con cariño is at the core of the translanguaging classroom, where the languages of bilingual students are no longer conceived as separate but as working juntos. The translanguaging classroom recognizes not just a harmonious cariño, but an "armed love" to "fight, to denounce, and to announce" (Freire, 2008, p. 209). The language practices of bilinguals work con cariño to fight

[1]See especially Valenzuela, 1999; see also Bartlett and García, 2011; Bartolomé, 2008; García et al., 2013; and Johnson, 2013.

against their representation as autonomous languages in which bilingual practices are considered "illegitimate." Teaching from a con cariño stance begins with embodying a *moral ethic of cariño* (Lomelí, 2023) as a practice in one's own approach to teaching.

3. *Como familia* refers to how translanguaging classrooms are like familias, always acting together to promote the well-being of the whole, but sometimes also struggling with each individual member. It also refers to language practices that, like families, sometimes act juntos and sometimes as separate individuals. Furthermore, como familia refers to how pláticas/conversations in classrooms cannot just be about content or language, but also need to be about sharing inner truths, connecting deeply and feeling (Flores-Dueñas, 1999; Johnson, 2013).

4. *Con acompañamiento* (Sepúlveda, 2011) means that teachers in translanguaging classrooms accompany youth as they share stories and experiences. Further, the act of teaching con acompañamiento includes "not only 'being' with another, or feeling with another, but also 'doing' with another" (Goizueta, 2001, p. 206). Teachers in translanguaging classrooms set up instruction so that they and their students are always languaging and learning juntos. The students' voices are never just in English or Spanish; they are experienced con acompañamiento.

The translanguaging stance—understanding that the language features of your students' bilingual repertoires always function juntos—is the first step toward setting up a translanguaging classroom. This stance extends to understanding that language, literacy, and content are learned juntos, that students' home and school experiences go juntos, and that critical consciousness is developed juntos with meaningful learning. A translanguaging stance considers how teachers' perspectives and practices might be embodied juntos in their pedagogical practices. Further, this stance provides *pedagogical clarity*, which is the increased consciousness that teachers have of their own practice (Johnson, 2021). Consistent with Freire (1974), once teachers have this consciousness, they increasingly rely upon it in teaching and decision making.

Valorización of Students' Experiences

Supporting students' socioemotional positions con respeto, con cariño, como familia, y con acompañamiento means valuing their language and cultural practices as strengths in learning. In this vignette from Carla's translanguaging unit, Cuentos de la tierra y del barrio, Carla displays her stance of valorización of bilingualism and bilingual students through her assessment practices.

During the lesson of el jardín, Carla and Sonia wanted to "valorar el conocimiento y apresamiento que tenían los estudiantes hacia el jardín de su vecindad" [validate the knowledge and appreciation that the students had of their community garden]. Throughout the translanguaging unit design cycle, Carla immersed her students in authentic activities, discussed their performances with them, gave them further opportunities to show what they knew, and supported them in new ways of demonstrating their learning. She put her own collaborative assessment of students' performances alongside that of students in their self-assessment and of the peer groups in which they worked. Finally, she had students show their families what they had learned and enabled family members to give feedback.

Carla knew that her students' socioemotional states were important to their learning throughout the stages of the translanguaging instructional design cycle, especially during assessment. She understood that she could not just design assessments that evaluated student work and identified their weaknesses. Rather, she designed dynamic and flexible assessments that informed her understanding of what her students knew and could do, which contributed to the students' socioemotional well-being. Carla put her students first, and her primary purpose in assessing was not for herself as a teacher or for the school or state, although each of these constituencies is important. Her primary purpose in assessing was to allow her students to learn. She knew students had to feel secure in their bilingual identities and they had to feel positive about their lives inside and outside school.

Carla's assessment is intimately tied to her instruction. For example, she selected stories and contexts with which students could identify. She honored students' bilingual voices and practices. All instruction and assessment stemmed from Carla's stance that her students' socioemotional well-being was central to their learning and that a translanguaging classroom offered them the spaces to fortify their bilingual identities.

A valorización stance requires you to first ask yourself as an educator: "How do I view my students' home language and cultural practices? Do I see the students' bilingualism as a problem or a resource?" Teachers in translanguaging classrooms need to answer these questions with a moral ethic of cariño and con respeto for who their students are and what they bring with them to the classroom community to nurture their capacities.

DESIGN: VALORIZACIÓN DEL TEXTO Y CONTEXTO

Designing a translanguaging classroom to support bilingual students' socioemotional standing involves attention to the classroom space and the instructional and assessment design. Having a valorización design can improve bilingual students' educational experiences by sustaining and strengthening socioemotional qualities developed at home and throughout the community. We return to Carla's and ***Stephanie***'s classrooms for examples.

Carla treated her students con respeto, con cariño, como familia, y con acompañamiento and made the world around them and the words on the page more comprehensible by putting forward opportunities to learn from meaningful and relevant multilingual and multimodal texts. Her translanguaging unit plan validated and supported the students' biliterate lived experiences by having them read, write, and discuss bilingual Latinx textos and contextos. This affirmed the students' socioemotional strengths as Latinx bilingual students.

Carla designed her (bi)literacy lessons by first selecting stories that facilitated the use of textos bilingües written by well-known Latinx authors—Sara Poot Herrera's *Lluvia de plata*, Sandra Cisneros's *Three Wise Guys: Un Cuento de Navidad*, and Rudolfo Anaya's *The Santero's Miracle*. One of the activities that Carla used during her literacy time was Cuéntame Algo, which began with her reading en voz alta a bilingual text to her students. Carla also invited guest speakers, such as family members and community leaders, to platicar about their cultural practices, thus extending to a much broader contexto. The Cuéntame Algo activity culminated with the students using translanguaging to develop and write their own cuentos from the barrio, which were then performed by the students with community participation.

Carla opened up a space that offered the students opportunities to use their translanguaging to communicate their ideas about relevant textos and contextos with her. This meant that students felt socioemotionally supported at all times.

Carla designed her literacy activities knowing that each text needed to be read within a larger context. Carla knew that reading *Lluvia de plata* would generate a discussion with her students because many were from Chihuahua, Mexico. Through the Cuéntame Algo literacy activity, the students used their bilingual voices and identities, which affirmed their socioemotional well-being. By promoting the use of translanguaging to communicate their thoughts, feelings, imaginings, and curiosity, Carla was helping her students develop strong identities as Chicanx/Latinx bilinguals, not simply as speakers of English as a second language or speakers of Spanish as a **heritage language** who were not up to the standards of a so-called "native speaker" of one or the other language. Rather than identifying with labels that seem truncated, deficit-oriented, or dated (e.g., second, heritage), Carla's students are developing a sense of who they are as bilingual Americans. They are starting to view bilingual languaging as authentic and fuller than monolingual performances in one or the other language. Carla's design recognizes and draws out the students' dynamic bilingualism as a resource to be nurtured.

Stephanie's teaching with valorización was always present in her translanguaging classroom as well, even though she did not speak her students' home languages. Stephanie acompaña her students con cariño y respeto, as they provide socioemotional support for each other in learning. As demonstrated in earlier chapters, she involved all of her students in creating a public service announcement (PSA) for the school community, regardless of their levels of oral and written English.

Stephanie required every student in the group to participate in the presentation of their collaboratively created PSAs. To scaffold this work, she provided sentence frames to each group to help them prepare and encouraged them to act out with their bodies what they wanted the audience to feel. Stephanie explained to Noemí that she should do her best to explain the group's choice in English but that she could use Spanish, as well as images, to expand on or clarify ideas.

After students had presented to the class, Stephanie made copies of students' PSAs and asked her school principal if students could post them around the school. The principal agreed and even asked Stephanie if two students would explain the project to the community during the school's morning announcements. Stephanie asked Mariana and Luis to work together to come up with an explanation of the PSA assignment in both Spanish and English that they would read during the announcements the following week.

In Stephanie's instructional design, acompañamiento was always present as she designed lessons with appropriate scaffolding and mediation from other people and material resources. She grouped students for support. She provided students, especially emergent bilinguals like ***Noemí***, with sentence starters, frames, and translations as needed. She urged her bilingual students to use the full features of their linguistic repertoires to express their ideas. At the end of the preceding vignette, the students show what it means to acompañarse—with ***Mariana*** and ***Luis*** accompanying each other as they collaborated in sharing with the school community their PSAs in both English and Spanish. Students in Stephanie's class were never left to feel insecure about their identities, their understanding, or their language use. They were always acompañados.

There are many ways to set the course of the translanguaging corriente to build and strengthen bilingual students' socioemotional well-being within your instructional and assessment design:

- Group students con acompañamiento, as they would be in a familia, con cariño, y respeto, to encourage and foster their different strengths and insights.
- Open up a dialogue space that engages teacher and students in discussion about their insights and experiences inside and outside the classroom with all their language resources.
- Encourage the bilingual voices of community and families in the lessons using multilingual and multimodal texts, and invite family members to become the classroom's familia.
- Place students at the center of learning and teaching by encouraging them to draw on their bilingual language practices at school.
- Have students share with the entire school community their bilingual understanding, as well as their language and cultural practices.

These translanguaging pedagogical strategies are only effective within the context of an instructional design of valorización. Embodying valorización requires educators to have love and sensitivity toward their students. Carla's and Stephanie's translanguaging stances are then what shape their instruction with humanity.

The translanguaging design for instruction and assessment is central to the translanguaging classroom; it is what makes it different from a traditional monolingual or bilingual classroom. Designing instruction to set the course of the translanguaging corriente means that you enact a translanguaging stance to carefully plan its components—the grouping of students, elements of planning (big ideas and questions, content objectives, language objectives, translanguaging objectives, texts, culminating project), design cycle (explorar, evaluar, imaginar, presentar, implementar), and pedagogical strategies. It also means including the voices of others, taking into account the difference between content and language and between general linguistic and language-specific performances, and giving students opportunities to do tasks with assistance from others and other resources when needed. The translanguaging design is the structure that makes the translanguaging classroom purposeful and strategic.

SHIFTS: CHANGING COURSE TO VALORAR

Good teaching is not always planned. In the same way, a good translanguaging classroom does not always follow a strictly planned translanguaging design. Most of the moment-by-moment shifts that teachers make have to do with following the flow of the translanguaging corriente, and most of those on-the-spot moves have to do precisely with ensuring students' socioemotional well-being so that they can learn. For example, recall that when Carla was reading *Lluvia de plata*, ***Moisés*** shared the following:

> Esta parte que leí me gusta porque los trabajadores que construyeron el ferrocarril le llamaban al tren que venía de Kansas a Chihuahua "si te cansas." Yo creo que no sabían cómo decir Kansas entonces para recordar cómo decirlo solamente mencionaban "si te cansas." [This part that I read I liked because the workers who built the railroad would call the train coming from Kansas to Chihuahua "si te cansas"/"if you get tired." I think they did not know how to say Kansas, so to remember how to say it they would mention "si te cansas."]

Carla hadn't planned the larger contexto that emerged in this interaction. However, she could see that the play on words was familiar to the students in the broader contexto of the community. Her students felt valorados when they heard the expression "si te cansas." When one student said, "es como mi familia habla" [like my family speaks], Carla went with the flow. She responded not by immediately going back to her lesson plan, but by encouraging other stories. The dialogue that ensued not only affirmed the students' bilingual socioemotional identities, but also gave Carla further insight into how her bilingual students and their families practiced (bi)literacy.

To separate languages and identities is indeed to segregate and maintain bilingual students as the "other." Carla's shifts were encouraged by her valorización stance, which enabled her to deeply understand her students' socioemotional strengths and work as their ally in the translanguaging classroom.

Translanguaging teachers can use different kinds of unplanned moves to respond to the translanguaging corriente and affirm bilingual students' socioemotional well-being:

- Exemplify a valorización stance with love and sensitivity toward students' corriente.
- Listen to students and their cuentos, using all their language practices.
- Respond to students' performances in ways that are intimately tied to what students are doing, with whatever language practices.
- Value what students and families have to say (and how they say it) sufficiently to depart from your planned lesson (and your planned language use) as necessary.
- Be willing to change course when students' and families' cuentos bring perspectives and language choices other than the one of your lesson design.

The *shifts* that you make in response to the translanguaging corriente are important. You can use them intentionally and strategically, for example, to valorizar students' experiences, mobilize texts, and seize significant learning moments.

TRANSLANGUAGING AND SOCIAL JUSTICE

Teaching for social justice means working alongside your students to create a better and more equitable world. It means enabling students—especially those who have been historically marginalized—not only to read the word and the world (Freire & Macedo, 1987), but also to write and *rewrite* it using their own voices and unique ways of knowing. These acts of reading and (re)writing are, of course, intimately tied to language, as teachers develop the necessary *ideological* and *political clarity* (Bartolomé, 2008) "to recognize the structural relationships between schools and society that largely determine the successes and failures of students" (p. 376).

Teaching for social justice requires recognizing additional forces and flows that are so often intertwined with the translanguaging corriente. As Kate has written elsewhere (Seltzer, 2025), "these corrientes of power and, specifically, raciolinguistic ideologies which '[co-construct] language and race in ways that frame the language practices of racialized communities as inherently deficient' (Flores, 2019, p. 53) . . . are also ever-present, and thus, also rise to the surface when teachers invite students' translanguaging." Thus, social justice encompasses, as mentioned in Chapter 2, racial and cognitive justice. A translanguaging pedagogy has the potential to disrupt these additional corrientes of power hierarchies and ideologies that racialize bilingual speakers and construct them as deficient and ignorant (García et al., 2021). By raising the critical consciousness of teachers and students, a translanguaging pedagogy can also provide a measure of cognitive justice, ensuring that education does not simply reproduce the values and knowledge systems of the powerful Global North (Santos, 2018).

For emergent bilinguals, being able to share their experiences and produce academic work that contributes to a larger sociopolitical conversation can only be achieved when they have access to all of their linguistic and knowledge system resources. For those bilinguals who are proficient in English, translanguaging enables them to put their whole selves into what Stephanie's students call la lucha, the struggle for social, racial, and cognitive justice that is carried out through the work of the translanguaging classroom.

We advocate taking up language not simply as an autonomous system of structures, but as "a series of social practices and actions that are embedded in a web of social relations" (García & Leiva, 2014, p. 201). Hence, when we *language*, we are performing a series of social practices that link us to what we want and who we believe we are. Translanguaging goes even further than this idea of *languaging* and acknowledges that within these social practices there are inequalities produced by the social position of speakers. Thus, opening up space for students to language flexibly also means opening up space for a discussion of power relations among social groups at school and in society. To break through the boundaries of language in the ways that society has constructed them, as English and Spanish for example, is also to break ties with the status quo, enabling teachers to embrace new bilingual and other social and epistemological realities. This, in turn, could lead to the transformation and empowerment of students and teachers, as well as to more authentic learning.

Teaching students to view the world with justice in their hearts requires a new lens that recognizes that there is no "neutral" approach to content and that traditional textbook explanations are often lacking. Social justice-oriented educators work with students to challenge the status quo. This kind of education opens students' eyes to silent hegemonies, prepares them to resist subordinate positions, and pushes them to work toward educational and societal change.

Translanguaging pedagogical practices focus on contesting the colonial production of knowledge and subjectivities so as to think from and with subaltern racial/ethnic/sexual bodies (Grosfoguel, 2007). Though *all* students need and deserve this kind of deep and meaningful education, a translanguaging decolonial education is especially important for historically marginalized students who may also have been racialized. Drawing bilingual students' attention to their own languages and practices and to how those languages are viewed by the school community and society at large can open their eyes and awaken what Freire (1970) called *conscientização*, or critical consciousness.

To move Latinx bilingual students to action, educators must use the approaches—and *languaging*—that encourage and support students on their journeys toward critical consciousness and the awakening to the presence of raciolinguistic ideologies. Taking up a translanguaging stance, enacting translanguaging designs, and flowing with shifts in your classroom provide means of working toward this goal.

Teachers who educate for social, racial, and cognitive justice infuse all parts of their teaching with authenticity, criticality, and the energy that catalyzes action. Rather than set aside specific time for this kind of teaching, teachers can encourage the flow of the translanguaging corriente as they work toward social justice.

Si como educadores amorosos podemos ver más allá de los ojos físicos al niño como un TODO en lugar de ver dos monolingües, separando sus prácticas lingüísticas y por ende sus fortalezas en un idioma, habremos logrado dar un paso gigante hacia la justicia social acompañando a nuestros estudiantes mientras se desafían posturas ideológicas profundamente arraigadas.

[If as loving educators we can see beyond the physical eyes to the child as a WHOLE instead of seeing two monolinguals, separating their language practices and therefore their strengths in a language, we would have taken a giant step towards social justice by accompanying our students as they challenge deeply entrenched ideological stances.]

—Leyda de Valdespino, classroom teacher, Omaha Public Schools

Learning and Critical Consciousness

In translanguaging classrooms, teachers facilitate and foster their students' development of conscientização, or critical consciousness (Freire, 1970; Palmer et al., 2019). They also know that to develop this kind of lens, students must use all of their language practices at all times. Teachers' own critical consciousness is a major part of their stance, which in turn helps them go with the flow of the translanguaging corriente and set a course toward social, racial, and cognitive justice. We now return to Stephanie's classroom to consider how teachers can help each student grow the kind of consciousness necessary to participate in la lucha:

Throughout her unit "Environmentalism: Then and Now," Stephanie incorporated readings about Latinx historical figures who were given little treatment in the standards-aligned textbook. For example, though the textbook gave a short autobiography of César Chávez and briefly outlined his role in fighting for workers' rights, Stephanie and her students felt it was too cursory for such an important voice in la lucha. Stephanie decided to devote several days to learning about Chávez's life and commitment to both the environmental movement and the fight for human rights.

Stephanie did research of her own and found several websites that had readings about Chávez in English and Spanish. Because she wanted her students to get a full picture of Chávez, rather than the flat rendering she found in the textbook, Stephanie found articles that examined Chávez's legacy from different angles. Some were glowing retellings of his role in the movement. Others highlighted criticism about Chávez and looked at the controversies around his life and work. While some of the readings she found were in Spanish, many were only in English. Thus, Stephanie knew she would have to use different kinds of strategies to help her students—especially emergent bilinguals like Noemí and Luis—access the texts. She knew that her students could handle the content of such nuanced, complex readings; they just needed the language support to do so.

Stephanie's social justice stance is clearly at work as she imagines her approach to a new topic. Stephanie and her students—whose opinions and ideas always inform her choices—identified a gap in their textbook: to them, César Chávez was underrepresented. Rather than simply move on to other content, Stephanie wanted to address the injustice by educating her students about this important figure, who also happened to be Chicano. She believed that providing her students with more information on Chávez would not only expand their knowledge of the unit topic but also help them think critically about why certain people are placed on the margins, rather than at the center, of social studies textbooks.

While the "what" (the varied readings on Chávez's legacy) was very important to Stephanie, the "how" was equally important. This meant providing many of the readings in English and Spanish and encouraging students to use translanguaging to delve deeply into these readings. By approaching this topic with a translanguaging stance, which is *itself* a social justice stance, Stephanie made space for students to access texts, voice their opinions and ideas, and connect with history in a more meaningful way. This kind of access not only made the classroom more engaging, but also opened the doors for Stephanie's students—especially emergent bilinguals—to see themselves as both invited into and important to academic discourse.

Designing Social Justice

Your classroom design—everything from the physical space to instruction and assessment—is where translanguaging for social justice becomes a reality. When your stance informs how you design your classroom, you set up opportunities for students to use all of their language practices at all times and to work together as a community to become agents for change.

Approaching Instruction with a Social Justice Lens Here we focus on Stephanie's planning process as she begins a new unit of instruction. This insider view of one teacher's design provides insight into the kind of thinking that leads to the creation of a social justice-oriented translanguaging unit.

First, Stephanie looked at the New York State Social Studies Standards. She thought about the resources she already had—and the understandings she wanted the class to grasp—and, again, found standards that met her students' needs. For example, Stephanie knew she wanted her students to use their understanding of environmentalism and sustainability to locate a problem in the school or community and come up with possible solutions. With this in mind, she found a standard that asked students to prepare a plan of action that defines an issue or problem, suggest alternative solutions or courses of action, evaluate the consequences for each alternative solution or course of action, prioritize the solutions based on established criteria, and propose an action plan to address the issue or resolve the problem. This standard—along with ones that asked students to explain how technological advances affect people, places, and regions, understand the nature of scarcity and its link to economics, and explore how citizens influence public policy—helped Stephanie align her vision to those standards that would help structure her students' learning.

Teaching in a translanguaging classroom means that *you* use the standards, not the other way around. This also extends to teaching for social, racial, and cognitive justice. Stephanie knew that she wanted her unit on the environmental movement to culminate in an action-based project that pushed students to imagine a more sustainable and environmentally conscious community. Rather than start from the textbook or from a set of standards, Stephanie started with her own social justice vision and found standards to support that vision. The standards helped Stephanie align and organize her instruction; they did not dictate what she would teach. By encouraging students to meet standards and engage with the curriculum using all of their language practices, and providing them with opportunities to language critically, you are also offering them increased access to academic success and the chance to extend their existing understanding to new learning experiences.

Holistic, Authentic, and Enriching Assessment Assessment should also reflect a social justice orientation. Carla designed assessments to activate her bilingual students' critical multilingual awareness (Ascenzi-Moreno, 2018; Ascenzi-Moreno & Seltzer, 2021) by providing students the opportunity to use their entire linguistic repertoire. Because so much of students' educational experience is tied to measuring their performances, it is important that what students know and can do is authentically represented. If students are to remain engaged in the work of the classroom and in their own learning, they must feel that their teachers (and others) see their potential. When we assess our students holistically, in a way that enriches—rather than stifles—their learning, we are engaged in an act of social justice. In Carla's classroom, this belief resulted in incorporating families, the students themselves, and peer groups into the assessment process. The following excerpt looks at the use of the *Family Assessment Tool: La conexión* (see Appendix 8.4).

Carla evaluates her students with multiple assessment tools, including her own, students' self-assessments, and their family members' assessments, to get a more complete picture of students' full potential. She used the Family Assessment Tool: La conexión to enrich her students' data folders by including the voices of family members and students. In la conexión, families provide Carla with feedback about what they learned from their children about different instructional topics. For example, after an activity in which students learned how to "put a jardín to sleep," families ask their children to show them or tell them what they learned that day. Parents wrote down what their children expressed in either Spanish or English and their children returned the handouts to Carla the next day.

La conexión refers not just to the connection between what students learn at school and what they show their families at home, but also to the connection and integration of home and school learning, practices, and understanding. This type of assessment practice reflects the assumption that knowledge is not simply deposited into students and then measured on a standardized test. Rather, authentic assessment is based on students' performances at school, at home, and in the community.

These types of assessment tools also invite families—arguably the very first "assessors" of their children—into the conversation around their children's progress and growth. Rather than mystifying assessment by distancing it from students and their families, la conexión and tools like it send the message that students' growth is *everyone's* responsibility and can be measured in various ways by different people. In addition to spanning the common gap between in-school assessments and the kind of learning that goes on at home, this type of assessment gives students multiple opportunities to demonstrate what they know. Instead of measuring students' knowledge in discrete ways, often using English-only tools, the translanguaging design for assessment provides insight into the whole child, making assessment more just.

Setting the Course with and for Social Justice There are many ways that teachers can set the course of the translanguaging corriente to work with, and for, social justice:

- Involve your students in decision making about curriculum and language use as well as the day-to-day workings of the classroom.
- Provide students with a variety of choices for demonstrating their learning and make space for them to justify those choices (e.g., let students make decisions about what language to use in a piece of writing and have them support that choice).
- Give students freedom to display their understandings in different, multimodal ways.
- Make projects and other assessments as authentic and local as possible, and include students' multiple ways of knowing in all classroom work so that they are better able to demonstrate their learning (e.g., flexible language use for meaning making, culturally relevant assignments, projects that encourage students to go into the community).

Enacting a Democratic Classroom

In the science class where ***Justin***—the ESL teacher—co-teaches, students speak a number of different languages, most of which he does not speak. This presents a particular challenge and requires creativity and flexibility on Justin's part, two characteristics that are reflected in his translanguaging shifts. As discussed in Chapter 7, in addition to gauging his students' comprehension and engagement and making on-the-spot shifts in response to their performances, Justin helps students understand new content by making some translanguaging moves that shape the conversation:

Justin was going over students' homework for their science class. As he discussed the topic, heredity, he got the sense that his students, especially Fatoumata and Yi-Sheng, who had recently arrived, did not understand what he was explaining. There were blank looks, some off-task behavior, and very little participation. Rather than plow forward, he stopped and asked students to talk to one another in Spanish, Mandarin, French, Vietnamese, Tagalog, or any of their languages about whether they looked like people in their families or not. Though he did not speak most of these languages, Justin could tell from the shift in energy in the room and the excited conversations that students were engaged. After they had spoken to one another, Justin asked them to share some of their ideas in English. Danilo, with the help of his Tagalog-speaking classmates, said that he had dark skin, but his sister was fair and even had freckles. A student translated for Fatoumata that though both her parents had brown eyes, she had green eyes, but no one knew why. Some students shifted the conversation to the many names for different skin colors in Spanish. Jumping off from these comments, Justin connected the idea of looking like (or not looking like) a family member to the work students had done that day with Punnett squares. Suddenly students started to make connections to concepts like dominant and recessive alleles, phenotype, and genotype that they had not tapped into before.

Justin's translanguaging shifts provided students with *access* to the new content. By talking with one another in their home languages, students were able to move from the abstract concept of heredity to the specific, relatable question about whether they looked like people in their families. As has already been discussed, providing emergent bilinguals with access to academic content is part of creating a social justice-oriented classroom. By granting all students, and especially those who are often left out of academic conversations, access to content, you are creating a more just classroom that focuses on students' strengths and potential.

In addition to increasing access through his translanguaging shifts, Justin also made his classroom more democratic by allowing his students' connections and interests to shape the conversation about content. Justin did not know that his students knew so much about a science topic like phenotype (even if they did not know what it was called). It was only through his flexibility that this kind of knowledge was released in the classroom, making content-area learning more interesting and connected to students' own experiences. Suddenly, Justin was not the sole "keeper of knowledge" in the classroom—his role as expert was shared with his students, who then used their own "local" knowledge and experiences to help the class understand these science topics in a more meaningful way. This kind of moment helped students see that their opinions, ideas, and stories were welcome and important to the academic conversation.

There are many ways that teachers can go with the flow of the translanguaging corriente and stimulate action for social justice:

- Have students turn and talk, brainstorm, free write, or make connections in their home languages so that they can better access content in a new language.
- Remember that your students are your greatest linguistic resource! Ask them for on-the-spot translations or explanations of content-area vocabulary or concepts and then have them (or a peer) translate what they said back into the new language.
- Elicit students' stories, experiences, and connections to new content whenever possible. This helps create a strong classroom community and makes space for students to teach one another through their own experiences.
- Have students share their own linguistic resources with others. This helps students see the languages of others as a resource and promotes linguistic tolerance and commitment to the struggle against linguistic discrimination.

When educators take up translanguaging in their classrooms, we can begin to challenge injustices experienced by bilingual students at school and in society.

CONCLUSION

We have seen how a translanguaging classroom works to leverage bilingual students' socioemotional strengths to learn. The valorización stance described is enacted in instruction con respeto, con cariño, como familia, y con acompañamiento. Teachers can support bilingual students' socioemotional well-being and their social standing through their choices of textos and contextos, as well as the ways they encourage students to interact with those texts and contexts. Teaching with translanguaging to enhance bilingual students' learning is itself an act of social justice—releasing voices, languaging practices, experiences, and knowledge other than the dominant ones of the classroom.

In translanguaging classrooms, the bureaucratic labels for students—ELL, LTELL, SIFE, student with disability—do not define them. All students are given opportunities to use their own resources to engage in learning. The curriculum is not watered down or considered remedial; the instruction is not piecemeal and unimaginative. ***Jennifer***, in Carla's classroom, may have been labeled as having a learning disability, yet Jennifer performs competently in both English and Spanish in this translanguaging classroom because of the affordances she is granted there.

We also emphasize that translanguaging classrooms do not simply work for individual bilingual student's success. Remember that a translanguaging classroom goes beyond traditional definitions of a monolingual or bilingual classroom. And a teacher in a translanguaging classroom goes beyond the definitions of a monolingual or a bilingual teacher. Translanguaging has the potential to develop bilingual students' sense of critical consciousness. Translanguaging classrooms can prepare teachers and students juntos to identify inequities at school and in society and then challenge and potentially transform them.

REFLECTION QUESTIONS AND ACTIVITIES

1. How does translanguaging open up space to support and leverage bilingual students' socioemotional development?
2. How does the translanguaging corriente relate to social justice? In what ways is translanguaging itself an act of social justice?
3. How can translanguaging contribute to the valorización of students' socioemotional strength? Describe the elements of valorización and how translanguaging contributes to each element.

TAKING ACTION

1. Look closely at a unit plan or lesson that you have implemented in your class (ideally the unit that you have developed as you work through this book).
    - How does your unit reflect con respeto, con cariño, como familia, y con acompañamiento?
    - How does your unit relate to your students' socioemotional well-being?
    - How does your unit work to advance social justice?
    - What action steps can you take to ensure that your translanguaging unit designs and assessments advance bilingual students' content and language learning, leverage their bilingualism, promote stronger socioemotional identity, and work toward social justice?

Afterword

Nelson Flores, University of Pennsylvania

I began my career as an educator with a strong belief in the power of education to promote social transformation. In particular, as an ESL teacher, I saw one of my primary responsibilities being to work toward the dismantling of cultural and linguistic hierarchies in my classroom. A few years into my experience, I had the opportunity to work in a collaborative team-teaching experience with an equally idealistic ELA teacher named Kate Seltzer at a high school in the Bronx serving a predominantly African American and Latinx student population. Many of our Latinx students were bilingual, with the bulk of these bilingual students officially classified as English learners. All of our students, including those officially classified as English learners, also came to our class with a range of linguistic resources in English, which was the official language of instruction. We sought to leverage all of these linguistic resources to support our students in meeting the academic demands of the New York State ELA standards. This included both us and our students fluidly using both English and Spanish as part of our meaning making in the class. This also included resisting the ideology that English was treated as a static set of prescriptivist rules with students being encouraged to critically reflect on their English language choices in class assignments in ways that navigated and resisted dominant linguistic conventions. In short, while we didn't have the words for it at the time, what we were attempting to do was to implement a translanguaging pedagogy.

This is just one illustration of the many educators who reflexively adopt translanguaging pedagogy as part of their efforts to affirm, build on, and extend their students' cultural and linguistic practices. That said, as is the case with many other educators relying on their instinct as they engage in these efforts, our pedagogy was inconsistent, with little cohesiveness to our approach beyond our strong commitment to empowering our students through challenging cultural and linguistic hierarchies. There are many things I would do differently now based on the insights I have developed over the years through explicitly engaging with the concept of translanguaging as a theory of language and the implications of this theory for education. This points to the importance of needing to move beyond a *reflexive* translanguaging pedagogy that consists of educators instinctively doing what feels right to them toward a *reflective* translanguaging pedagogy where educators are consciously embracing the re-orientation to language that translanguaging theory entails and translating this into a translanguaging pedagogy that fits their unique contexts and student populations.

Indeed, a desire to develop this more reflective pedagogical approach was a strong motivating factor in my decision to pursue doctoral studies. It was during my doctoral studies that I had the opportunity to take a class with Ofelia García, who first introduced me to the term translanguaging as a theory of language with profound educational implications. I was first introduced to the term through reading page proofs of what would become *Bilingual Education in the 21st Century: A Global Perspective*. While I had no idea how much of an impact this book would have on the field, I immediately felt its impact on both my sense of my own bilingualism and the type of educator that I yearned to be. Reading this book offered me much more than a name for what Kate and I were trying to do in our collaborative team teaching. It also offered me a cohesive re-orientation of language that begins from the premise that all linguistic borders are ideological, with the policing of these borders being a key mechanism in the marginalization of bi- and multilingual communities. However, it left me with many questions about how to apply these theories in practice for my students as well as for other New York City students.

I had the opportunity to oversee the beginning of efforts to answer this question in my year as project director of the CUNY-New York State Initiative on Emergent Bilinguals. This included working with CUNY faculty and doctoral students to develop monthly leadership seminars for school leaders, on-site school visits to support them in developing and implementation action plans that sought to adopt a translanguaging pedagogy in their school, and the development of supplemental materials to support educators in becoming more reflective about their engagement of translanguaging pedagogy. When the first edition of *The Translanguaging Classroom* came out in 2016, I remember seeing it as, in many ways, a culmination of the work that many of us had undertaken over the years to translate translanguaging theory into a concrete teaching resource for educators. On a personal level, I saw many kernels of the earlier reflexive translanguaging pedagogy that I developed in collaboration with Kate in ways that are further fleshed out into a reflective translanguaging pedagogy that brings more cohesiveness and systematicity to what we were working to do together all of those years ago. I could see the ways that a major contributor to this increased cohesiveness and systematicity was the theoretical foundation laid out in *Bilingual Education in the 21st Century* that the CUNY-NYSIEB team sought to further develop into concrete resources that supported educators in moving from reflexive to reflective translanguaging pedagogy. One of these resources that proved to be especially interesting to the local educators that we were working with at the time was *Translanguaging: A CUNY-NYSIEB Guide for Educators*, that Kate co-authored with Christina Celic. Through this work I began to truly appreciate the transformative potential of translanguaging pedagogy when theory was strongly connected with practice in ways that were thorough and comprehensive without being prescriptive.

While I learned so much from my engagement with translanguaging as a theory of language and pedagogy, I still had many questions as I undertook the work of supporting educators in enacting translanguaging pedagogy in their schools. This led me to new insights just as the first edition of *The Translanguaging Classroom* was being finalized. In particular, another motivating factor in my decision to pursue doctoral studies that a translanguaging pedagogy left unaddressed was the fact that most of the students I taught as a high school ESL teacher were born and raised in the United States and described themselves as more comfortable in English than in Spanish. I initially found myself describing these students through a deficit lens. In particular, using theories that I had learned in my own teacher education, I concluded that they had mastered "social" language in both English and Spanish but had failed to master "academic" language in either of them. It was the disconnect between this deficit framing and my desire to create classrooms that affirmed, built on, and extended students' existing cultural and linguistic practices that sent me looking for answers. Translanguaging as a theory of language that pointed to the ideological nature of all language borders offered me a point of entry for beginning to critically interrogate this dichotomous framing of language and the deficit perspective that it recruited me to adopt of my students. Gradually, I came to the realization that these deficit perspectives were not objective but rather ideological and that their roots were in longstanding colonial logics that framed racialized communities as inherently linguistically deficient as part of their dehumanization. It was this insight that would eventually move me in collaboration with Jonathan Rosa to develop a raciolinguistic perspective that argued that we cannot truly create pedagogical approaches that affirm, build on, and extend the cultural and linguistic practices of racialized students unless we center race in our analysis.

Yet Jonathan and I were never alone in insisting on the need to consider race in discussions of transformative language education in general or translanguaging pedagogy specifically. We were inspired by the many educators and teacher educators we have worked with who have long sought to make these links. While I have had the great privilege of working closely with some of these (teacher) educators, such as Ofelia García and Kate Seltzer, I have also had the privilege of connecting with others both nationally and internationally by sharing research that has sought to lay out a raciolinguistic perspective on translanguaging. Susana Johnson is one of these (teacher) educators. It was she who invited me to present at a translanguaging institute held in Albuquerque, New Mexico, in 2023. There, I had the opportunity to meet and learn about the Córdova sisters, two former New Mexican teachers fired for teaching ethnic studies to their predominantly Latinx student population in 1997. Susana's decision to place front and center struggles for ethnic studies in a conference focused on translanguaging was an important reminder that translanguaging can and must center race or risk becoming a tool for the continued maintenance of the racial status quo. It is also an important reminder that educators have been working to challenge both racial and linguistic oppression for many generations now. In this way, we might think of a raciolinguistic perspective as adding a reflective perspective on the co-naturalization of race and language that brings cohesion to the reflexive ways that many (teacher) educators have sought to make these links across the generations.

Jonathan and I first laid the foundation for this reflective raciolinguistic perspective in our 2015 article "Undoing Appropriateness: Raciolinguistic Ideologies and Language Diversity in Education," with the first edition of *The Translanguaging Classroom* published soon after in 2016. To see the ways that this raciolinguistic perspective has been taken up in the second edition of this amazing resource makes a powerful case against the argument made by some critics that a raciolinguistic perspective has little relevance to classroom practice. Throughout the chapters, we see the importance not just of creating space for educators and students to strategically use their entire linguistic repertoire to make meaning in the classroom (what translanguaging pedagogy is typically assumed to mean) but also of providing spaces for educators and students to reflect on the ways that their listening practices and the listening practices of their colleagues may reflect the hegemonic position of the White listening subject (which adds a raciolinguistic perspective to translanguaging). This White listening subject frames the bilingualism of affluent White students as an asset while framing the bilingualism of racialized students as a liability. It frames dual-language education as a form of gifted education for the "right" (White) kids and as not a good fit for "those" (racialized) kids. It dichotomizes language into "academic" and "social" language and characterizes the home language practices of racialized students as social language that provides little foundation for the academic language demanded in U.S. classrooms. *The Translanguaging Classroom* shows that creating space for educators and students to engage in this type of critical reflection lays the foundation for developing transformative pedagogical practices that shift the goal of (language) education away from teaching students the "codes of power" as a disembodied set of objective linguistic features toward engaging students in exploring language as a creative force that they can mold in ways that reflect their unique styles, identities, and voices as part of broader anti-oppressive political struggles.

As I have sought to further develop a raciolinguistic perspective on translanguaging over the years, I have shared my ideas with many educators around the country. They have always embraced the conversation with open arms. Rather than feeling devalued, they have felt affirmed by the acknowledgment of the real structural constraints that they confront as educators working with low-income racialized students in under-resourced schools. Rather than feeling like they were being called racist, they have appreciated the opportunity to reflect on the biases in their listening practices as part of developing new pedagogical approaches that resist these biases. Rather than seeing little relevance to their teaching, they have appreciated being able to discuss how to navigate the tension between pressures to meet the language demands of their curriculum while positioning the home language practices of their students as legitimate both inside and outside of the classroom. But perhaps most importantly, while they appreciate my assertion that there are no easy answers or magic bullets for how to resolve these tensions, they desperately yearn for more practical resources that they can use to support their efforts in addressing these tensions. I am happy that I can now tell them that the second edition of *The Translanguaging Classroom* moves beyond the reflexive understanding of the co-naturalization of race and language that many (teacher) educators have used to inform their work toward a more reflective understanding that extends translanguaging theory and pedagogy in ways that make race central rather than implied.

Glossary

academic language Has traditionally referred to ways of using language that align with the expectations of schools and standardized assessments. This book understands the term as ideological (Flores & Rosa, 2015; Valdés, 2004), reflecting deficit perceptions of multilingual learners rather than objective linguistic fact.

additive bilingualism The traditional view of bilingualism as adding one whole language to an existing whole language.

autobiographical translanguaging portraits A form of classroom-based assessment that invites students to visually represent their language use, providing them with the opportunity to take a critical perspective on their languaging and reflect on the meanings of their language practices.

bilingual education Using two languages for instructional purposes. *See also* **dual-language bilingual education** and **transitional bilingual education**.

bilingual zone of proximal development Offering assistance to students bilingually to mediate their learning and stretch their performance (Moll, 2013).

biliteracy Being able to use two or more languages to read, write, and engage in other forms of literacy.

convergent biliterate model A model of biliteracy where the interaction with a written text follows the language of the text but where minority literacy practices are calqued (copied) on majority literacy practices.

convergent monoliterate model A model of biliteracy where the text is only in the dominant language, but the interactions around the text can occur using the minority language.

flexible multiple model A model of biliteracy that uses two languages together to interact with texts written in both languages and in other media, according to a bilingual flexible norm capable of both integration and separation.

separation biliterate model Uses only the specific language in which the text is written to interact with that text, according to appropriate sociocultural and discourse norms.

biliteracy acompañamiento At all times, even when students are reading or producing monolingual texts, they are using all their language resources, including the other language, to make meaning.

code-switching Switching back and forth between language codes that are regarded as separate and autonomous. It considers language only from an *external perspective* that looks at bilinguals' language behavior as if they were two monolinguals in one.

cognitive justice Conceptualized by decolonial scholar Santos (2018) to refer to the process of including and centering the epistemologies and ways of knowing and languaging of diverse groups, thus disrupting the supremacy of Eurocentrism.

continua of biliteracy A theoretical model conceived by Hornberger (2003) that posits an L1/L2 continuum in which bilingual learning is maximized when students can draw from all their existing language skills in two languages.

corriente Spanish word for current, used here to indicate different and fluid language and cultural practices that flow through classrooms, even when invisible.

critical consciousness The understanding and awareness that there are social, political, and ideological aspects to the content and language students are learning in school.

critical metalinguistic awareness Refers to the ability to consciously reflect on the nature of language.

critical multilingual awareness The awareness of and ability to draw from one's full repertoire of understandings and practices to render a linguistic performance appropriate for a task.

critical race theory (CRT) An academic framework that emerged primarily from legal studies that is used to understand and challenge the intersection of race, law, and power structures.

dual-language bilingual education (DLBE) A type of bilingual education where the objective is for students to become bilingual and biliterate and achieve academically through two languages.

two-way These DLBE programs, by definition, include equal numbers of students who are learning English and students learning the language other than English.

dynamic bilingualism In opposition to **additive bilingualism**, dynamic bilingualism posits that the linguistic features of what are considered two languages are entwined and adapt to the communicative circumstance at hand.

emergent bilingual(s) Refers to those students whose bilingualism is emerging. In this book, the term is mostly used to refer to students who are developing English, but it can also be used to refer to students developing the language other than English.

English as a second language (ESL) Programs of instruction for emergent bilinguals where only English is used.

pull-out ESL programs where teachers take out a small group of emergent bilinguals for intensive English work.

push-in ESL programs where teachers work collaboratively with classroom teachers to support emergent bilinguals in the English-medium mainstream classroom.

structured English immersion Considered an ESL program in which instruction is in English only. It is only for emergent bilinguals, and teachers modify the language used and the curriculum.

experienced bilinguals Refers to those students who can use two or more languages with relative ease, although their performances vary according to task, modality, and language.

heritage language Refers to minority language(s) learned at home and/or to minority language(s) that are culturally/ethnically affiliated with one's family/community.

general linguistic performance(s) Refers to the ability to use language without focusing on specific conventions associated with one or another national language. This includes, for example, the ability to use language to express complex thoughts, joke, argue, and explain.

intrapersonal voice Refers to the inner voice of bilingual people, which always draws on an integrated repertoire of linguistic and other features to make meaning and can be tapped into as students learn in school, regardless of the language of instruction.

juntos Spanish word for together, used here in relation to the **translanguaging stance** to refer to the teacher's core beliefs that a bilingual student has one language system with features that need to be leveraged together/juntos.

language features Lexical and structural features of language, such as words, phonemes (sounds), morphemes (word endings), tense systems, pronoun systems, case distinctions, gender distinctions, syntactic structures, discourse markers, and so forth.

language(s) other than English (LOTE) Refers to any languages other than English.

language repertoire(s) Refers to the totality of linguistic features that individual speakers have, without identifying them as one language or another.

language-specific performance Focuses on linguistic performance with language features that have been preapproved for school use: standard grammar, vocabulary, and usage.

leverage To use something to gain a desired effect and maximum advantage; in this book appears in connection with the use of the home language to amplify learning and gain a higher return.

long-term English language learners (LTELLs) Term used to identify students who were designated as English learners when they entered the school system and have yet to be categorized as fluent, usually after 7 years.

monoglossic ideology A belief that languages are autonomous wholes, and thus bilingualism is just two separate languages. It is the opposite of heteroglossia, the Bakhtinian concept that recognizes different voices regardless of what society deems appropriate language.

multilingual ecology Refers to the ways in which the different language practices of a community are reflected in schools and classrooms. It can refer to visual features (e.g., bulletin boards, signage, posters, and student work in multiple languages) and audible features (e.g., talk, announcements, and songs).

named language According to Otheguy, García, and Reid (2015), named languages are socially **constructed** categories, often tied to nation-states, that are used to label and separate linguistic practices under names like "Spanish" or "English." They argue that these categories reflect ideological boundaries rather than linguistic realities, as people's ways of languaging often transcend these labels.

racial justice Refers to the the fair treatment of people of all races, resulting in equitable opportunities and outcomes for everyone. It also refers to the dismantling of any policies and practices that maintain or reinforce differential outcomes by race.

raciolinguistic ideologies A concept put forth by Nelson Flores and Jonathan Rosa (2015) to explore the conflation of "certain racialized bodies with linguistic deficiency unrelated to any objective linguistic practices . . . raciolinguistic ideologies produce racialized speaking subjects who are constructed as linguistically deviant even when engaging in linguistic practices positioned as normative or innovative when produced by privileged white subjects" (p. 150).

semiotic Refers to the signs and symbols that, in addition to linguistic features, are a part of one's meaning-making system.

social justice Refers to the equitable treatment of all people within a society as well as the pursuit of eliminating inequalities based on categories such as race, gender, or disability.

students with incomplete/interrupted formal education (SIFE) Refers to immigrant emergent bilingual students who have not received an adequate education in their countries of origin and therefore have low literacy in their home language.

transitional bilingual education A type of bilingual education where the home language is used progressively less and less, until a student is deemed fluent in English and can transfer to a monolingual classroom. The goal is for these emergent bilinguals to achieve academically in English as they develop English for academic purposes.

- **early-exit** Refers to transitional bilingual education programs where students are transferred to monolingual instruction as soon as they are deemed fluent in English.
- **late-exit** Refers to transitional bilingual education programs where, although English is progressively used more frequently, students are not transferred until they finish the program of instruction, usually at the end of elementary school.

translanguaging The theory that posits that bilinguals have one unitary language system that enables them to use all the language features fluidly. It also refers to the pedagogy that leverages that fluid language use.

classroom Refers to the space built collaboratively by the teacher and bilingual students as they leverage their different language practices to teach and learn in deeply creative and critical ways.

corriente The flow of students' bilingual language practices, which is always present wherever we find bilingual students, even in so-called English-only classrooms.

design The planning of the classroom space, the elements of instruction and assessment, and the strategies to be used with bilingual students.

instructional design cycle Refers to the planning of the sequencing of instruction into five stages: explorar, evaluar, imaginar, presentar, and implementar.

evaluar Encourages students to explore a new topic or theme, follow their natural interests and questions, and build their background knowledge.

explorar Encourages students to think critically about the content they are exploring, thus developing their critical consciousness and critical literacies.

imaginar Encourages students to use what they have learned in the explorar and evaluar stages to imaginar something new, including new ideas and new ways of using language to learn.

presentar Involves students in peer editing, conferencing, rewriting, and presenting their work, with attention both to content and to the choices they make about language.

implementar Invites students to move their work from the classroom to the larger community, applying what they learned in authentic ways.

objectives Planned ways of leveraging bilingualism and ways of knowing so that students can better access both content and language practices valued in school.

pedagogy/pedagogical practices Refer to the ways teachers can scaffold students' engagement with content and language, engage students in ways that deepen their understandings, and enact their translanguaging stances through daily design choices that make space for and leverage la corriente.

rings Described by Sánchez et al. (2017) as ways of providing students with scaffolding, differentiation, and various ways of connecting what they already know and can do with both language and content to what is expected of them in the classroom.

shifts Refer to the many moment-by-moment decisions that teachers have to make all the time.

spaces Refer to spaces that explicitly invite the language practices of bilingual communities, enabling students to language flexibly and creatively as they learn and make meaning of new content and language.

stance Refers to the belief that bilingual students' different language practices need to be leveraged together and performed collaboratively with others.

zone of proximal development In this zone, students can learn and do *more* than they can on their own because of the "boost" they receive from their peers (Vygotsky, 1978).

References

American Educational Research Association, American Psychological Association, and National Council on Measurement in Education. (2014). *National Council on Measurement. The standards for educational and psychological testing.* American Psychological Association.

Anaya, R. (2004). *The Santero's miracle.* University of New Mexico Press.

Anya, U. (2021). Critical race pedagogy for more effective and inclusive world language teaching. *Applied Linguistics, 42*(6), 1055–1069.

Anzaldúa, G. (1987). *Borderlands/La Frontera: The new Mestiza.* Aunt Lute Books.

Arellano, B. (2022). *New Mexico's biliteracy seal: A new study examines who earns biliteracy seals and whether earning a seal impacts college outcomes.* Regional Educational Laboratory Program.

Ascenzi-Moreno, L. (2018). Translanguaging and responsive assessment adaptations. *Language Arts, 95*(6), 355–369.

Ascenzi-Moreno, L., García, O., & Lopez, A. (2023). Latinx bilingual students' translanguaging and assessment. In S. Melo-Pfeifer & C. Ollivier (Eds.), *Assessment of plurilingual competence and plurilingual students: Educative issues and empirical approaches* (pp. 48–61). Routledge.

Ascenzi-Moreno, L., & Seltzer, K. (2021). Always at the bottom: Ideologies in assessment of emergent bilinguals. *Journal of Literacy Research, 53*(4), 468–490. https://doi.org/10.1177/1086296X211052255

Baker, C. (2001). *Foundations of bilingual education and bilingualism.* Multilingual Matters.

Bartlett, L., & García, O. (2011). *Additive schooling in subtractive times: Bilingual education and Dominican immigrant youth in the Heights.* Vanderbilt University Press.

Bartolomé, L. (2008). Authentic cariño and respect in minority education: The political and ideological dimensions of love. *International Journal of Critical Pedagogy, 1*(1), 1–17.

Bauer, E. B., Colomer, S. E., & Wiemelt, J. (2020). Biliteracy of African American and Latinx kindergarten students in a dual-language program: Understanding students' translanguaging practices across informal assessments. *Urban Education, 55*(3), 331–361. https://doi.org/10.1177/0042085918789743

Bodrova, E., & Leong, D. J. (2019). *Tools of the mind: The Vygotskian approach to early childhood education* (2nd ed.). Merrill/Prentice Hall.

Busch, B. (2010). School language profile: Valorizing linguistic resources in heteroglossia situations in South Africa. *Language and Education, 24*(9), 283–294.

Busch, B. (2012). The linguistic repertoire revisited. *Applied linguistics, 33*(5), 503–523. https://doi.org/10.1093/applin/ams056

Canagarajah, S. (2011). Translanguaging in the classroom: Emerging issues for research and pedagogy. In L. Wei (Ed.), *Applied linguistics review* (Vol. 2, pp. 1–27). De Gruyter Mouton.

Canagarajah, S. (2013). *Translingual practice: Global Englishes and cosmopolitan relations.* Routledge.

Carini, P. (2000). Prospect's descriptive processes. In M. Himley & P. Carini (Eds.), *From another angle: Children's strengths and school standards. The Prospect Center's descriptive review of the child* (pp. 8–20). Teachers College Press.

Celic, C. (2009). *English language learners day by day K–6. A complete guide to literacy, content-area, and language instruction.* Heinemann.

Celic, C., & Seltzer, K. (2012). *Translanguaging: A CUNY-NYSIEB guide for educators.* https://www.cuny-nysieb.org/wp-content/uploads/2016/04/Translanguaging-Guide-March-2013.pdf

Cervantes-Soon, C. (2018). Using a xicana feminist framework in bilingual teacher preparation. Toward an anticolonial path. *The Urban Review, 50*(5), 857–888.

Chávez-Moreno, L. (2024). A literature review of raciolinguistics in dual-language bilingual education. In J. Freire, C. Alfaro, & E. de Jong (Eds.), *The handbook of dual language bilingual education* (pp. 254–265). Routledge.

City University of New York - New York State Initiative on Emergent Bilinguals (Eds.). (2020). *Translanguaging and transformative teaching for emergent bilingual students: Lessons from the CUNY-NYSIEB project.* Routledge.

Cioè-Peña, M. (2022). TrUDL, a path to full inclusion: The intersectional possibilities of translanguaging and Universal Design for Learning. *TESOL Quarterly 56*(2), 799–812. https://doi.org/10.1002/tesq.3074

Creese, A., & Blackledge, A. (2010). Translanguaging in the bilingual classroom: A pedagogy for learning and teaching? *The Modern Language Journal, 94,* 103–115.

de los Ríos, C., & Seltzer, K. (2017). Translanguaging, coloniality, and English classrooms: An exploration of two bicoastal urban classrooms. *Research in the Teaching of English, 52*(1), 55–76.

Delavan, M. G. (2024). Gentrification of dual language bilingual education: Defining types, historical evidence, and alternatives. In J. Freire, C. Alfaro, & E. de Jong (Eds.), *The handbook of dual language bilingual education* (pp. 235–253). Routledge.

Díaz, E., & Flores, B. (2021). How teachers unknowingly organize failure for children of color by creating "zones of negative development." In *Handbook of Latinos and education* (pp. 299–308). Routledge.

Durán, L., & Hikida, M. (2022). Making sense of reading's forever wars. *Phi Delta Kappan, 103*(8), 14–19. https://doi.org/10.1177/00317217221100003

Escamilla, K., Hopewell, S., Butvilofsky, S., Sparrow, W., Soltero-González, L., Ruiz-Figueroa, O., & Escamilla, M. (2014). *Biliteracy from the start: Literacy Squared in action.* Caslon.

España, C., & Herrera, L. Y. (2020). *En comunidad: Lessons for centering the voices and experiences of bilingual Latinx students.* Heinemann.

Espinosa, C., & Ascenzi-Moreno, L. (2021). *Rooted in strength: Using translanguaging to grow multilingual readers and writers.* Scholastic.

Fitts, S. (2006). Reconstructing the status quo: Linguistic interaction in a dual-language school. *Bilingual Research Journal, 30*(2), 337–365.

Flores, N. (2014, July 19). Let's not forget that translanguaging is a political act. *The Educational Linguist.* https://educationallinguist.wordpress.com/2014/07/19/lets-not-forget-that-translanguaging-is-a-political-act/

Flores, N. (2019). Translanguaging into raciolinguistic ideologies: A personal reflection on the legacy of Ofelia García. *Journal of Multilingual Education Research, 9*(1), Article 5.

Flores, N. (2020). From academic language to language architecture: Challenging raciolinguistic ideologies in research and practice. *Theory into Practice, 59*(1), 22–31.

Flores, N., Lewis, M. C., & Phuong, J. (2018). Raciolinguistic chronotopes and the education of Latinx students: Resistance and anxiety in a bilingual school. *Language and Communication, 62*, 15–25.

Flores, N., & Rosa, J. (2015). Undoing appropriateness: Raciolinguistic ideologies and language diversity in education. *Harvard Education Review, 85*(2), 149–171. https://doi.org/10.17763/0017-8055.85.2.149

Flores, N., & Schissel, J. (2014). Dynamic bilingualism as the norm: Envisioning a heteroglossic approach to standards-based reform. *TESOL Quarterly, 48*(3), 454–479.

Flores, N., Tseng A., & Subtirelu, N. (Eds.). (2020). *Bilingualism for All?: Raciolinguistic Perspectives on Dual Language Education in the United States.* Multilingual Matters.

Flores-Dueñas, L. (1999). Plática as critical instruction: Talking with bilingual students about their reading. *Educational Considerations, 26*(2), 44–49.

Freire, J. A., Gambrell, J., Kasun, G. S., Dorner, L. M., & Cervantes-Soon, C. (2022). The expropriation of dual language bilingual education: Deconstructing neoliberalism, whitestreaming, and English-hegemony. *International Multilingual Research Journal 58*(2), 121–133.

Freire, P. (1974). *Education for critical consciousness.* Continuum.

Freire, P. (1970). *Pedagogy of the oppressed.* Herder and Herder.

Freire, P. (2008). Teachers as cultural workers: Letters to those who dare teach. In M. Cochran-Smith, S. Feiman-Nemser, D. J. McIntyre, & K. E. Demers (Eds.), *Handbook of research on teacher education: Enduring questions and answers in changing contexts.* Routledge.

Freire, P., & Macedo, D. (1987). *Literacy: Reading the word and the world.* Praeger.

Frieson, B. L. (2022). Remixin' and flowin' in centros: Exploring the biliteracy practices of Black language speakers in an elementary two-way immersion bilingual program. *Race Ethnicity and Education, 25*(4), 585–605.

García, O. (2009). *Bilingual education in the 21st century: A global perspective.* Wiley/Blackwell.

García, O. (2011a). Educating New York's bilingual children: Constructing a future from the past. *International Journal of Bilingual Education and Bilingualism, 14*(2), 133–153.

García, O. (2011b). From language garden to sustainable languaging: Bilingual education in a global world. *Perspectives*, Sept/Oct, 5–10.

García, O. (2012). Theorizing translanguaging for educators. In C. Celic & K. Seltzer (Eds.), *Translanguaging: A CUNY-NYSIEB guide for educators.* https://www.cuny-nysieb.org/wp-content/uploads/2016/04/Translanguaging-Guide-March-2013.pdf

García, O. (2013). From diglossia to transglossia: Bilingual and multilingual classrooms in the 21st century. In C. Abello-Contesse, P. Chandler, M. D. López-Jiménez, M. M. Torreblanc López, & R. Chacón Beltrán (Eds.), *Bilingualism and multilingualism in school settings* (pp. 155–178). Multilingual Matters.

García, O. (2014). Countering the dual: Transglossia, dynamic bilingualism and translanguaging in education. In R. Rubdy & L. Alsagoff (Eds.), *The global-local interface, language choice and hybridity* (pp. 100–118). Multilingual Matters.

García, O., & Cervantes-Soon, C. (2023). Best practices to support the literacy development of bilingual learners. In L. Morrow, E. Morrell, & H. Casey (Eds.), *Best practices in literacy instruction* (7th ed., pp. 335–353). Guilford Press.

García, O., Flores, N., Seltzer, K., Li, W., Otheguy, R., & Rosa, J. (2021). Rejecting abyssal thinking in the language and education of racialized bilinguals: A manifesto. *Critical Inquiry in Language Studies, 18*(3), 203–228.

García, O., & Kleifgen, J. (2018). *Educating emergent bilinguals: Policies, programs and practices for English learners* (2nd ed.). Teachers College Press.

García, O., & Kleifgen, J. (2020). Translanguaging and literacies. *Reading Research Quarterly, 55*(4), 553–571. https://doi.org/10.1002/rrq.286

García, O., & Kleyn, T. (Eds.). (2017). *Translanguaging with multilingual students: Learning from classroom moments.* Routledge.

García, O., & Leiva, C. (2014). Theorizing and enacting translanguaging for social justice. In A. Blackledge & A. Creese (Eds.), *Heteroglossia as practice and pedagogy* (pp. 199–216). Springer.

García, O., & Wei, L. (2014). *Translanguaging: Language, bilingualism and education.* Palgrave Macmillan Pivot.

García, O., Woodley, H. H., Flores, N., & Chu, H. (2013). Latino emergent bilingual youth in high schools: Transcaring strategies for academic success. *Urban Education, 48*(6), 798–827.

Gibbons, P. (2009). *English learners, academic literacy, and thinking: Learning in the challenge zone.* Heinemann.

Goizueta, R. S. (2001). *Caminando con Jesus: Toward a Hispanic/Latino theology of accompaniment.* Orbis.

Goodman, K., Goodman, Y., & Flores, B. (1979). *Reading in the bilingual classroom: Literacy and biliteracy.* National Clearinghouse for Bilingual Education.

Gort, M. (2015). Transforming literacy learning and teaching through translanguaging and other typical practices associated with "doing being bilingual." *International Multilingual Research Journal, 9*(1), 1–6.

Gort, M., & Sembiante, S. F. (2015). Navigating hybridized language learning spaces through translanguaging pedagogy: Dual language preschool teachers' languaging practices in support of emergent bilingual children's performance of academic discourse. *International Multilingual Research Journal, 9*(1), 7–25.

Grosfoguel, R. (2007). The epistemic decolonial turn. Beyond political-economy paradigms. *Cultural Studies, 21*(2–3), 211–223.

Grosjean, F. (1982). *Life with two languages.* Harvard University Press.

Gutiérrez, K. D. (2008). Developing a sociocritical literacy in the third space. *Reading Research Quarterly, 43*(2), 148–164.

Gutiérrez, K. D., Morales, P. Z., & Martinez, S. C. (2009). Remediating literacy: Culture, difference, and learning for students from nondominant communities. *Review of Research in Education, 33,* 212–245.

Hamman-Ortiz, L. (2023). Cultivating a critical translanguaging space in dual language bilingual education, *International Multilingual Research Journal, 18*(2), 119–139. https://doi.org/10.1080/19313152.2023.2277101

Haugen, E. (1953). *The Norwegian language in America: A study of bilingual behavior.* University of Pennsylvania Press.

Heller, M. (1999). *Linguistic minorities and modernity: A sociolinguistic ethnography.* Longman.

Herrera, S. G. (2022). *Biography-driven culturally responsive teaching: Honoring race, ethnicity, and personal history.* Teachers College Press.

Hornberger, N. (1990). Creating successful contexts for bilingual literacy. *Teachers College Record, 92*(2), 212–229.

Hornberger, N. (Ed.). (2003). *Continua of biliteracy. An ecological framework for educational policy, research, and practices in multilingual settings.* Multilingual Matters.

Hornberger, N. (2005). Opening and filling up implementational and ideological spaces in heritage language education. *Modern Language Journal, 89*(4), 605–609.

Hornberger, N. H., & Skilton-Sylvester, E. (2000). Revisiting the continua of biliteracy: International and critical perspectives. *Language and Education: An International Journal* 14(2), 96–122.

Hruby, G. G. (2020). Language's vanishing act in early literacy education. *Phi Delta Kappan, 101*(5), 19–24.

Johnson, S. I. (2013). *Dual language teachers' changing views of Spanish literacy teaching and learning as influenced by critical dialogue* [Unpublished doctoral dissertation]. University of New Mexico.

Johnson, S. I. (2021). Cultivating pedagogical clarity: Dual-language bilingual education teachers' changing views of literacy practices as influenced by critical dialogue. In E. G. Murillo et al. (Eds.), *Handbook of Latinos and education* (pp. 365–382). Routledge.

Johnson, S. I., & García, O. (2023). Siting biliteracy in New Mexican borderlands. *Journal of Latinos and Education, 22*(5), 1913–1928.

Kabuto, B. (2022). *Becoming bilingual readers: Identity, translanguaging, and biographic biliteracy profiles.* Routledge.

Kibler, A., Valdés, G., & Walqui, A. (Eds.). (2021). *Reconceptualizing the role of critical dialogue in American classrooms. Promoting equity through dialogic education.* Routledge.

Lee, J. S., Hill-Bonnet, L., & Gillispie, J. (2008). Learning in two languages: Interactional spaces for becoming bilingual speakers. *International Journal of Bilingual Education and Bilingualism, 11*(1), 75–94.

Linquanti, R., & Cook, H. G. (2013). *Toward a "common definition of English learner": A brief defining policy and technical issues and opportunities for state assessment consortia.* Council of Chief State School Officers. http://eric.ed.gov/?id=ED542705

Lippi-Green, R. (2012). *English with an accent: Language, ideology and discrimination in the United States* (2nd ed.). Routledge.

Lomelí, K. (2023). The moral ethic of cariño: A culturally competent approach to working with immigrant-origin students. *Association of Mexican American Educators Journal, 17*(2), 11–34.

MacSwan, J. (2017). A multilingual perspective on translanguaging. *American Educational Research Journal, 54*(1), 167–201. https://doi.org/10.3102/0002831216683935

MacSwan, J. (2022). Codeswitching, translanguaging, and bilingual grammar. In J. MacSwan (Ed.), *Multilingual perspectives on translanguaging* (pp. 1–44). Multilingual Matters.

Mahoney, K. (2017). *The assessment of emergent bilinguals: Supporting English language learners.* Multilingual Matters.

Makoni, S., & Pennycook, A. (2007). *Disinventing and reconstituting languages.* Multilingual Matters.

Martínez, R., Hikida, M., & Durán, L. (2015). Unpacking ideologies of linguistic purism: How dual language teachers make sense of everyday translanguaging. *International Multilingual Research Journal, 9*(1), 26–42.

Martínez, R. A., Vieyra, V. M., Ahmad, N. B., & Stovall, J. L. (2022). Prefiguring translingual possibilities: The transformative potential of translanguaging for dual language bilingual education. In M. T. Sánchez & O. García (Eds.), *Transformative translanguaging espacios* (pp. 95–112). Multilingual Matters.

May, S. (Ed.). (2013). *The multilingual turn: Implications for SLA, TESOL and bilingual education*. Routledge.

McTighe, J., & Wiggins, G. P. (2013). *Essential questions: Opening doors to student understanding*. Association for Supervision and Curriculum Development.

Menken, K. (2008). *English learners left behind: Standardized testing as language policy*. Multilingual Matters.

Mignolo, W. (2000). *Local histories/global designs: Essays on the coloniality of power, subaltern knowledges and border thinking*. Princeton University Press.

Moll, L. (2013). *L.S. Vygotsky and education*. Routledge.

Moll, L. C., Amanti, C., Neff, D., & González, N. (1992). Funds of knowledge for teaching: Using a qualitative approach to connect homes and classrooms. *Theory into Practice, 31*(2), 132–141.

Neville, M., & Johnson, S. I. (2022). "My literacies expand over two languages": Language and literacy autobiographies as justice-oriented teacher education. *Journal of Adolescent & Adult Literacy, 66*(2), 111–121.

Ortiz, P. (2018). *An African American and Latinx history of the United States*. Penguin Random House.

Otheguy, R., García, O., & Reid, W. (2015). Clarifying translanguaging and deconstructing named languages: A perspective from linguistics. *Applied Linguistics Review, 6*(3), 281–307. https://doi.org/10.1515/applirev-2015-0014

Otheguy, R., & Stern, N. (2011). On so-called Spanglish. *International Journal of Bilingualism, 15*(1), 85–100.

Palmer, D., Cervantes-Soon, C., Dorner, L., & Heiman, D. (2019). Bilingualism, biliteracy, biculturalism, and critical consciousness for all: Proposing a fourth fundamental goal for two-way dual language education. *Theory into Practice, 58*(2), 121–133.

Palmer, D., & Henderson, K. (2016). Dual language bilingual education placement practices: Educator discourses about emergent bilingual students in two program types. *International Multilingual Research Journal, 10*(1), 17–30.

Palmer, D. K., & Martínez, R. A. (2013). Teacher agency in bilingual spaces: A fresh look at preparing teachers to educate Latino/a bilingual children. *Review of Research in Education, 37*, 269–297.

Palmer, D. K., Martínez, R. A., Mateus, S. G., & Henderson, K. (2014). Reframing the debate on language separation: Toward a vision for translanguaging pedagogies in the dual language classroom. *Modern Language Journal, 98*(3), 757–772.

Paris, D. (2012). Culturally sustaining pedagogy: A needed change in stance, terminology, and practice. *Educational researcher, 41*(3), 93–97. https://doi.org/10.3102/0013189X12441244

Paris, D., & Alim, H. S. (2017). *Culturally sustaining pedagogies: Teaching and learning for justice in a changing world*. Teachers College Press.

Pearson, P. D., Palincsar, A. S., Biancarosa, G., & Berman, A. I. (Eds.). (2020). *Reaping the rewards of the Reading for Understanding Initiative*. National Academy of Education.

Perez, B., & Torres-Guzmán, M. E. (1992). *Learning in two worlds: An integrated Spanish/English biliteracy approach*. Longman Publishers.

Popham, J. (2008). *Transformative assessment*. Association for Supervision and Curriculum Development.

Przymus, S. D., & Lindo, E. J. (2021). Dual-language books as a red herring: Exposing language use and ideologies. *The Reading Teacher, 75*(3), 317–327. https://doi.org/10.1002/trtr.2063

Reyes, M. de la L. (1992). Challenging venerable assumptions: Literacy instruction for linguistically different students. *Harvard Educational Review, 62*(4), 427–447. https://doi.org/10.17763/haer.62.4.d522623315485031

Ruiz, R. (1984). Orientations in language planning. *NABE Journal, 8*(2), 15–34.

Sánchez, M. T., & García, O. (Eds.). (2022). *Transformative translanguaging Espacios: Latinx students and teachers rompiendo fronteras sin miedo*. Multilingual Matters.

Sánchez, M. T., García, O., & Solorza, C. (2017). Reframing language allocation policy in dual language bilingual education. *Bilingual Research Journal 41*(1), 37–51. https:// doi.org/10.1080/15235882.2017.1405098

Santos, B. de Sousa. (2018). *The end of the cognitive empire*. Duke University Press.

Schissel, J. (2019). *Social consequences of testing for language minority bilinguals in the U.S.* Multilingual Matters.

Seltzer, K. (in press). "My students would never write something like that for me": Evolving a critical translanguaging stance toward writing with secondary ELA teachers. In M. Gort, M. Zapata, K. Seltzer, & M. Gomez (Eds). *Translanguaging Perspectives on Writing Development and Pedagogy: Learning from Findings Across Teaching and Learning Contexts*. Information Age Publishing.

Seltzer, K. (2019). Reconceptualizing "home" and "school" language: Taking a critical translingual approach in the English classroom. *TESOL Quarterly, 53*(4), 986–1007.

Seltzer, K., & de los Ríos, C. V. (2021). *Understanding translanguaging in U.S. literacy classrooms: Reframing bi/multilingualism as the norm* [Policy brief]. James R. Squire Office of Policy Research in the English Language Arts. NCTE.

Sepúlveda, E. (2011). Toward a pedagogy of acompañamiento: Mexican migrant youth writing from the underside of modernity. *Harvard Educational Review, 81*(3), 550–619.

Street, B. (1984). *Literacy in theory and practice* (Vol. 9). Cambridge University Press.

The Reading League (TRL) and the National Committee for Effective Literacy (NCEL). (2023). *Joint statement: Understanding the difference: The science of reading and implementation for English learners/emergent bilinguals (ELs/EBs).* https://multilingualliteracy.org/wp-content/uploads/2023/10/Joint-Statement_SOR-EL_EB.pdf

Tian, Z., Aghai, L., Sayer, P., & Schissel, J. (Eds.). (2020). *Envisioning TESOL through a translanguaging lens: Global perspectives.* Springer.

Valdés, G. (1996). *Con respeto: Bridging the distances between culturally diverse families and schools.* Teachers College Press.

Valdés, G. (2004). Between support and marginalisation: The development of academic language in linguistic minority children. *International Journal of Bilingual Education and Bilingualism, 7*(2-3), 102–132. https://doi.org/10.1080/13670050408667804

Valdés, G. (2017). Entry visa denied: The construction of symbolic language borders in educational settings. In O. García, N. Flores, & M. Spotti (Eds.), *Handbook of language and society.* Oxford University Press.

Valenzuela, A. (1999). *Subtractive schooling: U.S.–Mexican youth and the politics of caring.* State University of New York Press.

Vertovec, S. (2007). Super-diversity and its implications. *Ethnic and Racial Studies, 30*(6), 1024–1054.

Vygotsky, L. S. (1978). *Mind in society: The development of higher psychological processes.* Harvard University Press.

Walqui, A. (2006). Scaffolding instruction for English learners. A conceptual framework. *International Journal of Bilingual Education and Bilingualism, 9*(2), 159–180.

Wei, L. (2010). The nature of linguistic norms and their relevance to multilingual development. In M. Cruz-Ferreira (Ed.), *Multilingual norms* (pp. 397–404). Frankfurt, Germany: Peter Lang.

Wei, L. (2011). Moment analysis and translanguaging space: Discursive construction of identities by multilingual Chinese youth in Britain. *Journal of Pragmatics, 43*, 1222–1235.

Wei, L. (2013). Conceptual and methodological issues in bilingualism and multilingualism research. In T. K. Bhatia & W. C. Ritchie (Eds.), *The handbook of bilingualism and multilingualism* (2nd ed., pp. 26–51). Wiley Blackwell.

Wei, L. (2014). Who's teaching whom? Co-learning in multilingual classrooms. In S. May (Ed.), *The multilingual turn: Implications for SLA, TESOL and bilingual education* (pp. 167–190). Routledge.

Weinreich, U. (1953). *Languages in contact: Findings and problems.* New York: Linguistic Circle of New York.

Williams, C. (1994). *Arfarniad o ddulliau dysgu ac addysgu yng nghyd-destun addysg uwchradd ddwyieithog* [An evaluation of teaching and learning methods in the context of bilingual secondary education] [Unpublished doctoral dissertation]. University of Wales, Bangor.

Williams, C. (2002). *A language gained: A study of language immersion at 11–16 years of age.* University of Wales, School of Education. http://www.bangor.ac.uk/addysg/publications/Ennill_Iaith.pdf

Wright, W. E., Boun, S., & García, O. (Eds.). (2015). *The handbook of bilingual and multilingual education.* Wiley-Blackwell.

Index

Page numbers followed by *f*, *t*, and *b* indicate figures, tables, and boxes, respectively.